GEORGE CHAPMAN

A Critical Study

Millar MacLure

UNIVERSITY OF TORONTO PRESS

247134

English

Title-page of *The Whole Works of Homer*, with the portrait of Chapman (Bodleian Library). See p. 158.

GEORGE CHAPMAN: A CRITICAL STUDY

TO MY WIFE

NOTE ON TEXTS AND ABBREVIATIONS

For my own and the reader's convenience, I have used the standard modern editions of Chapman's poems, plays and (with the exception of one or two short pieces) translations, with consequent inconsistencies in spelling, italicization and punctuation. When it has been necessary in reproducing the Chapman text, and generally in other quotations, I have followed the usual practice of normalizing i/j, u/v, and contractions with m or n. The following abbreviations are used in text and notes:

Poems: The Poems of George Chapman, ed. Phyllis Brooks Bartlett (New York, 1941).

Tragedies: The Plays of George Chapman, ed. Thomas Marc Parrott (reprinted New York, 1961). I: *The Tragedies.*

Comedies: The Plays of George Chapman, ed. Thomas Marc Parrott (reprinted New York, 1961). II: *The Comedies.*

Homer: Chapman's Homer, ed. Allardyce Nicoll, Bollingen Series XLI (New York, 1956). 2 vols.

PREFACE

Many years ago, I wrote a short interpretation of Chapman's *The Shadow of Night* which I laid aside, deciding that I needed to know more. I still do not know enough, but I have found that others share my interest in Chapman and my estimate of his importance, and this has encouraged me to attempt something more ambitious. At this writing, there exists no book-length study of Chapman in English, and no study in any language which provides a detailed critical discussion of all his work: poems, plays, translations. This is a general survey of the man and his work based on the present state of our knowledge, and I hope that it will not only be useful in that way, but may invite other scholars to discover facts which may qualify or even invalidate some of my conclusions.

I wish I could have written a different kind of book. Chapman is not much read, and I have tried to exhibit his powers and weaknesses by extensive quotation; he has an esoteric vocabulary, which I have imperfectly translated; he is full of marginal stuff and irritable attention to detail, and so, I fear, am I. He deserves the kind of concentrated critical homage which Beckett, in a little book, accorded to Proust. But I can claim that the reader will find all of Chapman here. I have neither cut anything for the sake of a thesis, nor added anything for the sake of a striking analogy.

My necessary indebtedness to the authorities, early and late, is indicated in the notes. I have used the excellent bibliographies of Chapman in Douglas Bush, *English Literature in the Earlier Seventeenth Century* (Oxford, 1962), in Jean Jacquot, *George Chapman* (Paris, 1951), in Marcello Pagnini, *Forme e Motivi nelle Poesie e nelle Tragedie di George Chapman* (Florence, 1957), as well as S. A. Tannenbaum's *Concise Bibliography* (New York, 1938) with its *Supplement* (1946).

I have profited especially from M. Jacquot's admirable book, from the articles by Peter Ure and D. J. Gordon, and from H. C. Fay's thesis. My essential disagreements with Ennis Rees and George de F. Lord do not inhibit my respect for their careful and serious readings of Chapman.

In the course of research and writing I have incurred many obligations, personal and professional. I am particularly obliged to Peter Ure, F. D. Hoeniger and H. G. Robertson, who read parts of the manuscript and made many searching and helpful comments, and to the (anonymous) readers for the University of Toronto Press. The staffs of the North Library of the British Museum and of the Cambridge University Library have been, as always, gracious and helpful, and my introduction to the unique facilities of the Warburg Institute Library I owe, with other good offices, to J. B. Trapp.

The initial work on this book was undertaken on a leave of absence from my College, during the tenure of a post-doctoral fellowship from the Canada Council. I have also received assistance from the fund for grants in aid of research of the University of Toronto. This work has been published with the help of a grant from the Humanities Research Council of Canada using funds provided by the Canada Council and with assistance from the Publications Fund of the University of Toronto Press.

I am especially grateful to Miss F. G. Halpenny, Managing Editor of the University of Toronto Press, and to R. M. Schoeffel of the Editorial Department, for their assistance in preparing the manuscript for the press.

M.M.

Victoria College, University of Toronto
April 1, 1966

CONTENTS

GEORGE CHAPMAN: A CRITICAL STUDY

I · THE POET IN THE WORLD

N A CHANCERY SUIT of 1617, arising from George Chapman's money troubles, one Roger Jones deposed that Chapman "hath made dyvers playes and written other books, but whether he may be termed a Poet or not this deponent . . . doth not know."[1] An ambiguous remark, but at least it is symbolic of the bad luck which made Chapman's life unhappy and his shade a precarious tenant on the middle slopes of Parnassus. He was unlucky in his patrons, the protectors of his career, and generally speaking, he has been ill-served by his critics, the custodians of his fame.

"Wretched man . . . borne/To want, and sorrowe, and the vulgars scorne,"[2] he did not deserve his difficulties: he could hardly have foreseen Essex's fall, Prince Henry's early death (for all poets a sorrow, for Chapman a catastrophe), Somerset's disgrace; he was not in trouble with the stage censorship more often or more seriously than many of his fellows. "A person of most reverend aspect, religious and temperate, qualities rarely meeting in a poet" (so Anthony Wood, reporting the tradition), he was incapable of policy and subject to melancholy; of an "uncourtlie and sillie [i.e. unsophisticated] disposition," as he told Lady Walsingham; in his head and heart, said Davies of Hereford, the "treasures of arte," but in his hand "too little coyne." "Poetry, in this latter Age," wrote Jonson coldly, "hath prov'd but a meane *Mistresse*, to such as have addicted themselves to her, or given their names up to her family. They who have but saluted her on the by . . . shee hath

---

[1]C. J. Sisson and Robert Butman, "George Chapman, 1612–22: Some New Facts." *MLR* XLVI (1951), 185.

[2]*Poems*, p. 179.

done much for, and advanced in the way of their owne professions (both the *Law* and the *Gospel*)."[3] Chapman was wholly dedicated to "the divine discipline of Poesie"—we may imagine that even when hacking out *The Old Joiner of Aldgate* he told himself that he was serving the muse of comedy—and indeed out of the paradox of his intimations of greatness and the meanness of his estate (with some recollection of Erasmus' *Enchiridion* too) he created the moral "figure" which recurs obsessively in his work, of life divided between an "outward" world of riches, "opinion" and "policy," and an "inward" world of spiritual and poetic vision. But if his highmindedness compels our admiration, his poetic practice makes it very hard to be fair to him. His methods of composition have inevitably tempted his critics to let his poems dramatic and undramatic, and his Homeric commentary, dissolve into the conventional, much-foxed divisions of the common-place books from which he worked them up. Then, having observed that he is a scholarly poet, they are forced to admit that his scholarship is not of the first rank; having searched him for ideas, they discover that the ideas as such are neither original nor particularly profound. Furthermore, his passionate assertion that his "strange Poems" are only for "searching spirits," his dark hints at esoteric meanings, and other such ambiguous giving-out in which he delighted, have encouraged scholars to seek him in the shadow of night, to chase his emblems through the flowering thickets of neoplatonic occultism (where indeed some of them are to be found), and sometimes to lose him altogether in a wasteland of political topicalities.

All this is too bad, and needs to be reformed. He was, after all, an eccentric and powerful personality, a great melancholic in an age which cultivated that temper, and an important poet in an age of important poets. But (to adapt Bacon's famous triad) though he was a "full" man, he was neither "ready" nor "exact," and so he missed then, and still misses, the sympathetic attention which has been accorded to others, his contemporaries, of inferior but more assimilable powers.

Chapman might well have seen his career as an emblem of that irreconcilable feud between Virtue and Fortune which is a recurring topic in Renaissance art and speculation, with himself as Herculean Virtue, full of labours, having chosen the hard high road of "good

---

[3]Anthony à Wood, *Athenae Oxonienses*, ed. P. Bliss (London, 1813–20), II, 576; *Poems*, p. 132; John Davies of Hereford, *The Scourge of Folly* (1611), "To my highly vallued Mr George Chapman, Father of Our English Poets"; *Ben Jonson*, ed. C. H. Herford, Percy and Evelyn Simpson (Oxford, 1925–52), VIII, 622.

life,"[4] though crying out upon the whore Occasion whose forelock, stretched upon the wind of Time, always eluded his grasp but offered its silken rope to time-servers, chapmen, and politicians. Epictetus, the table-book of his later years, may have taught him to distinguish between those things which are in our power and those which are not, but it is a hard lesson, and if the old man's querulousness of the "Invective" against Jonson may be admitted as evidence, he was never able to attain to the religious calm of his Cato.

We know very little of Chapman's private life, and the chances are poor that we shall find out more. As we should expect, we have next to nothing from his first life, from what in these days we call the formative years. He was thirty-five when he published *The Shadow of Night* (1594), and by that age most of us have arranged the past to suit our open covenants with fate. When he composed his gnomic epistle to Matthew Roydon, that curious intellectual for whom diplomatic adulation (by Thomas Nashe, Robert Armin and the sheaf-gatherer Francis Meres) and the timely disappearance of manuscripts combine to create a minor eminence which he may or may not have deserved,[5] setting the crabbed and pretentious sentences before his hymns, he had, it seems, resolved to appear as the inspired poet, full of lore, and anxious to claim a place on the periphery of what he supposed to be a secret circle of noble adepts ("most ingenious *Darbie*, deepe searching *Northumberland*, and skill-embracing *heire of Hunsdon*") whom he did not presume to approach directly (depending on Roydon's "report"), but to whom he addressed a seemly dedication at one remove, imagining their studies congenial to his own.[6] They had read, he hoped in effect, the same books. The dedication, and the poems, complete with glosses almost as conspicuously coy as E.K.'s and as learnedly unhelpful as those attached to *The Waste Land*, smell pungently of candle-wax. Where did it burn? Anthony Wood's testimony, echoed by Warton, that "he spent some time in Oxon, where he was observed to be most excellent in the Lat. and Greek tongues, but not in logic and philosophy,"[7] hence taking no degree, remains unsupported and sounds in any case like inference from the works, though

[4]See R. Wittkower, "Chance, Time and Virtue, " *JWCI* I (1937-8), 318-9 & plate 52a; cf. Chapman's "Virgils Epigram of this letter Y," *Poems*, pp. 234-5.

[5]*DNB*, s.v. "Matthew Roydon"; Roydon's *Friends Passion for his Astrophel* is reprinted in *The Pembroke Booklets*, First Series (Hull, 1905).

[6]*Poems*, pp. 19, 422.

[7]*Athenae Oxonienses*, II, 576; Thomas Warton, *History of English Poetry*, ed. W. C. Hazlitt (London, 1871), IV, 321-2.

it is perhaps consistent with his bitter references to "Academickes"
who

> ever rate
> A man for learning, with that estimate
> They made of him, when in the schooles he liv'd;
> And how so ere he scatter'd since, or thriv'd,
> Still they esteeme him as they held him then,

or with his assertion that "decrees" (that is, the inward laws of inspired
truth) are not "degrees," and that love or virtue and integrity is the
only "argument of all truth . . . without which all is sophisticate and
adulterate, howsoever painted and splinted with degrees and languages."
"Artsmen," he says elsewhere, merely "stuffe their windy memories."[8]
These remarks ring with the scorn of the creative artist for the
academic drudge. When he comes to defend his translation of Homer
against the "learned," he seems to say that he has been wholly self-
taught. They cannot believe, he says,

> That one not taught like them, should learne to know
> Their Greeke rootes, & from thence the Groves that grow,
> Casting such rich shades, from great *Homers* wings,

and adds,

> He's the best Scholler, that through paines and vows,
> Made his own Master onely; all things know's.[9]

We may decide that whether or not he went up to university, briefly and
unhappily a brilliant or indifferent misfit, he was and thought of
himself as a self-made scholar. He displays all the crankiness of a man
who works confidently from his own bookshelf; his learning sticks out;
he is always full of the last books he has read.

The university, then, did not enter into his sorry scheme of things,
nor show the way to holy orders, an obvious career for the younger son
of a substantial yeoman, with probable good connections through his
cousins the Grimestons or the distinguished Sir Ralph Sadler, the
trusted servant of the Queen and Burghley, in whose household, by
his own testimony, his "youthe was initiate."[10] Later he became very

---

[8]*Poems*, pp. 242, 245, 369; dedicatory epistle to Bacon, in *The Georgicks of Hesiod*
(1618).

[9]*Ibid.*, p. 417.

[10]For the Grimeston connection, see Jean Jacquot, *George Chapman, 1559–1634,
sa vie, sa poésie, son théâtre, sa pensée* (Paris, 1951), ch. I; Chapman's early life is

pious, and must always have been serious, too serious perhaps to listen to any but the nonconformist call to be a poet.

The silent time remains to tease our powers of conjecture. Was he perhaps a schoolmaster, as Hine surmised, a grumpy and frustrated young pedant, Holofernes in the making? We do not know. He borrowed money from the usurer John Wolfal in 1585, perhaps to equip himself for adventure on the continent, and so took the first step into the morass of debt through which he seems to have floundered all the rest of his life. At some time or times between 1585 and 1600 he was, a process informs us, "byonde the seas," and that he served in the Low Countries, as Jonson did, is as certain as any inference can be, supported by the "Nimigan" simile in the "Hymnus in Cynthiam" and other familiar references to those wars.[11] We think of war as a long apprenticeship to routine and initiation into the impersonality of danger—but that is scientific war; the quasi-religious wars of the 1590's in the Netherlands and in northern France were amateur affairs, bloody tourism for the gentry, graduate courses for Fluellens, and squalid suffering for other ranks. Chapman grew to hate war as much as Erasmus: perhaps he knew more about it; the engraving in the *Whole Works of Homer* shows us a soldier's face, bearded like the pard. We do not know when he began to be aware of Homer, but Homer taught him the glory of arms first, the Achillean virtues, and then, after reflection, the lessons of inward peace, the perils of the "banefull wrath" which gives rein to "th' impious lust of Mars."

"Best men are long in making," he said later in his own defence against "meer Artists" on the one hand and "Academickes" on the other, and the man who broke into print in 1594 was not yet a "compleat" man. But he thought he had found the way to that perfection: in the epistle to Roydon he calls it "the deepe search of knowledge." The "skil" it takes so long to learn is not academic but therapeutic, working the subjugation of the affections to the judgment; it is identical with what he later deifies as "Learning." Here he compares it, politely, with studies esoteric and also ennobling indulged in by Roydon's patrons, "to the admirable luster of their true nobilitie." The hints point to mystical mathematics and alchemy. It is well known that Ralegh and the "wizard Earl" Northumberland were both

---

discussed by Jean Robertson, "The Early Life of George Chapman," *MLR* XL (1945), 157–65, and Mark Eccles, "Chapman's Early Years," *SP* XLIII (1946), 176–93.

[11]R. L. Hine, *Hitchin Worthies: Four Centuries of English Life* (London, 1932), pp. 48–69; Eccles, 184; Jacquot, pp. 13–16; *Poems*, pp. 38, 341, 415.

interested in alchemy, and in 1593 Northumberland was praised by George Peele as a patron of secret and noble arts,

> (Leaving our Schoolemens vulgar troden pathes)
> And following the auncient reverend steps
> Of Trismegistus and Pythagoras.[12]

These disciplines were thought of as purifying too, in their highest reaches, and Chapman's "heavenly familiar," the tutelary daimon who taught him to write (and incidentally filled up some pages in the variorum edition of Shakespeare's *Sonnets*) is very like the good angel who was supposed to preside over the meditations of the alchemists.[13]

This analogy, however imprecise (the very mention of alchemy is an invitation to imprecision), helps to characterize what Chapman at this time already thought "Learning" is and what it is not. It is not mere book-learning, that is clear. And here we come upon the first of many paradoxes in Chapman, for his first two productions, *The Shadow of Night* and *Ovids Banquet of Sense*, are very bookish and pedantic indeed. The former is apparently learned in the wrong sense, and the latter is almost a scientific poem, in which a good deal of currently accepted physiology is laboriously and often rather inharmoniously versified. The poet seems determined to appear well-read, full, like "men that all things learne, and nothing know," of "vast varied reading," to use his own contemptuous phrase. The glosses to *The Shadow of Night* are stuffed with *auctores*: Aratus (twice), Hesiod (four times), Plato, Homer (four times), Lycophron, Orpheus (four times), Pherecides (more of him in *Caesar and Pompey*), Callimachus (twice), Plutarch, Apollonius Rhodius, Strabo, Nicander, Euripides, Cicero. But M. Schoell has demonstrated, of course, that almost all these references were supplied by Natalis Comes, whose manual of "bookish and barbaric" mythology made pedantry portable for poets.[14] The "philosophical conceits" of the *Banquet*, on the other hand, far more "learned" in the ordinary sense, are very lightly glossed. Both poems are experiments. Chapman was trying, among other things, to find out how to put learning to the service of Learning, an art he never wholly mastered, even later on, with the powerful aids of Plutarch

[12]*The Honour of the Garter* (1593), sig. A3.
[13]See C. G. Jung, *Psychology and Alchemy*, Bollingen Series XX (1953), pp. 262–3 and fig. 137.
[14]F. L. Schoell, *Études sur l'Humanisme Continental en Angleterre* (Paris, 1926), *passim*; the phrase "bookish and barbaric" is applied generally to the handbooks by Jean Seznec, *The Survival of the Pagan Gods*, Bollingen Series XXXVIII (1953), p. 256.

and Epictetus. Also, it may be, he was already looking for the genre which would serve best to express the inchoate but powerful sentiments which impelled him to write in the first place. (He was anti-Aristotelian in his notion of the nature of poetic creation, and for him, consequently, a genre was an instrument and not an end; but of that more below.)

"Th'effect proper to perfect Learning," Chapman tells us in *The Tears of Peace*, is

> to direct
> Reason in such an Art, as that it can
> Turne blood to soule, and make both, one calme man.

But he was himself a divided man, and those who have interpreted his characters and symbols without taking this into account, like Ennis Rees in his book on the tragedies, have made a falsely homogeneous and sad hash of him. The schism in the soul would not be so relevant had he possessed "negative capability," in Keats's phrase; I am sure that Shakespeare was divided as many ways as an orange or as Montaigne, but he rested in the riddle, while Chapman (like Greville) was always irritably striving after reasons and conclusions and what he called "material instructions," so that the conflict keeps breaking through.

The art of turning "blood to soule" is figured in the act of poetic "making," and poetic gestation was for Chapman hard and strange. In that moving confessional epistle to Thomas Harriott, printed with *Achilles Shield* (1598), he found the image which most fitly characterizes the process and its results:

> O had your perfect eye Organs to pierce
> Into that Chaos whence this stiffled verse
> By violence breakes: where Glowworme like doth shine
> In nights of sorrow, this hid soule of mine:
> And how her genuine formes struggle for birth,
> Under the clawes of this fowle Panther earth;
> Then under all those formes you should discerne
> My love to you, in my desire to learne.[15]

Twice afterwards, in this same poem, he returns to this figure of light erupting from darkness, to "some gleames of wrastling fire" which "breake from [his] spirits oppression"—that is, from his earthy melancholy—and to the "flames/Of [his] prest soule." To Harriott, dwelling as he thinks in the serene "Sphere of fire" where "Reason moves," he uses the familiar (to them both) analogy of creative form

[15] *Poems*, p. 382.

working in chaos, "digesting" an "absolute body" out of disorder as the soul imposes *form* on the rebellious earth of the body, but the images carry more than the neoplatonic explanation; this is the cry of a spirit walking in darkness, but a spirit who has found, *nel mezzo del cammin di nostra vita,* his guide.

> For though I now consume in poesie,
> Yet *Homer* being my roote I can not die.

"On the hill/Next *Hitchins* left hand," he had already met his "Angell ... Starre and Fate," his Homer, who, "invisible, went prompting" him to do the work he was "born to do," the great translation.[16]

But the poems which he first published do not belong exclusively either to the "inward" world of his growing vocation or to that semi-private realm from which they were "learnedly" derived. It is, for example, conceivable and indeed probable that he kept up with what was being circulated or published, that the "Hymnus in Noctem" may be an "answer" to Prince Arthur's outcry against Night in *The Faerie Queene,* III, iv, 55–60, and that the *Banquet,* in intention probably and in effect certainly "more of a treatise than a debauch" (Bush), was inspired by a cranky reading of *Venus and Adonis,* 11. 427–46, an anticipatory banquet of the senses, as well as by its learned sources. It is typical of Chapman that he should choose to make himself conspicuous by a different kind of complaint of the world's vanity and a different kind of amatory poem, that he, the moony melancholy seer, should set himself against the temptations and flatteries of a "glitterand" House of Pride. But the conjectures which make him a protagonist in literary warfare and a propagandist for a court faction (for Ralegh vs. Essex) have still, in spite of the care, brilliance and erudition which created them, no satisfying substance.[17]

> No pen can any thing eternal wright
> That is not steept in humor of the Night

and

> Never durst poet touch a pen to write
> Until his ink were temper'd with Love's sighs

---

[16]*Poems,* pp. 174–5.

[17]The best recent summary of the evidence for the "Schoole of Night" is in Richard David's introduction to his New Arden edition of *Love's Labour's Lost* (5th ed., 1956), pp. xliv ff. See also M. C. Bradbrook, *The School of Night: A Study in the Literary Relationships of Sir Walter Raleigh* (Cambridge, 1936).

go together, but the narrow valley of the literary 1590's is full of echoes,
and the textual evidence for the "Schoole of Night" is weak enough to
trouble the whole theory.[18] Chapman was intimate with Roydon (or
wished to appear so), knew and revered Harriott for his occult studies,
admired Ralegh, dreamed of an "academy"; Shakespeare, in *Love's
Labour's Lost*, made fun of a courtier's "academy," of "the superior
persons who exalt learning above nature and common sense,"[19] and
that is all we really know. We may assume, I suppose, in a general way,
that Shakespeare the popular poet and rising playwright, vouched for
by "divers of worship," warmed by the sun of success and attempting
no *obvious* profundities, would have little in common with the obscure
melancholic stuffed with "literary" knowledge, vociferating against
the wickedness and disorder of the times, and pretending acquaintance
with marvellous and powerful folios. Chapman may have thought of
Shakespeare, in the middle '90's, as a "sugred" amatory versifier,
celebrating "loves sensuall Emperie" like the sonneteers—while *his*
mistress was "Philosophie"[20]—and as a journeyman of the theatre;
as one of "the wiser sort" (Gabriel Harvey's phrase) he may have been
pleased by *Lucrece* and *Hamlet*, but he has not told us. In fact, given
his strong confessional bent, fearless temper and intransigent opinions,
it is significant that he has told us nothing at all. If we cast him as the
"rival poet" of Shakespeare's *Sonnets*, assuming all the time that that
poet was not a fiction, a notable "feigning" in what is, after all, a kind
of problem play in sonnets, "that affable familiar ghost/which nightly
gulls him with intelligence" of no. 86 does sound a little like Chapman's
"heavenly familiar," and if we give any countenance at all to the
"Schoole of Night" we must perforce be struck by the reference to that
curious advisory committee of "compeers by night" who aid the rival
to shake out "the proud full sail of his great verse." But to what
person who might conceivably be "Mr. W. H." did Chapman, at any
time before 1609, address such verses or "fill up his line" with that
beloved countenance? In the present state of our knowledge we are
forced back upon hypothetical lost manuscripts, accepted at an unknown date by an unknown person, and that will not do. And besides,
as Dr. Rowse is the latest to remind us, there was Marlowe.

As early as 1595/6 Chapman was himself a theatrical journeyman

[18]See E. A. Strathmann, *Sir Walter Raleigh: A Study in Elizabethan Skepticism*
(New York, 1951), pp. 264–70, &c.

[19]David, p. xlviii.

[20]*Poems*, p. 83.

on Henslowe's books,[21] keeping his sail afloat, like so many others, by writing for the stage—then as ravenous for "material," in a small way, as television is now. His productive years were just beginning. His ambition was to write "absolute poems," that is, poems in which "high and harty invention" would be carried out in "fit" figures, and his various literary pursuits, while they were directed "outward" to his living, were also, it seems, prompted "inwardly" by the search for the perfect vehicle for his invention. He came nearest to it (setting aside the *Homer*) when "by strange instigation" (whatever that means) he set out to complete Marlowe's *Hero and Leander*.

Employing his "serious time in so trifeling a subject" (a nice bit of dedicatory double-talk), Chapman did his best to make the poem serious (in his terms) as a whole, but he also amplified its parts not only by multiplying the sententious lines with which Marlowe studded his narrative, but by opinionated digressions, topical similes and other incidental juvenalia. His continuation was written and published, after all, in the high tide of formal satire before the prohibition of 1599, and Chapman obviously tried to ride the flood too. Apart from some characteristic disquisitions on the physiology of the senses and especially the functions of the eye (e.g. III, 85–90, 235–38), of the "scientific" kind which forms the argument of the *Banquet*, we find Hero's chaste bosom invaded by passion as Essex stormed Cadiz in 1596 (III, 203–26), an attack upon "the worlds stale cunning" and upon "slick-tongde fame" which is "the drunken bastard of the multitude"; a pious wish that ladies would inform their beauties with virtue and so lead "affection prisoner"—in other words that they should practice "Learning" (IV, 112–21), and a Miltonic digression on the corrupt clergy:

> O lovely *Hero*, nothing is thy sin,
> Wayd with those foule faults other Priests are in;
> That having neither faiths, nor works, nor bewties,
> T'engender any scuse for slubberd duties;
> With as much countnance fill their holie chayres,
> And sweat denouncements gainst prophane affayres,
> As if their lives were cut out by their places,
> And they the only fathers of the Graces.
>
> (IV, 210-17)

More in the mode of Roman satire are the inflated similes in which,

[21]On Henslowe's relations with the dramatists, see R. A. Foakes and R. T. Rickert, eds., *Henslowe's Diary* (Cambridge, 1961), pp. xxiv ff.

failing decorum, Chapman compares Leander's fate to a "fleering slavish Parasite" who flatters his victim (VI, 19–34) and Leander in his *hubris* to "an emptie Gallant" who "hath seene the hot Low Countries, not their heat" (i.e. has not fought there),

> Observes their rampires and their buildings yet.
> And for your sweet discourse with mouthes is heard.
> Giving instructions with his very beard.
> Hath gone with an Ambassadour, and been
> A great mans mate in travailing, even to *Rhene*,
> And then puts all his worth in such a face,
> As he saw brave men make, and strives for grace
> To get his news forth.
>
> (VI, 115-23)

But Chapman was no satirist. He was capable of wit and grace, as the comedies show, and of heavy moral indignation, but he lacked the high-heartedness, the delight in being angry, which is the mark of the true satiric spirit, exemplified in his time by Thomas Nashe. The best satirists, from Juvenal to Mencken, are in love with anger. Chapman's best tone, in his dealings with the world, is cloudy panegyric touched with the heat lightning of condemnation. He detested pettiness, the small mind, whether expressed in trifling verses or in the little avaricious transactions by which most people live off each other. Having a taste for the grandiose, he was no connoisseur of the absurd—at least where moral issues were involved, and he could be moved by dreams and visions, his own or other men's. Hence the remarkable eloquence of his commendatory verses prefixed to the brilliant and unfortunate Laurence Keymis's *Relation of the second Voyage to Guiana* (1596), in which he commends Ralegh's imperial enterprise to the Queen and to the "*Patrician* Spirites" of hoped-for colonials, and condemns the slothful and the incredulous who do not see these wonderful possibilities of a golden future. The piled hyperboles, the assembled brass were not just banged out to order, for the poet's own preoccupations intrude from the beginning, where, as prelude to a sounding invocation to Clio, he announces the primacy of his own mental strife, the quarrel in him between contemplation and action:

> What worke of honour and eternall name,
> For all the world t'envie and us t'achieve,
> Filles me with furie [i.e. *furor poeticus*], and gives
> armed handes

> To my heartes peace, that els would gladlie turne
> My limmes and every sence into my thoughtes
> Rapt with the thirsted action of my mind?[22]

(Chapman had no left hand, no cool element in composition, and attributed to the most occasional verse from his pen a final importance. He lectures even the noble patrons to whom he addressed the complimentary sonnets to the *Homer*, which are far less conventional and diplomatic than the otherwise comparable little elegancies which Spenser placed before *The Faerie Queene*. In his dedications generally he seems to be talking to himself, and his obsequiousness is always in consequence grotesque.) The paradox of the Orinoco enterprise, which should yield "*Riches* with honour, *Conquest* without bloud," appealed to him, and his idealism was fired by the prospect of creating "a golden worlde in this our yron age." He is able, accordingly, to hold up to scorn those "that would be wise in Wisdomes spight," the "poysoned soules" of such as do not believe in the prospect of seeing "*vertue* rich:/Till *Honour* having golde, rob golde of honour," and to promise a new world to those who will follow the dream of "th'industrious Knight, the soule of this exploit." This is his final vision:

> And now a wind as forward as their spirits,
> Sets their glad feet on smooth *Guianas* breast,
> Where (as if ech man were an *Orpheus*)
> A world of Savadges fall tame before them,
> Storing their theft-free treasuries with golde,
> And there doth plentie crowne their wealthie fieldes,
> There *Learning* eates no more his thriftlesse books,
> Nor *Valure* Estridge-like his yron armes.
> There *Beautie* is not strumpet for her wantes,
> Nor *Gallique* humours putrifie her bloud:
> But all our Youth take *Hymens* lightes in hand,
> And fill each roofe with honor'd progenie.
> There makes *Societie* Adamantine chaines,
> And joins their harts with wealth, whom wealth disjoyn'd.
> There healthfull Recreations strowe their meades,
> And make their mansions daunse with neighbourhood,
> That here were drown'd in churlish *Avarice*.
> And there do Pallaces and temples rise
> Out of the earth, and kisse th'enamored skies,
> Where new *Britania*, humblie kneeles to heaven,

---

[22] *Poems*, p. 353.

The world to her, and both at her blest feete,
In whom the Circles of all Empire meet.[23]

The skyscrapers of South America, here unwittingly prophesied, were to be built on petroleum and coffee, and by other hands; Elizabeth gave her name only to Virginia, and Ralegh ("wrong'd soule of *Nature*") found his doom in his Eldorado, on the banks of which Keymis killed himself. Yet Chapman's Utopia, with its harmonious marriage of Art and Nature, its ideals reminiscent of the Roman *imperium* and its function to purify the ills of a sick society, deserves to be mentioned with the other utopian visions of the Renaissance, though in another light it is little more than a hymn to free enterprise and a promised paradise for younger sons. Chapman was a younger son.

He turned his talent as celebrator of heroic action nearer home in those crowded years at the end of the century, when Ralegh's star was down and Essex's blazed fitfully in a troubled sky. To Essex he dedicated his first labours in Homer: the *Seaven Bookes* of the *Iliad* and *Achilles Shield* of 1598. In the epistle to the first of these, after some important observations on poetry and Learning, he addresses Essex as "the most abundant President of true Noblesse," and "most true Achilles (whom by sacred prophecie Homere did but prefigure in his admirable object and in whose unmatched vertues shyne the dignities of the soule and the whole excellence of royall humanitie)," beseeching him not to let

the Pessant-common polities of the world, that count all things servile and simple that pamper not their own private sensualities, burying quick in their filthie sepulchres of earth the whole bodies and soules of honor, vertue and pietie, stirre [his] divine temper from perseverance in godlike pursute of Eternitie,[24]

that is, of that fame which the eternizing poet can give, though obscured by "his unfashionable habite of povertie that, like the poisoned mists of thawing mucpits, smokes from the horded treasure of souleless goldwormes." It is to be noted that those books of the *Iliad* translated in this volume (I, II, VII, VIII–XI) happen, by accident or design, to exhibit pointedly the injustice done to Achilles and the evil fortunes of the Greeks without him. The fulsome comparison of Essex to

[23] *Poems*, p. 357. For the relation of this poem to the *Masque of the Inner Temple and Gray's Inn*, see Appendix A.
[24] *Homer*, I, 504.

Creep | through
of the

Achilles may have prompted Shakespeare to a contrasting portrait in *Troilus and Cressida*. Chapman asks his hoped-for patron to defend him from the Blatant Beast, here characterized as "the doting and vitious furie of the two Atrides—Arrogancie and Detraction," and from his poverty, which "distracts invention necessarie even in translation—interrupts the industry of conceipt and the discourse of the soule," and commends the *Iliad* in Fluellen-like phrase "since it contaynes the true portraite of ancient stratagems and disciplines of war" having affinity to the Earl's "present complementes of field."[25] These appeals apparently failed of their effect, and Chapman renewed his suit in another dedicatory epistle, "humbly presenting [Essex's] Achillean vertues with Achilles' Shield," but characteristically, in his disappointment, taking no humble line at all but lecturing the Earl Marshal on the unsurpassable qualities of Homer, contemning the ignorance of those who, like "soule-blind Scaliger," have presumed to set Vergil over Homer and those who have no confidence in the capacity of English to convey "the coppie and elegancie of the originall," and remarking ominously, out of Ptolemy, that "he that had slight handes to entertayne Homer had as sleight braines to rule his common wealth." He struck back at other backbiters in the epistle "To the Understander," against such as had professed to find his dedication to the *Seaven Bookes* "darke and too much labored":

For all the affected labour bestowed in it, I protest two morninges both ended it and the Reader's Epistle: but the truth is, my desire and strange disposition in all thinges I write is to set downe uncommon and most profitable coherents for the time, yet further removed from abhorde affectation than from the most popular and cold digestion.[26]

His complaint is that no one will take the pains to understand him.

Lonely, despised, poor, his productions received with thoughtless censures, yet still straining after the ineffable, the prophetic, the absolute: this is the self-portrait he offers to Harriott in the verse-letter attached, as a kind of last resort, to *Achilles Shield*, with no apparent sense of the incongruity of dedicating a book to Essex and also to a distinguished protegé of his rival Ralegh. The applause of a rational soul, Chapman affirms, should "suffice the free and royall mind," but, alas,

> as the soule upon the flesh depends,
> Vertue must wait on wealth; we must make friends

---

[25] *Homer*, I, 506.
[26] *Ibid.*, I, 543–7, 548.

> Of the unrighteous Mammon, and our sleights
> Must beare the formes of fooles or Parasites.[27]

Professing unworldliness, the poet turns the dialogue of soul and body into an impassioned cry against the demands of the fleshly world, which chokes his creative mind, and on which as on a dunghill the "formall Clearkes" and "ignorants" seek gain and glory, keeping "a squeaking stirre/With cald on muses to unchilde their braines/Of Winde and vapor," while the true poet, his estate "[kept] under with all contempt," feeds upon his "spirits oppression" and is forced to such sleights as the adulation of noble (and probably heedless) prospective patrons.

The wonder is that this centripetal imagination, returning again and again to flourish with all the heavy colours of his rhetoric the central preoccupation with "good life" and the "informing" action of Learning upon corrupt nature—as, later, in *The Tears of Peace* and other poems to be discussed below—should be able to range at large over the wooden O of the popular stage, for which he was turning out, for the Admiral's men, a "humours" play (*An Humorous Day's Mirth*), "ij ectes of a Tragedie of bengemens plotte" (so begins the recorded association with Jonson, the fruits thereof unhappily lost), *The Blind Beggar of Alexandria*, which as we have it is diluted and travestied Marlowe, and some other pieces which have been sometimes speculatively identified as early versions of his extant plays, that is "the ylle[?] of A Womon," "the ffount of new facianes," "the world Rones A Whelles" or "all fooles but the foolle," and a "pastrall tragedie."[28] He apparently left Henslowe's stable after July, 1599, having collaborated, it seems, only with Jonson, though Greg wonders if he might have worked later on the "Biron" of October 1602,[29] having possibly "initiated the whole Jonsonian comedy of humours,"[30] and learned to adapt, topically and tropically, the Plautine intrigue to the popular stage of the day. He was sufficiently conspicuous to find a place among the masters of comedy and tragedy listed by the invaluable if tedious

[27]*Poems*, p. 381.

[28]*Henslowe's Diary*, ed. Foakes-Rickert, pp. 91, 99, 100, 122. It has been suggested by G. H. Wilkes that "the ffount of new facianes" is an early version of *Sir Giles Goosecap* ("Chapman's Lost Play, *The Fount of New Fashions*," *JEGP* LXII [1963], 77–81).

[29]*Henslowe's Diary*, ed. W. W. Greg (London, 1904), II, 250. His IOU to Henslowe for ten guineas, of October 24, 1598, was signed by him in both the Italian and English hands; see *ibid.*, I, 142.

[30]M. C. Bradbrook, *The Growth and Structure of Elizabethan Comedy* (London, 1955), pp. 144, 171.

Meres in 1598,[31] and sufficiently popular (and indigent) in 1602/3 to try his hand at a topical piece, "scenting out the makings of a play in certain odd proceedings in Newgate ... writing the play as a private venture and selling it in the best market," producing the now lost and hypothetically reconstructed *Old Joiner of Aldgate*. The whole wonderful farcical yarn has been spun out of documents in the Public Record Office and Somerset House by Professor Sisson,[32] but I must reproduce at least part of it here, to show Chapman's "outward" career in a light more garish than his favorite private dark affords.

It is the story of the heiress Agnes Howe, whose father seems to have negotiated for her betrothal with a whole flock of suitors, and overreached himself, while the sought-after Agnes was picked up with suspicious speed and unclerkly resource by Rev. John Milward of Christ Church.[33] In the legal processes by which Milward sought to hold and the disappointed suitor John Flaskett sought to break the lucrative contract, suits in which the interrogatories examined by Professor Sisson show "a tangled web of sturdy swearing to ... a bewildering mass of detailed circumstance," it appears that Flaskett arranged, while the case was *sub judice*,

that a stage play should be made & was made by one George Chapman upon a plott given unto him concerning ... Agnes Howe ... & the same under coulorable & fayned names personated, so made & contryved was sold to Thomas Woodford & Edward Pearce for xx marks to be played upon the open stages in divers playhouses in the citie of London to resemble and publish the dealing of [Agnes Howe's] father towards her concerning his practize with severall sutors to bestow her in marriage with one that might forgoe her portion.[34]

The play was acted by the Children of Paul's in February 1603; in May, Chapman was summonsed in the cause and in his sworn deposition affirmed himself not guilty of any conspiratorial action; he said he had sold the play to Woodford (described by Sisson as a "theatrical speculator") for £13.6s.8d—a very good price indeed—but that he never saw it acted, a characteristically diffident and lofty attitude. Of course it was well to profess a certain detachment in the circumstances; Flaskett, for example, saw the play but did not, he said, "make anie regarde or accounte of the same but as Toys & jests such as are acted in other Places." Perhaps the situation appealed to

[31]*Elizabethan Critical Essays*, ed. Gregory Smith (Oxford, 1904), II, 319–20.

[32]C. J. Sisson, *Lost Plays of Shakespeare's Age* (Cambridge, 1936).

[33]The preacher troubled by a cuckoo. See my *The Paul's Cross Sermons, 1534–1642* (Toronto, 1958), p. 226.

[34]*Lost Plays*, p. 58.

Chapman as a literary man, because the intrigues and counter-intrigues resembled so interestingly the involutions of Roman comedy; but the names which he attached to his characters—Snipper Snapper a barber for John Howe, Touchbox for Flaskett, Spitter Spatter for John Oswald (?)—at least suggest a capacity for good clean and lucrative fun.

If the reader feels any sense of inconsistency between the lonely inspired bard and the purveyor of popular and witty entertainments, he can find in the series of comedies which Chapman wrote for the Children of the Chapel (afterwards the Queen's Revels) some recurring themes not wholly out of keeping with the poetic personality which Chapman rather self-consciously displayed to his "understanders." The poet, unsocial, dumpish, "spirit-less," is fascinated by power (which as Rinaldo in *All Fools* says is Fortune's gift), by *confidence* (the slogan of the overpowering Tharsalio in *The Widow's Tears*), and the Hermes-figure of the lucid and protean trickster tends to dominate Chapman's comic scene. On the other hand, the themes of melancholy and entombment recur also, with the melancholy man presented either as malcontent or hermetic seer; the scholar Clarence in *Sir Giles Goosecap* looks like a self-portrait—or at least a portrait of one *persona* of the poet, for he despises the world, is of "mean estate," and pursued by envy and detraction while he studies the "black springs" of things. But his friend Momford says to him: "I tell thee, friend, the eminent confidence of strong spirits is the only witchcraft of this world," and perhaps in this dialogue we have the dramatization of an inner debate.

The story of *Eastward Ho* (1605) has been told often and well, and I do not propose to rehearse it here. The two most notable documents in the case are Jonson's report to Drummond about his (voluntary, he said) imprisonment with Marston and Chapman "for writing something against the Scots in a play," and his eloquent letter of appeal to Robert Cecil, with its reference to Chapman as "a gentleman (whose name may, perhaps, have come to your lordship) one Mr. George Chapman, a learned and honest man." Most scholars accept the learned and honest man's attribution to Marston of the offending clauses in III, iii, 40–47, which indeed sound like interpolations in a scene generally thought to be Chapman's work.[35] If the Chapman letters in the Dobell manuscript are genuine,[36] we have a rather

[35]*Ben Jonson*, IX, 636ff.

[36]Printed by Bertram Dobell as "Newly Discovered Documents of the Elizabethan and Jacobean Periods," in *The Athenaeum*, March 23, 30, April 6, 13, 1901, from the

ambiguous piece of additional evidence from an appeal of Chapman to the Lord Chamberlain Suffolk, who apparently intervened on behalf of the playwrights. In this letter Chapman says that the King's wrath is to his "most humble and zealous affection . . . so much the more stormye, by how much some of my obscured laboures have striv'd to aspire in stead thereof his illustrate favoure: and shall not be the least honor to his most Royall vertues."[37] To my ear at least, this— especially the last clause—sounds almost too much like Chapman to be true, but let that pass. If he did write it, it suggests that he was seeking from the King the patronage he later secured from Prince Henry, to whom he was already sewer in ordinary.

Now it may well be true, as Jonson and Chapman affirmed, that the offending passage was written by Marston, but Chapman could be temerarious too, as when, three years later, he introduced on the Blackfriars stage, in *The Tragedy of Byron*, the Queen of France quarreling with her husband's mistress, and giving her a box on the ear. The French ambassador La Boderie quite naturally protested, and upon his representations three of the players were arrested, but the author escaped.[38] How did he imagine he could get away with such stuff, or even with the passage from the fourth act of *The Conspiracy*, in which, apparently, Queen Elizabeth was shown pointing out to her visitor Byron the moral of the fall of Essex? His letter to (probably) the Master of the Revels in the Dobell collection provides us with a characteristic if unsatisfactory answer to the question. He complains:

I have not deserv'd what I suffer by your austeritie; if the two or three lynes you crost were spoken; my uttermost to suppresse them was enough for my discharge: To more then which no promyse can be rackt by reason; I see not myne owne Plaies; nor carrie the Actors Tongues in my mouthe. . . .

---

ms. now Folger 420423. The manuscript includes twelve letters or documents supposed by Chapman, but they are copies, not originals. On the provenance of the ms., see Dobell's description and Jacquot's note (p. 12), reproducing the opinion of Dr. Giles Dawson.

[37]As in *Athenaeum*, March 30, 1901, 403.

[38]See La Boderie's letter in E. K. Chambers, *The Elizabethan Stage* (reprinted Oxford, 1951), III, 257–8; and *Tragedies*, pp. 591–2. John B. Gabel, in "The Original Version of Chapman's *Tragedy of Byron*, *JEGP* LXIII (1964), 433–40, argues that the scene of altercation between the women was an *interpolation*, not necessarily written by Chapman, that Chapman's letter refers to an earlier prohibition of the Byron plays secured by La Boderie, and that the masque in Act II is also an interpolation. The argument is cogent, but Chapman did not, when printing the plays, reject the masque, and accordingly we may not reject it either, when considering the structure and meaning of *The Tragedy*.

This, we recall, was his excuse in the matter of *The Old Joiner*. He continues:

Whoever it were that first plaied the bitter Informer before the frenche Ambassador for a matter so far from offence; And of so much honor for his maister [Henry IV] as those two partes containe, perform'd it with the Gall of a Wulff, and not of a man.[39]

Intransigent, querulous, pulling over the velvet hand of the appeal the iron glove of self-justification: this is the Chapman tone.

He was, of course, much more conspicuous than at the time of the Flaskett business. He had produced his best comedy, *All Fools*, and his only resounding popular success in tragedy, *Bussy d'Ambois*; he had been (probably) portrayed upon the stage in the figure of Bellamont in Dekker and Webster's *Northward Ho* (1607; acted late 1605).[40] Bellamont is a poet and playwright upon whom the character Maybery offers to "bestow a piece of Plate . . . to bring [his] wife upon the stage" (sig. B2)—a hit at *The Old Joiner?*—and who has apparently written a tragedy of Caesar and Pompey (sig. E2v); he is "haunted by a Fury," i.e. *furor poeticus* (sig. E1), and is busy writing a "Tragedy of Astianax" to be presented in the French court, where at the performance he will stand "behind the Duke of Biron" (sig. E3). It is a slovenly portrait, whether Chapman sat for it or not, but it does strike off, by accident or design, what one comes to recognize as Chapman's curious combination of strength and vulnerability both in life and art. Here he was writing a series of tragic poems, secular oratorios upon sentences out of Plutarch, Seneca and Epictetus, distinguished alike for their moral seriousness and for what Webster above all admired in them, "that full and heightened style," and yet he was capable of such grotesqueries as the apparitions of *Bussy d'Ambois*, IV, ii, the unreadable, unactable humours of *Sir Giles Goosecap*, or the rash topicalities of the Byron plays—and capable, too, of rushing to the defence of the indefensible. So we find him, in *The Tears of Peace* and the Epistle Dedicatory to the *Iliads* of 1609, committing himself securely to "Learning, and her Lightner, Poesie," to that "circular" (his favorite word) existence in which art is the mirror of the moral order of its creator's being; but "the gaudie vulgar light/Burns up [his] good thoughts, form'd in temperate Night," and, thin-skinned as ever, he strikes all around him at "wolf-fac't worldlings"

[39]As in *Athenaeum*, April 6, 1901, 433.

[40]See Allardyce Nicoll, "The Dramatic Portrait of George Chapman," *PQ* XLI (1962), 215–28, who accepts the identification as "beyond question," and describes Bellamont as "a more or less faithful delineation of Chapman the poet."

and their "vainglorious bubbles and impieties," at the "stupide ignorants" who "whisper behind" him.[41]

Yet all apparently went well with him until 1612, when Prince Henry died. He was busy with his Homer, and with the composition of plays, had purged his melancholy with the tears of peace and emptied his commonplace book into the little volume called *Petrarchs Seven Penitential Psalms* (1612). The Homeric enterprise, to which he had been commanded by the Prince, was his chief concern; to gain the time for it he went heavily into debt, when, as he said, he might have been employed with some profit in writing more plays,[42] in expectation of £300 promised him on the completion of the translation. Then the blow fell: the money was not paid, the pension promised by the Prince on his death-bed was not forthcoming, the place of sewer in ordinary was not renewed, and the poet was "miserably lost."

Prince Henry died on November 6, 1612; his funeral was December 7. On December 11, Chapman's *Epicede* was entered for publication.[43] There is internal evidence that it was composed in haste: roughly the second half of its 640 lines is paraphrased, as Sidney Lee was the first to point out, from Politian's *Elegia sive Epicedion in Albierae Albitiae* (1546), an elegy on a fifteen-year-old girl, with appropriate addition of local references. The poem hardly counts among Chapman's more distinguished performances, but, written presumably in a tempest of genuine sorrow, it illustrates how he could see to read his favorite authorities (Ficino, Plutarch) even through his tears, and how the loss of his ideal, the "Incomparable Prince of Men," is so assimilated to the poet's generally mordant view of his times as to lend to a usually frigid genre the warmth, if not of a sacrificial flame, at least of an emotional bonfire. In this respect the elegy may profitably be contrasted with Donne's witty exercise upon the same occasion, his "Elegie upon the untimely death of the incomparable Prince Henry." For both Chapman and Donne, the Prince is imaged as the soul of the world, but Chapman not only cries out upon Death and Fate for "inverting" the world, but sets out a dismal picture of the "wilde Bore, Barbarisme" at large in a garden from which the "divine Ideas," the forming and civilizing influence of the Prince are withdrawn, where

> one wretched end
> Will take up all endeavours; Harpye Gaine,

---

[41]*Poems*, p. 195; *Homer*, I, 15.

[42]As in *Athenaeum* Apr. 6, 1901, 433.

[43]*Poems*, pp. 451–2. For a study of the elegies on Prince Henry see E. C. Wilson, *Prince Henry and English Literature* (Ithaca, 1946), pp. 128 ff.

> Pandar to Gote, Ambition; goulden Chaine
> To true mans freedome; not from heav'n let fal
> To draw men up; but shot from Hell to hale
> All men, as bond slaves, to his Turckish den,
> For Toades, and Adders, far more fit then men.[44]

This vision of anarchy, of the triumph of the base passions, is similar to the description of the enemies to "Learning" in *The Tears of Peace* (11. 402–408), the "inverted men," "whose soules no more contain/The actuall light of Reason, then darke beasts," who giant-like throw "goulden hils gainst heaven"; the Prince was the exemplar of true Learning, his mind enriched by "Heroique formes," inspiring the "holy rages" of poets, a prince of peace.

The argument of the elegy is carried forward in Chapman's usual cumbrous vehicle, trimmed with glosses, fuelled with borrowed similes, and (as noted above) enlarged by paraphrase and adaptation; the epistle, to his friend and creditor Henry Jones, is a page from the letter-book of a disappointed man. It begins (in accents reminiscent of *The Tears of Peace* (11. 1010–1015):

The most unvaluable and dismaiful loss of my most deare and Heroical Patrone, Prince HENRY, hath so stricken all my spirits to the earth, that I will never more dare, to looke up to any greatnesse; but resolving the little rest of my poore life to obscuritie, and the shadow of his death; prepare ever hereafter, for the light of heaven.[45]

He owes Jones money, and offers him this "publication of his gratitude," as an "unprofitable" kind of instalment on a debt which will be paid in full when God blesses his "future labours." This is presumably the "best deserving friende" Henry Jones to whom Chapman inscribed a copy of the *Iliads*, and who had often relieved him of money difficulties because "[Chapman] was a pleasant wittie fellow, & one whome [Jones] delighted [in] and loved." Chapman's debt to Jones was secured by a bond, guaranteed by his brother Thomas of Hitchin (described as a "man of good wealth") and entered into in this very month of November, 1612.[46] The complaint of the poet's poverty mingles with the resolution upon religious retirement in the occasional productions of the years following. In the epistle to Francis, Lord Russell which accompanies *Eugenia* (1614), he affirms that

[44]*Poems*, p. 257.
[45]*Ibid.*, p. 253.
[46]These transactions are described by Sisson and Butman, "*George Chapman, 1612–22*," 190.

"religious contemplation is the whole scopes, and setters up of my poore lifes rest"; in the verse-preface to *Pro Vere* (1622) he is still complaining of "the *Envies*, and *Infortunes*" following him. He was probably living in obscurity, perhaps at Hitchin, for part at least of the period during which the Homer and the translations of Musaeus (if this is not early) and Hesiod were completed, that is from about 1614 to 1620.[47] But, before that, seeking a replacement for Prince Henry in Robert Carr, Earl of Somerset, he wrote himself down an ass, it is sad to say, with *Andromeda Liberata*.

Late in 1613 the town was buzzing with the Essex-Somerset-Overbury scandal.[48] Consider the timing. On September 25, after a lengthy legal process conspicuous for its flouting of common justice, common sense and common decency, Lady Frances Howard secured the annulment of her marriage to the Earl of Essex, alleging his impotence; Sir Thomas Overbury had died in the Tower ten days before; on November 3, Carr was created Earl of Somerset; on December 26 he was married to Lady Frances, who wore her hair loose, being accredited a virgin by a committee of sad and serious matrons. Chapman's poem was entered on March 16, and published while the affair was still fresh, though not yet given the fillip of the Overbury murder case, the continued allegory and not so dark conceit of the work being that Andromeda (Lady Frances), bound to a barren rock (Essex), to be the spoil of the sea-monster (the savage multitude), is rescued by Perseus (Somerset), and happy generation issuing in a "renowned Progenie" is to be looked for.

The poem, is, of course, much more than this: in this inflated and fuliginous production Chapman mounted his most elaborate and sustained attack upon "Opinion" and the monster multitude, an attack complete with vanguard, the crabbed prose preface "to the prejudicate and peremptory reader" and the fulsome couplets of the epistle dedicatory to Somerset; and rearguard too, the "free and offenceles justification" for the poem which he was forced to publish in the same year. *Nihil a veritate nec virtute remotius quam vulgaris opinio*, says the title page. *Andromeda Liberata* is, in fact, a poetic editorial, aimed at "such as backebite the highest."

Having translated his "Argument" word for word from Natalis

---

[47]*Poems*, pp. 271, 339; Sisson and Butman, 190.
[48]There is a condensed account in Jacquot, pp. 51–4; the best account is still in S. R. Gardiner, *History of England from the Accession of James I to the Outbreak of Civil War, 1603–1642* (London, 1883–7), II, chs. xvii, xx.

Comes, he begins his address to the Earl and Countess with a pronouncement which serves as "sentence" to the whole,

> As nothing under heaven is more remov'd
> From Truth & virtue, then *Opinions* prov'd
> By vulgar *Voices*: So is nought more true
> Nor soundly virtuous then things held by few:
> Whom *Knowledge* (entered by the sacred line,
> And governd evermore by grace divine)
> Keepes in the narrow path to spacious heaven,
> And therefore, should no knowing spirit be driven
> From fact, nor purpose; for the spleens prophane
> Of humours errant, and Plebeian,[49]

and continues, after a fine passage on the "soules Pulse, *Poesie*," with a disquisition on the *forming* power of the soul to subdue the passions (adapted from Ficino, *Comm. in Convivium Platonis*) and of the soul's "Regent" Reason to order the "civill bodie of a man." These noble activities he professes to find exemplified in the characters of the pair to whom he "humbly and faithfully" presents his poem, a poem not for the "ungodly Vulgars" who are dismissed in the first 26 lines of it as "in nought but misrule regulare," and unable, being poisoned by spleen, to perceive the innocence which has been demonstrated by "Joves ballance" in the hands of "Kings and their Peeres." Thereafter he develops his narrative, punctuating it at first with such *sententiae* as

> *No truth of excellence was ever seene,*
> *But bore the venome of the Vulgars spleene*

or

> *With noblest names and bloods is still embrewd*
> *The monstrous beast, the ravenous multitude,*

these being the following squibs of his initial explosion, harping on the divine innocence of his Andromeda ("bound to a *barraine* Rocke") and leading up to a devastating analysis of public opinion and its power (11. 161–214), so perceptive, so prophetic of the *News of the World* and the slander sheets that one can forgive its author such enormities as

> And now came roring to the tied, the Tide,

which just precedes it. The monster coming up from the sea to devour Andromeda bears "in one masse mixt" the image of the people,

[49] *Poems*, p. 305.

"greedie of disastrous sights/And newes," for whom "any ill/Is to their appetites, their supreme good," men of a spiced conscience who welcome innovation and cosily gloat over the troubles of the great. But suddenly appears Perseus, the ideal man, and the poet rises to a commendation of his "corporeall grace," the mirror of his mind, and to a highly technical description of his "temperate corporature," the perfect mixture of the elements in him; from that to a comparably technical description of the astrological influences which bore upon the attraction of this Venus to this Mars; from that, finally, to a celebration (based on Ficino) of the omnipotence of Love:

All things submit to Love, but love to none.

The poem swings jerkily from one paradox to another: "he dies that loves"; "himselfe in her he found"; he is a "Homicide" who "man to be borne lets"—a dangerous observation that, as it turned out, but then the whole poem was absurd, what with its "Parcarum Epithalamion," a hymn to generation, and its "apodosis," in which the poet commends to his noble patron the achievement of "Persean victories" over avarice, atheism, barbarism, the monsters who "kill the Man-informing Arts."

Yet, forced by scandalous interpretations to justify it, Chapman rose above the occasion, and (perhaps disingenuously) uttered from the muddle of this low business his most resonant statement of the esoteric nature of high poetic speech, in the prose preface to *A Free, and Offenceles Justification* (1614), an argument anticipating that of his friend Henry Reynolds in *Mythomystes*. The theory is in itself generally important and interesting, and I shall deal with it at length below; in the immediate circumstances, Chapman grounds his case on the inevitable *ambiguity* of poetic speech, which the mob "giving up their understandings to their affections," and "evermore baying lowdest at the most eminent Reputations," have wilfully and maliciously misinterpreted, "straining the Allegorie past [its] intentionall limits, [to] make it give blood." The poet will have nothing of their gross opinions; he has never written for the many at any time; in this case he has reason to believe that his poem has "already past the test of some of the most Judiciall and Noble of this Kingdome," and he retires "within the Castle of [his] Innocence." His conscience is clear:

The Loves of the right vertuous and truly noble, I have ever as much esteemed, as despised the rest: finding ever of the first sort, in all degrees, as worthy as any of my rancke, till (having enough to doe, in mine owne necessary ends, hating to insinuate and labour their confirmation, and encrease of opinion, further then their owne free judgements would excite and direct them) I still met with undermining laborers for them selves, who (esteeming all worth their own, which they detract from others) diminisht me much in some changeable estimations . . . whose supplies yet farre better have still brought me unsought: and till this unequall impression opprest me, I stood firme up with many, now onely, with God and my selfe. For the violent hoobub, setting my song to their owne tunes, have made it yeeld so harsh and distastefull a sound to my best friends, that my Integritie, even they hold, affected with the shrill eccho thereof, by reflexion; receiving it from the mouths of others.[50]

Chapman's syntax does not need embarrassment or passion to complicate it, but these causes are superadded here. I find this a very moving paragraph. He says two things which may well excite the admiration of any fair critic: first, that the praise and love even of the best is no good unless it is freely given; second, that the kind of esteem which can be turned away by popular opinion is worthless— but it hurts to lose it. Later he says: "If my whole life were layd on the racke, it could never accuse me for a *Satyrist* or *Libeller*, to play with worthie mens reputations." This is very fine too, and yet the uneasy thought worms its way back beneath the palisade of all this protest: how could he have written what he did without seeing how exposed it all was to false constructions? The "Dialogus," which follows,[51] may tell us.

"Your *Perseus* is displeasd," begins the accuser *Pheme* (Rumour), "and sleighteth now/Your worke, as idle, and as servile, yow." That hurt, badly, the poet who believed in the perhaps reversible proposition that a just man is a free man.[52] "Can I seeme servile to him," he cries, "when ahlas/My whole *Lifes freedome*, shewes I never was?" His friends, it appears, have forsaken him; well, "let them flie," their motives are subtle, but he is "made of downe right, flat simplicitie." He goes on to escape from the word "homicide" by a quotation from Ficino, and from "bound to a *barraine* rocke" by the angry observation that only "barraine Malice" could ever think of this epithet being applied to a man (i.e. to Essex). If we are to take all this as it appears, Chapman either did not realize how far even "the prejudicate and peremptory reader" would be happy to go in interpreting his lines, or, he simply decided to go the whole way with Carr, come what would— "one may be worth all."

[50] *Poems*, p. 329.
[51] *Ibid.*, pp. 332–5.
[52] Cf. the epigraph to *The Tragedy of Caesar and Pompey, Tragedies*, p. 342.

I prefer the second alternative. I see Chapman as the sort of man who passionately and irrevocably espouses the cause of a patron the more because that patron has obvious imperfections and is obviously vulnerable. Having seized on what quite honestly he takes to be a virtue in his patron (or employer, leader), he rallies the more to that virtue as he finds it a seeming vice to others, and stubbornly clings to his commitment long after he comes to recognize its futility or even its danger, to himself or to the object of his devotion. Be this as it may, Chapman stuck faithfully to Somerset, dedicating his *Odysses* "To the most noble, now living restorer of the Ulyssean Temper; of solide vertue the most secret, and therein sacred Sustainer; of Popular Vapor the most open, profest, and Heroicall Contemner; of all True Honor the most Truth-like, unalterable, and invincible Deserver,"[53] as also his *Crowne of all Homers Worckes* (1624?). Both in this epistle and in his dedicatory poem to Somerset before *Pro Vere* (1622), Chapman speaks of Somerset's "calme Retreate" from the ill and babble of the world; this action, forced upon his patron after his release from the Tower in 1622, the poet characteristically regards as evidence of the "free minde"; it was a course he favoured himself as a fruit of virtue, though, as we have noted, his own "retirements" may have been politic as well as pious. It is also possible that in *The Tragedy of Chabot* (written c. 1612, revised c. 1622), Chapman asserted the innocence of Somerset in the political allegory of the play.[54] For his part, Somerset helped to "sustaine/A *Life*, that other subtler *Lords* disdaine[d],"[55] but by how much in cash has not transpired.

The querulous note which runs through all these documents was by this time habitual. He had aged into evil days, verminous times, was surrounded by evil tongues. "Bright ELIZA's blessed raigne," which passed all "fore Races, for all sorts of Men,/Schollers, and Souldiers, Courtiers, Counsellours," was long gone—that was written in that year of disgrace 1622.[56] The handsome folios of the *Homer*, the work he was born to do, stood in the stationers' shops, followed by the Musaeus, the *Georgics* of Hesiod, the *Batrachomyomachia* and Homeric Hymns, and Juvenal's Fifth Satire; but the performer of all these labours seems to have been lonely, poor, and testy to the end. A fog of anticlimax drifts about the last days of the collaborators in *Eastward Ho*; perhaps James, out of his knowledge of *goetia*, laid a

[53]*Homer*, II, xii.
[54]Described by N. D. Solve, *Stuart Politics in Chapman's Tragedy of Chabot* (Michigan, 1929).   [55]*Poems*, p. 339.
[56]*Ibid.*, p. 340; for the events of 1622 see Gardiner, *History . . . 1603–1642*, iv.

slow curse on them for defaming his Scots. The worst was that Jonson and Chapman, strong spirits both, traders in learned compliment, fellow-contemners of the mob, of chapbook poets and gaudy syco-phants, fell away from each other in the end. They had been friends for years (Jonson told Drummond that "Chapman and Fletcher were loved of him"), collaborators more than twice, if Chapman's was the "second pen" which shared in the first draft of *Sejanus*, for which he wrote his most elegant commendatory poem,[57] were both learned with-out "degrees"—except Jonson's honorary ones. Here perhaps a prophecy of the breach, for Jonson stood much upon his triumphs, spread himself in his great days, and got to think of himself as an institution, in the provision of masks for the court and otherwise. It has been suggested[58] that Chapman knew about Jonson's marginalia on the *Homer*,[59] and that they would cause him more irritation than could be drowned in a friendly cup of canary. But this is very doubtful, and besides the comments are not extensive, being a few casual and semi-jocular notes of misinterpretations (e.g., opposite the reference to Horace in the prose preface: *male intellexisti Horatium, mi Chap-manne*; and to the notes on *Il.* III. 213: *o quam inepte haec omnia, et sequentia*), and objections to Chapman's abuse of J. C. Scaliger, marked tersely *scurriliter*. Jonson told Drummond that he had by heart "a piece of Chapmans translation of ye 13 of the Iliads, which he [thought] well done." No, the trouble more likely arose, as Herford and Simpson suspected, because Chapman sided with Inigo Jones,[60] who had produced the pageant for the Middle Temple mask of 1613, to whom he dedicated his translation of Musaeus, and who may be the "just friend" appealed to at 1. 149 of the "Invective wrighten by Mr. George Chapman against Mr. Ben: Johnson."[61] It appears that the pretensions of Jonson's "Execration upon Vulcan," written upon the loss of his library in 1623, grated on Chapman, and he wrote these violent lines in "reply." We have no reason to believe that Jonson ever saw them.

Chapman had the "Execration" before him as he wrote.

> Your sacred deske
> (The wooden fountayne of the Mightye Muses)
> (Alas) is burned,

---

[57] *Poems*, pp. 358–63; see *Ben Jonson*, I, 34.
[58] By Phyllis Bartlett, in *Poems*, p. 477.
[59] In his copy of the *Whole Works*, in the Fitzwilliam Museum, transcribed by Percy Simpson, *TLS*, March 3, 1932, 155.
[60] *Ben Jonson*, X, App. xxiv.
[61] *Poems*, pp. 374–8.

he observes nastily, and goes on to quote from Jonson's rueful card-index to his shelves. But he seems to have looked back grimly at his own poem to *Sejanus* too, and in deliberate anger reversed the judgment of Jonson set forth there. There, he compared Jonson to "the wealth-contracting Jeweller" who gathers his "Pearles and deare Stones, from richest shores & streames" (i.e. from Tacitus, &c.), cuts and sets them in his own "Goulden Verse," thus providing a dignified apologia for Jonson's learned method in writing Roman tragedy; he explained Jonson's delay in writing tragedy as the "vertuous selfe-mistrust" of his "chaste *Muse*"; he associated himself with his subject in disdain of the poet-hating multitude; and he wished his friend well in their common ideal, "not making *Fame* our object, but *good life*" (his touchstone, we remember, for true "Learning"). In the "Invective," he tells his "just friend" that Jonson "onlye reading showed," tells Jonson that his scenes were "Labord and Unnaturall"; he accuses him in every line of arrogance and self-adulation, and of courting cheap praise, "all mens Admirations"; and ends, or breaks off rather, with this finger-wagging observation:

> If of mans true and worthiest knowledge rude,
> Whiche is to knowe and be, one Compleat man,
> And that not all the swelling Ocean
> Of Artes and sciences, cann poure both In;
> If that brave skill, then when thou didst begine
> To studdye letters, thy great witt had plide
> Freelye and onlye thy Disease of pride
> In vulgar praise, had never bound thy . . .

However we take it, it is a sad affair.

It would be pleasant to believe William Oldys' tradition that "Chapman was much resorted to latterly by young persons of parts as a poetical chronicle; but was very choice who he admitted to him, and preserved in his own Person the dignity of Poetry—which he compared to the flower of the Soul, which disclaims to open its leaves to the eye of a smoking taper."[62] But there were no "sons of George." Like Jonson in his "Elegie on My Muse;" he might have cried:

> What's left a Poet, when his Muse is gone?
> Sure, I am dead, and know it not.

He died in May, 1634, and was buried in the churchyard of St. Giles in the Fields. Whether his monument (by Inigo Jones) was slow in

---

[62]Oldys ms. note in B.M. copy of Gerard Langbaine, *An Account of the English Dramatick Poets* (1691), p. 58.

erection or not, William Habington, in a poem "To [his] honoured Friend and Kinsman, R. St. Esquire" [1635?], complained

> that *Chapmans* reverend ashes must
> Lye rudely mingled with the vulgar dust,

and hoped that someone "devout to Poesie" would move his corpse inside the "warme Church."[63] Chapman is still commemorated by a stone set against the west wall of the eighteenth-century church, in a corner.

Chapman, writes M. Jacquot, summing him up judiciously, was "une nature orgueilleuse," "convaincu de l'opposition de la vie spirituelle et du monde," religious but "vraisemblablement un ancien soldat."[64] Both Habington and Wood use the word "reverend"; Jonson (in his verses before the Hesiod) calls him "worthy and honour'd" friend. He was a good man.

[63] *The Poems of William Habington*, ed. K. Allott (Liverpool, 1948).
[64] Jacquot, p. 58.

OR FICINO, Plato was *medicus animarum*; for Chapman, following his preceptor, books were physic, not lumber. The unsympathetic modern, following in the deep footsteps of M. Schoell, may find the borrowings lumpish and undigested (with definite overtones of Ovid's *rudis indigestaque moles*), but even Comes' *Mythologiae*, barbarous and pedantic as it (with Giraldi and Cartari and the emblem-books) appears to the modern Hellenist, provided a vocabulary for "philosophical" thought, a dense texture of cosmological symbol analogous to the anthropological lore available to the twentieth-century "learned" poet. But Ficino *informed* Chapman's mind in another sense, was the source of what it is not absurd to call a regimen of mental health, a compass for the soul's voyage, which he never wholly abandoned.[1] The fog and the exaltation of neoplatonism, and the longing to be a sage standing in God's holy fire, were his; also the melancholy and evangelical zeal smouldering (in a cold climate), and, alas, the appalling eclecticism and imprecision of the most unphilosophic of philosophical movements, which sought wisdom and became contented with rhetoric. (Except for Epictetus, and I cannot see that Chapman did more with Epictetus than search him like a Puritan for proof-texts, his main sources in "moral philosophy," Plutarch's *Moralia*, Erasmus' *Adagia*, Cicero's *De Officiis*, are monuments of eclecticism, full of high general sentence—as is Seneca—and particular copy-book paradox,

---

[1]Cf. Sears Jayne, "Ficino and the Platonism of the English Renaissance," *Comparative Literature* IV (1952), 214–38; Ernst Cassirer, *The Platonic Renaissance in England* (London, 1953), p. 111: "Chapman lives so completely in the matter and thought of Ficino's work that his own poems are often no more than versifications or poetic paraphrases of well-known teachings of the Florentine philosophy." (An over-statement: note the implications of "well-known.")

and for any man with an Elizabethan grammar school training the combination was irresistible. But this is blurring the picture.) It was the occultism of the Florentines which attracted him first, and afterwards the platonic idealism, supported by the individualistic ethics of stoicism—always seductive to one who lives—or thinks he lives—in an age of disintegrating values. Chapman began by dreaming of an English Academy, and ended as lonely as Milton.

As we stumble over the miscellaneous furniture of Chapman's mind, touched by the fitful gleams of candle and moon in *The Shadow of Night*, we can at least begin to classify it with the aid of the authorities on the neoplatonic tradition, though there are some odd local touches and provincial aberrations.

The epistle to Roydon[2] is not an introduction to the poem ("this poore and strange trifle") but to the kind of mental activity of which the poem is presumably evidence, "that *Herculean* labour," "the deepe search of knowledge," undertaken in a "rapture of delight" and having as its effect the subjugation of the "monstrous affections to most beautiful judgement." The poet announces his rejection of the "profit-ravisht" world, of the outward world of the senses and the passions, and his dedication to the contemplative life of inward vision and purification, the life of soul-forming: in the Ficinian sense, "philosophy."

The subject-matter of this discipline is not defined: Chapman implies that such is the learning entertained by the "school of night," and, as I have already noted, these studies were reputedly in the occult sciences, alchemical and mathematical, designed to warm what Chapman calls "freezing science," frozen, one supposes, in the Aristotelian categories. The epistle emphasizes the mental or spiritual posture of the initiates who pursue secret things "with invocation, fasting, watching; yea not without having drops of their soules like an heavenly familiar." This is the condition of *creative* melancholy, the Saturnian state of the night-blooming seer.

All those who have invented anything great in any of the nobler arts [wrote Ficino] did so especially when they took refuge in the citadel of the Soul, withdrawing from the body. . . . Therefore Aristotle writes that all outstanding men in any art were of melancholy temper, either born so or having become so by continual meditation. . . . The melancholy humor invites and helps the soul to gather itself into itself.[3]

2 *Poems*, p. 19.
3 Quoted in P. O. Kristeller, *The Philosophy of Marsilio Ficino* (New York, 1943), pp. 304–5. See also Lawrence Babb, "The Background to *Il Penseroso*," *SP* XXXVII (1940), 257–73. The definitive study of melancholy as malady and temperament,

Such are Bruno's "heroical spirits" and such the true professors of *magia*. Such, too, is the solitary meditating alchemist, engaged on the Divine Work—which like Chapman's hymns begins in Chaos and ends with a phoenix—whose secret is revealed to the sage either in dreams or by "familiars." Such is the "superior being" symbolized in Dürer's "Melancolia," which is associated with night and the moon.[4] The Aristotelian doctrine quoted by Ficino makes possible an equation between *furor melancolicus* and *furor divinus*,[5] and opens the way for a theory of poetic inspiration, which, incidentally, Chapman obviously assumes here without stating it directly.

For Chapman the pose was congenial because the condition was constitutional—no doubt of that at all, even without the evidence of the probably spurious sonnet to *All Fools*.[6] He was perfectly aware that melancholy is malignant as well as creative: witness Byron's "adust and melancholy choler" and the melancholy of Count St. Anne in *Monsieur D'Olive*, as contrasted with the "holy fury" of the scholar Dowsecer in *An Humorous Day's Mirth*, and the linking of "proud Melancholie" with lunacy and "direct Madnesse" in the epistle to *Sejanus*.[7] The postscript to his *Masque* is illuminating in this connection:

The Hill of the Muses (which all men must climb in the regular way to Truth) is said of old to be forked. And the two points of it, parting at the top, are *insania* and *divinus furor*. *Insania* is that which every rank-brained writer and judge of poetical writing is rapt withal, when he presumes either to write or censure the height of poesy, and that transports him with humour, vain glory, and pride, most profane and sacrilegious; when *divinus furor* makes gentle and noble the never-so-truly inspired writer.[8]

Here the context is purely literary, and the conventional idea extrapolated to make a characteristic invective; but the most sympathetic

---

and its relation to the iconography of Saturn, is Raymond Klibansky, Erwin Panofsky and Fritz Saxl, *Saturn and Melancholy* (London, 1964). For "creative" melancholy see especially Part III. The authors, in their incidental references to melancholy in English Renaissance poetry, cite Daniel, Donne and Milton, but not Chapman.

[4] See the comment on Bruno's views in relation to the Ralegh circle in Philip Henderson, *Christopher Marlowe* (London, 1952), p. 46; on *magia*, see H. C. Agrippa, *De Occulta Philosophia*, I, lx; III, iii; E. Panofsky, *Albrecht Dürer* (4th ed., Princeton, 1955), pp. 156, 160. Jacquot thinks (p. 22) that Chapman's "familiar" is derived from the idea of a δαίμον in the *Mysteries* of Iamblicus, as translated by Ficino.

[5] Panofsky, *Dürer*, pp. 165–7.

[6] Printed in *Comedies*, p. 725.

[7] *Poems*, p. 360.

[8] *Comedies*, p. 444.

reader, looking at Chapman from the outside, as it were, is aware of what we should now call a kind of manic-depressive alternation in him, for which the best contemporary diagnosis is that of Thomas Walkington:

The melancholic man is said of the wise to be *aut Deus aut Daemon*, either angel of heaven or friend of hell, for in whomsoever this humour hath dominion, the soule is either wrapt up into an *Elysium* and paradise of blisse by a heavenly contemplation, or into a direfull hellish purgatory by a cynicall meditation.

And André de Laurens adds:

When this humour groweth hot, by the vapours of blood, it causeth as it were, a kind of divine ravishment, called *Enthousiasma*, which stirreth men up to plaie the Philosophers, Poets, and also to Prophesie.[10]

Melancholy and rage are "noble passions":[11] they inform *The Shadow of Night*.

The theme of melancholy will recur, for it is one main clue to Chapman, but it is especially appropriate as an introduction to this poem, which is among other things Chapman's *Il Penseroso*. What else it is probably derives in part from the poet's recollection of Ficino's four "furies," ascending from that *furor poeticus* which tempers the various parts of the soul, to *mysteria* or "skil" of nature's secrets, to *vaticinium*, the moral and prophetic power, to *amor*, in which art converses with the divine majesty.[12] Certainly the poet assumes the presence in the poem of all these powers, though most of its modern readers are not willing to grant it any power at all, and find it, professing "form" as its subject, formless and amorphous beyond bearing.[13]

The Shadow of Night, a poem in two hymns, "Hymnus in Noctem" and "Hymnus in Cynthiam," each with its gloss mainly giving the sources for the epithets and mythological similes, belongs to a genre of didactic verse more widely practised by the continental humanists

[9] *The Opticke Glasse of Humours* (1607), f. 64v.
[10] *A Discourse of the Preservation of the Sight* (1599), p. 85.
[11] E. Wind, *Pagan Mysteries in the Renaissance* (London, 1958), p. 69.
[12] *Marsilio Ficino's Commentary on Plato's Symposium*, trans. Sears Jayne (Columbia, Mo., 2nd ed., 1944), pp. 231–2.
[13] So Schoell: "La pensée reste amorphe et ne progresse selon aucune règle"; and C. S. Lewis: "The 'In Noctem' suffers from having that amorphous subject which never attracts a good writer and always exposes a bad one: the general state of the world today." But Janet Spens calls *The Shadow of Night* a "dream-fugue" (*ESEA* [1925], 161). The chief detailed study is R. W. Battenhouse, "Chapman's *The Shadow of Night*: An Interpretation," *SP* XXXVIII (1941), 584–608, to which I am considerably indebted.

of the Renaissance than by English poets, though Chapman seems to have had some imitators.[14] These quasi-"scientific" (in the arcane sense), quasi-allegorical productions, with a mythological vocabulary and a theological or cosmological ("Uranian") interest, addressed often—as Chapman's is—to fit audience though few,[15] lie historically and thematically between such antiquities as the Orphic hymns (which Chapman may have known about) and the immensely popular and influential work of Du Bartas. But however much *The Shadow of Night* may display the hermetic panoply of its kind, it is at once simpler in its "messages" and more complicated in its detail than, say, Spenser's *Hymns*; simpler because it gives voice to a set of obsessions rather than an imaginative vision, and with the complication of imperfection rather than of profundity.

Between them the two hymns deal with the two sorts of "temporal beatitude" according to Ficino: the contemplative (*religio*) and the active (*justitia*).[16] The first hymn is contemplative, concerned with poetic wisdom and its enemies; the second turns to the life of action, to politics and morals. The first is concerned with art, the second with nature.

A pleasantly discursive essay might be written on Night and the poetic sensibility in English literature, taking into account Drummond, Milton, Young, Thomson, Dylan Thomas and others; but it would have to begin with Chapman, the first, I think, to sing of

> darkness aiding intellectual light,
> And sacred silence whisp'ring truths divine,

a theme to which he returned appropriately and elegantly in the "vigiliae" of *Eugenia*:

> Now to the Nestfull woods, the Broode of Flight
> Had on their black wings brought, the zealous Night,
> When Fames friends, op't the windowes they shut in,

---

[14]See, e.g., Odette de Mourgues, *Metaphysical, Baroque & Précieux Poetry* (Oxford, 1953). Among English poems with some likenesses to *The Shadow of Night*, one may mention Drayton's *Endimion and Phoebe* (1595), Thos. Edwards' *Cephalus and Procris* (1595), which opens with "a paraphrisis of the Night," and has some verbal echoes of Chapman, and perhaps Nathaniel Baxter's *Sir Philip Sidney's Ourania* (1606), a Bartasian cosmological poem set in the frame of Cynthia-worship.

[15]Cf. Nuysement (*Les visions hermétiques*): "Je parle aux entendus, esloignez-vous, prophanes, Cor mon âme s'esleve aux plus secrets arcanes," quoted in de Mourgues, p. 42.

[16]E. Panofsky, *Studies in Iconology* (New York, 1939), p. 138.

To barre Daies worldly light; and Mens rude Din;
In Tumults raisd about their fierce affaires,
That deafen heaven to their distracted praiers,
With all the vertues; Grave Religion
That slept with them all day, to ope began
Her Eares, and Red Eyes; hearing every way
The clocks, and knells of Cities, and the Bay
Of Countrie Dogs, that mock mens daily Carck,
And after them, all night, at shadowes barke.
　　Though all Fames brazen Gates, and windowes stoode
Ope day and night, yet had her tendred broode
Close in their private chambers, their owne fashion,
Silence, and Night, doe best fit Contemplation.[17]

Behind all this lies the paradox, adhered to by religious mystics and occultists alike, that Night fosters the inward wisdom, the knowledge of divine things, by blotting out the sense impressions by which we receive the knowledge of ordinary life; and, since the senses are the sources of corruption of the soul and of mistaken knowledge, Night purifies the mind, acts as a purge for pure spirits, as Michelangelo put it. The poet goes altarwards by owl-light, in this half-way house.[18]

But Chapman's "vaste présence maternelle," as M. Jacquot felicitously terms it, is more deeply mythologized, out of Natalis Comes of course, collecting the Hesiodic and other sources, but also with a hint (perhaps) of the Orphic theogony, or (also perhaps) from Pico; Battenhouse describes it as a primitive metaphysical darkness which is not evil.[19] Since the argument of the "Hymnus in Noctem" depends on the antithesis of a "forming" or shaping soul working upon a shapeless and resistant matter, one thinks at once of the microcosmic analogy in Ficinian philosophy between soul-body and celestial-mundane realms, in which man is "a rational soul participating in the divine mind, employing a body,"[20] and consequently Chapman's Night resembles the neoplatonic *nous*, of which, for Chapman at least, the psychological equivalent would be the "higher" soul, what he calls

---

[17]*Poems*, p. 282.

[18]Michelangelo, sonnet xliv. See also Valeriano, *Hieroglyphia sive de sacris Aegyptorum*, &c [1575], fol. 146v, on Athena's bird, and a curious composition collected by Dornavius, *Amphitheatrum . . . joco-seriae*, &c. (1619), I, 699–718.

[19]On Orphism, cf. W. K. C. Guthrie, *The Greeks and their Gods* (Beacon Paperbacks, 1955), ch. XI; the hint in Pico is suggested by Wind, p. 66n.; Battenhouse, "Chapman's *Shadow of Night*," 585–6. On the Orphic *nox*, see Frances A. Yates, *Giordano Bruno and the Hermetic Tradition* (London, 1964), p. 177.

[20]Panofsky, *Studies in Iconology*, p. 137.

(at 1. 11) his "working soule," which, the senses being "bound," can control

> The court of skil, compact of misterie,
> Wanting but franchisement and memorie
> To reach all secrets.
> ("HN," 11. 13–15)

Following Du Bartas,[21] the poet invokes Night "rempli d'images fabuleuses," matrix of all the cosmic host, and also his heavenly Muse to whom he prays for tears to weep "the shipwrecke of the world," for verbal artillery to "breake harts" with "the threates of vertue." Then he introduces the paradox upon which the hymn is grounded: such is the orderless state of the world, that

> when unlightsome, vast, and indigest
> The formelesse matter of this world did lie,

and Night filled every place with her divinity, there was more perfection than now:

> Chaos had soule without a bodie then,
> Now bodies live without the soules of men,
> Lumps being digested; monsters, in our pride.

Men are fallen into a second night, "a stepdame Night of minde," *Nox mentis* (Comes), where the soul is "defamde" and the intellectual faculties are blind. The poet describes an inverted world, or world of confusion: "religious curb, that manadgd men in bounds" (cf. "Ceremony" in *Hero and Leander*) is cast away, and men are turned by self-love into "Calydonian bores," or their "manless" natures are by ambition and "selfe-desire" shrunk into lumps.

> If then we frame mans figure by his minde,
> And that at first, his fashion was assignd,
> Erection in such God-like excellence
> For his soules sake, and her intelligence:
> She so degenerate, and growne deprest,
> Content to share affections with a beast,
> The shape wherewith he should be now indude,
> Must beare no signe of mans similitude.
> ("HN," 11. 123–130)

It is therefore the function of "Promethean Poets" to figure forth in living verse such creatures as centaurs and harpies, to show men what they have become; or, like Orpheus, show the force of human wisdom

---

[21]Jacquot, p. 63n.

"in calming the infernall kinde,/To wit, the perturbations of his minde." The poet is a shaper, being "enobled with a deathlesse love /Of things eternall."

The paraphrase of the argument is indeed pedestrian, nor does the poem advance, as a didactic poem should, to a conclusion. It just smoulders on like an ill-lit fire, from which some repetitive and barely-glimmering flames start up and die in smoke. "Heavenly contemplation" and "cynical meditation" alternate: for example, beginning at 1. 171, two similes, the first of the painter's "counterfet," the second of rural dancing (which reminds one of the great image in *East Coker*), exhibit further the deformity and shapelessness of beastly men; this is followed by a graceful aubade and evening-song ending with the proclamation of "scilence, studie, ease, and sleepe." The poet invokes the Eumenides, "chast daughters" of Night, and then in a passage reminiscent of *The Faerie Queene*, I, ix (Spenser's Despair is a melancholy intellectual too), consecrates himself to brooding solitude:

> Rich-tapird sanctuarie of the blest,
> Pallace of Ruth, made all of teares, and rest,
> To thy blacke shades and desolation,
> I consecrate my life; and living mone,
> Where furies shall for ever fighting be,
> And adders hisse the world for hating me,
> Foxes shall barke, and Night-ravens belch in grones,
> And owles shall hollow my confusions:
> There will I furnish up my funerall bed,
> Strewd with the bones and relickes of the dead.
> Atlas shall let th' Olimpick burthen fall,
> To cover my untombed face withall.
> And when as well, the matter of our kind,
> As the materiall substance of the mind,
> Shall cease their revolutions, in abode
> Of such impure and ugly period,
> As the old essence, and insensive prime:
> Then shall the ruines of the fourefold time,
> Turnd to that lumpe (as rapting Torrents rise)
> For ever murmure forth my miseries.
>   ("HN," 11. 268–87)

With such invocations of the return of the *prima materia* the poem assumes an apocalyptic tone, appropriate to its prophetic function; and, sermon-like, its closing passages constitute an exhortation to the "living spirits" of like minds, that they should shun the light of base affections, reject the "idolatrous desire of gold," and "create in serious truth,/A bodie figur'd to [their] vertues ruth," to "fall worm-like on the ground,"

> And from th'infectious dunghill of this Round,
> From mens brasse wits, and golden foolerie,
> Weepe, weepe your soules, into felicitie.

Night sends from her ivory gate "sweet Protean dreames," but from the port of horn "graver dreames inspir'd with prophesies":

> All you possess with indepressed spirits,
> Indu'd with nimble, and aspiring wits,
> Come consecrate with me, to sacred Night
> Your whole endevours, and detest the light,
> Sweete Peaces richest crowne is made of starres,
> Most certaine guides of honord Marinars,
> No pen can any thing eternall wright,
> That is not steept in humor of the Night.
> ("HN," 11. 370–377)

The poem thus becomes an appeal to would-be poets to emulate the "invocation, fasting, watching" of its preface, and to restore to a failing art its sacred fire. Yet the larger apocalyptic context is resumed in the conclusion: the Moon rises (heavy with epithets from the handbooks), and the poet prays for the presence of this gracious empress, "Till vertue flourish in the light of light," and the "revolutions" cease in the stillness envisioned at the end of the "Mutabilitie Cantos."

The "Hymnus in Noctem" is as tedious, as repetitious, as inflated as an evangelical sermon—which in a sense is what it is; Chapman is preaching the mantic, zealous, intuitive, visionary gospel of his neoplatonic sources. Yet the quality of the imagery is not of the refined, sleek or smooth pastoral sort which one might naturally associate with a mode so sophisticated as this. The impression is rather of "broken shapes of heroic grandeur," as Elizabeth Holmes noted,[22] and the objects of external nature, where they appear, are rough and massive, of the kind we associate with the romantic temperament, though Chapman's shades, precipices, and torrents were not inspired by any Alpine journey, but by the bleak and surrealistic landscapes of emblem books.

The "Hymnus in Cynthiam" is less formless, more chaste in

[22]Elizabeth Holmes, *Aspects of Elizabethan Imagery* (Oxford, 1929), p. 72. See also the characterization of Chapman's style by Marcello Pagnini, *Forme e Motivi nelle Poesie e nelle Tragedie di George Chapman* (Firenze, 1957), p. 65: "Il discorso poetico del Chapman contiene un'energia possente, grandiosa...."

expression, more intellectual and hence more difficult, more decorated, in fact more Spenserian, than its companion piece. Cynthia is first of all Queen Elizabeth:

Some call her Pandora: some Gloriana: some Cynthia: some Belphoebe: some Astraea: all by several names to express several loves: Yet all these names make but one celestial body, as all these loves meet to create but one soul.[23]

The analogy with Ralegh's "Cynthia," with Jonson's *Cynthia's Revels* (1600), which was written not for "ev'rie vulgar, and adult'rate braine" but for those who with Crites despise vanity and the "groveling thoughts" which dwell on the flesh, is obvious enough, and the adulation of "the mortal moon" is familiar to every reader of Elizabethan poetry. The "historical allegory" of the Hymn is most conspicuous in the first 120 lines, in such passages as

> In perfect circle of whose sacred state,
> The circles of our hopes are compassed:
> All wisedome, beautie, majestie and dread,
> Wrought in the speaking pourtrait of thy face,

or, expressing an oft-repeated fear:

> So (gracious Cynthia) in that sable day,
> When interposed earth takes thee away,
> (Our sacred chiefe and soveraigne generall,)
> As chrimsine a retreat, and steepe a fall
> We feare to suffer from this peace, and height,
> Whose thancklesse sweet now cloies us with receipt,

and especially in the conclusion of the first part:

> No otherwise, (O Queene celestiall)
> Can we beleeve Ephesias state wilbe
> But spoile with forreine grace, and change with thee.
> The purenesse of thy never-tainted life,
> Scorning the subject title of a wife,
> Thy bodie not composed in thy birth,
> Of such condensed matter as the earth,
> Thy shunning faithlesse mens societie,
> Betaking thee to hounds, and Archerie
> To deserts, and inaccessible hills,[24]
> Abhorring pleasure in earths common ills,

---

[23]From the prologue to *Old Fortunatus*, quoted in Frances A. Yates, "Queen Elizabeth as Astraea," *JWCI* IX (1947), 27.

[24]Borrowed from the generation and habit of Spenser's Belphoebe, *FQ*, III, vi.

Commit most willing rapes on all our harts:
And make us tremble, lest thy soveraigne parts
(The whole preservers of our happiness)
Should yeeld to change, Eclips, or heaviness . . .[25]
  Then set thy Christall, and Imperiall throne,
(Girt in thy chast, and never-loosing zone)
Gainst Europs Sunne directly opposit,
And give him darknesse, that doth threat thy light.[26]
("HC," 11. 95–109, 116–119)

This is very Spenserian, and so (by anticipation, for Spenser's Fifth Book was not yet published) is the implied identification with Astraea, presiding goddess of *iustitia* in a golden age, who, departing, leaves a fallen bestial world; the poet cries:

Discend againe, ah never leave the earth.

But the moral and religious allegory is of course dominant. Cynthia is the soul of the world, a purifying and shaping spirit dwelling in Night,[27] cutting off "all desire/Of fleshly sports," and figuring "the forces of the mind,"

An argument to ravish and refine
An earthly soule, and make it meere divine.

From the symbolic narrative which follows the poet excludes the

flesh confounded soules
That cannot beare the full Castalian bowles,
Which sever mounting spirits from the sences,[28]

and asserts, announcing a "dark saying," that this "deep fount" though it "shadows night," will display to "purest eyes" the "bowells of these misteries." This narrative (11. 170–399), interrupted from time to time by explanatory gnomic *sententiae*, is "hieroglyphic," and in interpreting it I confess to some impurity of vision, though the general idea is, as M. Jacquot observes, neither difficult nor new: the

[25]"Eclips" here obviously does not mean death; cf. Shakespeare's sonnet 107.

[26]Cf. Yates, "Queen Elizabeth as Astraea," 73 and plates 17 a & b: "a moon of imperial reform" versus the papal and Spanish symbols.

[27]See Battenhouse, "Chapman's Shadow of Night," 598, citing the moon as symbol of the world-soul in Plotinus (*Enneads*, V, vi, 4). Chapman's Cynthia is analogous to either Ficino's *anima mundana* or translunary presence, or his *spiritus mundanus*, through which the cosmic soul operates upon the corruptible realm of matter. I think the latter. Cf. Panofsky, *Studies in Iconology*, pp. 132–6.

[28]A probable hit at the Ovidian epigraph to *Venus and Adonis*, as has been frequently noted.

allegory is a "pageant of earthly desire" (Battenhouse), teaching that "ceux qui s'abandonnent à leurs passions ne peuvent connaître le contentement de l'âme" (Jacquot). Such is the face of the mystery, but not, I fear, its bowels. There is a curious fascination, to be noted again in *Ovids Banquet of Sense*, with the prolongation and peril of amorous pursuit, with "licorous hast" which never reaches its object, calling for a psychological explanation which only a perverse ingenuity could document from later poems.

The Moon is the goddess of Night; in the day she is but a shadow of night. She descends, accordingly, unaccompanied by her usual attendants, ocean nymphs and foresters (as she is Luna and Diana),

> but doth beget
> By powrefull charmes, delightsome servitors
> Of flowres, and shadows, mists, and meteors:
> Her rare Elysian Pallace she did build
> With studied wishes, which sweet hope did guild
> With sunnie foyle, that lasted but a day:
> For night must needs, importune her away.
>
> (11. 173–79)

This house of *illusions*, which is like Spenser's House of Pride a deceitful palace faced with "golden foile," is framed by "Forme" in likeness of a "pyramis," and from it the goddess herself takes "the pleasures of the day"; of a meteor she frames "a goodly Nimph" Euthimya (in *The Tears of Peace*, contentment or peace of the soul; here possibly sensual satisfaction), and to her

> gives all the raines
> Of wished pleasance; frames her golden wings,
> But them she bindes up close with purple strings,
> Because she now will have her run alone,
> And bid the base, to all affection.
>
> (11. 213–17)

Contentment is heavenly, pursued by night; but men pursue her by day through their appetites, hence she "bids the base," i.e. challenges the affections. The pageant is completed by the creation out of the same vapours of hunters and their hounds who are set to pursue Euthimya. Chapman elucidates the emblem thus:

> Wealth faunes on fooles; vertues are meate for vices,
> Wisedome conformes her selfe to all earths guises,
> Good gifts are often given to men past good,
> And Noblesse stoops sometimes beneath his blood.
>
> (11. 228–31)

Chased by the hounds (whose names come from Comes' "De Ac-
taeone") the nymph first turns into a panther, symbol of beautiful
but fierce attraction, and a moon-creature too,[29] who leads them into
a vast thicket, the "blind shade" of those who have offended the
goddess in her *nocturnal* majesty, a hell for sensual men:

> But preasing further, saw such cursed sights,
> Such AEtnas filld with strange tormented sprites,
> That now the vaprous object of the eye
> Out-pierst the intellect in facultie.
> Basenesse was Nobler than Nobilitie:
> Fur ruth, (first shaken from the braine of Love,
> And love the soule of vertue) now did move,
> Not in their soules (spheres meane enough for such)
> But in their eyes:[30] and thence did conscience touch
> Their harts with pitie: where her proper throne,
> Is in the minde, and there should first have shone:
> Eyes should guide bodies, and our soules our eyes,
> But now the world consistes on contraries.
>
> (11. 309–21)

Men's rational souls, then, the hunters, urging their steeds, the
spirited passions, follow the dogs, the base affections, into confusion
and fear; the panther turns into a boar next, having led the chase into
a "fruitfull Iland" (England?) filled with beauteous dames, where
"bewtie strikes fancie blind," and there the hunters follow her through
"noblest mansions,/Gardens and groves." But day is over, the goddess
mounts again into her sphere,

> And leaves us miserable creatures here.

It should be noted that the goddess herself joins in the hunt of the
panther (11. 248–9). As there are two Nights, there are two aspects
of Cynthia, who is, Chapman says, empress

> Of what soever the Olympick skie
> With tender circumvecture doth embrace,

and in the *active* life of day participates in the "spirited" life, though
all that is created by day belongs to mutability:

> Thus glories graven in steele and Adamant
> Never supposd to waste, but grow by wasting,
> (Like snow in rivers falne) consume by lasting.

---

[29]On this significance of the panther see La Primaudaye, *The French Academie*
(1586), p. 831.

[30]Cf. "And your cleare eyes the Spheres where *Reason* moves," epistle to Harriott,
Achilles Shield; and "Hymnus in Noctem," 11. 364–5.

So the poet summons her to return in her other majesty, in which she presides over the inner life; instead of a temple of day called "Pax Imperij," let there be "reextructed" her Ephesian temple of *intellectual* beauty, for "in-sight illustrates; outward braverie blindes," and Cynthia's temple is built in the "vertuous parts" of fair ladies; wisdom is "the mindes true bewtie," which dims the fire of the sun, and quenches base desire. Cynthia loved Endymion (the poet) for his "studious intellect," searching the secrets of nature "and all Astrologie." Finally, the goddess is invoked as Hecate in wonder of her power.[31]

The opposition of day and night, sense and soul, is settled in *The Shadow of Night* by the victory of "in-sight" over the inverted and "indigest" bravery of the outward world, in spite of the dangers of wrath in the first hymn and of concupiscence in the second. But *Ovids Banquet of Sense* (1595) has a different mythos, and the resolution remains in doubt. Nevertheless the two poems are complementary: the dominant motif of *The Shadow of Night* is fire striking out of darkness, but the *Banquet* is a daylight poem, with a promised darkness within it, clear only to "a radiant, and light-bearing intellect." A coda to the two poems is provided by "A Coronet for his Mistresse Philosophie," the ring of ten sonnets, characteristically "circulare," in the 1595 volume.

Since the dominant figure of the *Banquet* is postponement, one may be forgiven a somewhat leisurely approach to it, beginning with the prefatory letter to Roydon, which, as Chapman's first piece of explicit literary criticism, deserves some consideration. This preface looks backward as well as forward; apparently the poet has been accused of darkness, and he begins with a complaint and proclamation:

Such is the wilfull povertie of judgements . . . wandring like pasportles men, in contempt of the divine discipline of Poesie, that a man may well feare to frequent their walks: The prophane multitude I hate, & onlie consecrate my strange Poems to these serching spirits, whom learning hath made noble, and nobilitie sacred.[32]

---

[31] Cf. *As You Like It*, III, ii, 2: "thrice-crowned queen of night"; *Metamorphoses*, VII, 177: *diva triformis*.

[32] *Poems*, p. 49. Among contemporaries repeating the topos, cf. Abraham Fraunce, *The third part of the Countesse of Pembrokes Yuychurch* (1592), sig. B 2: "[Readers] that are better borne and of a more noble spirit, shall meete with hidden mysteries of naturall, astrologicall, or divine and metaphysicall philosophie, to entertaine their heavenly speculation"; and William Vaughan, *Poems, with the tenth Satyre of Iuvenal Englished* (1646): "To you alone, whose more refined *Spirits* out-wing these dull Times, and soare above the drudgerie of durty *Intelligence*, have I made sacred these

(He had all kinds of precedent for such a statement, but its pomposity invites satiric rejoinder, such as this of Marston, in which the third line quoted seems to refer to the *Banquet*:

> I am too mild, reach me my scourge againe,
> O yon's a pen speakes in a learned vaine,
> Deepe, past all sence. Lanthorne & candle light,
> Here's all invisible, all mentall spright.
> What hotchpotch, giberidge, doth the Poet bring?
> How strangely speakes, yet sweetly doth he sing. . . .
>   This affection,
> To speake beyond mens apprehension,
> How Apish tis. When all in fustian sute
> Is cloth'd a huge *nothing*, all for repute
> Of profound knowledge, when profoundnes knowes
> There's nought contained, but only seeming showes.[33])

Chapman then proceeds to define and defend his own kind of "clearness" on grounds which, as Miss Tuve has observed, are as old as the discipline of rhetoric. Poetry is by definition a "shadowing"; that it should be "as perviall as Oratorie, and plainnes her speciall ornament, were the plaine way to barbarisme." What is required "in absolute Poems" is not *energia* but *enargia*,

not the perspicuous delivery of a lowe invention; but high, and harty invention exprest in a most significant, and unaffected phrase.[34]

The analogy is with "perspective" in painting, and it is delightfully ambiguous:

It serves not a skilfull Painters turne, to draw the figure of a face onely to make knowne who it represents; but hee must lymn, give luster, shaddow, and heightening; which though ignorants will esteeme spic'd, and too curious, yet such as have the judiciall perspective, will see it hath motion, spirit, and life.

The distinction between the board-room portraits of past presidents and a Holbein or Rembrandt is clear enough, but one remembers also the Elizabethan fascination with "perspectives" and realizes that

---

fancies." See the discussion in Robert Ellrodt, *Les Poètes Métaphysiques Anglais*, Seconde partie (Paris, 1960), pp. 136–7.

[33] *The Scourge of Villanie* III, ix, in *Poems*, ed. A. Davenport (Liverpool, 1961), p. 160.

[34] See Rosemond Tuve, *Elizabethan and Metaphysical Imagery* (Chicago, 1947), pp. 30–2; on poetry as "Shadowing," cf. Thomas Wilson, *The Arte of Rhetorique* (1553), fol. 104v.; on *enargia* see Puttenham, *Arte of English Poesie*, III, iii. On covert wisdom in emblem books, see Robert J. Clements, *Picta Poesis* (Rome, 1960), ch. 5.

Chapman is speaking by analogy about verbal structures for which one needs a special angle of vision or "key" and which appear grotesque to the uninstructed observer. He goes on to note that what is "with a little endevour serched, ads a kinde of majestie to Poesie," and concludes this part of the argument:

Obscuritie in affection of words, & indigested concets, is pedanticall and childish; but where it shroudeth it selfe in the hart of his subject, utterd with fitnes of figure, and expressive Epethites; with that darknes wil I still labour to be shadowed.

Here he is of course very sound—and very close to Jonson:

Whatsoever looseth the grace, and clearness, converts into a Riddle: the obscurity is mark'd, but not the valew. That perisheth, and is past by, like the Pearle in the Fable. Our style should be like a skeine of silke, to be carried, and found by the right thred, not ravel'd, and perplex'd; then all is a knot, a heape.[35]

But the ambiguity in the painting metaphor suggests something else, more esoteric, which runs through the whole epistle. "My strange poems," open to "sacred" spirits; "high" invention; the secret which adds "majestie" to poetry—these hints, and then an explicit statement:

... rich Minerals are digd out of the bowels of the earth, not found in the superficies and dust of it; charms made of unlerned characters are not consecrate by the Muses which are divine artists, but by Evippes daughters, that challengd them with meere nature, whose brests I doubt not had beene well worthy commendation, if their comparison had not turnd them into Pyes.[36]

The poet creates "charms," that is "hieroglyphics," by sacred influence; he goes on to address the special powers of the initiate Roydon, who has been "acquainted long since with the true habit of Poesie"— that is, with its allegorical or "shadowing" character rendered illustrious by elegant and fitting figures, but who now since his "labouring wits endevour heaven-high thoughts of Nature," has "actual meanes to sound the philosophical conceits" that the poet's "new pen so seriously courteth." Whether the "new pen" refers to both *The Shadow of Night* and the *Banquet*—Chapman was not an established poet—is not clear; but since the prefaces to both poems are addressed to Roydon, it is likely that he is announcing a new kind of poetic utterance in this poem, and that the apology for the fitness of his

[35]*Ben Jonson*, VIII, 624.
[36]The myth is recounted in Ovid, *Metamorphoses*, V, 294 ff. The "rich minerals" image is from Erasmus' *Adagia*; see Schoell, p. 88.

figures and his "expressive Epethites" refers primarily to the allegorized mythological ornament of *The Shadow*, which is almost totally absent from this poem.

Chapman's most complete statement of the doctrine of poetic hieroglyphics is set out in the "free and offenceles Justification" of *Andromeda Liberata*, where it forms the foundation of his plea for liberty of prophesying in the dubious circumstances already described.

As *Learning* [he begins], hath delighted from her Cradle, to hide her selfe from the base and prophane *Vulgare*, her ancient Enemy; Under divers vailes of *Hieroglyphickes*, Fables, and the like; So hath she pleased her selfe with no disguise more; then in misteries and allegoricall fictions of *Poesie*.

These poetic mysteries have priority of time and power and have ever been held in reverence, as concealing "some sappe of hidden Truth," either of divinity or "the grounds of naturall, or rules of morall Philosophie,"

ever (I say) enclosing within the Rinde, some fruit of knowledge howsoever darkened; and (by reason of the obscurity) of ambiguous and different construction. Εστι τε φύσει ποιητικὴ ἡ συμπάσα αἰνιγματώδης, &c.
Est enim ipsa Natura universa Poesis aenigmatum plena, nec quiuis eam dignoscit. Plat. in Alcib. 2.[37]

Here we have the combination of the didactic and the secretive which, as Wind observes, is a prime rule of neoplatonic pedagogy. The poet as inspired priest of a natural religion protects his arcana by hedges of metaphor (*figurarum umbraculis*), as the inspired writers of the Old Testament couched their oracles in mysterious terms (*dissimulata autem et occultata*) and hid holy things under incongruous symbols.[38] The general theory of the dark saying in poetry and commendation of its "cryptic pomp" are repeated over and over by sixteenth-century English writers, and every reader will have his own analogues, from Sidney down, to add to mine,[39] but Chapman's

---

[37] *Poems*, p. 327. Cf. Henry Reynolds, *Mythomystes*, in *Critical Essays of the Seventeenth Century*, ed. J. E. Spingarn (Oxford, 1957), I, 157–60.

[38] Wind, *Pagan Mysteries*, pp. 140 (following Ficino), 157; cf. Pico on the esoteric character of poetry, summarized in J. W. H. Atkins, *English Literary Criticism: The Renaissance* (London, 1955), p. 28, and Dionysius the Areopagite, quoted in Wind, p. 20.

[39] See, e.g., Thomas Nashe, *Works*, ed. McKerrow-Wilson (Oxford, 1958), I, 25: "I account of Poetrie, as of a more hidden & divine kind of Philosophy, enwrapped in blinde Fables and darke stories, wherein the principles of more excellent Arts and morall precepts of manners . . . are contained." (Note that this parallels Chapman's assertion of the double intention, ethical and "scientific.") William Golding,

"charms" or "philosophical conceits" are in intention at least *mysteria*, "mystères littéraires," of the kind transferred by the neoplatonic academies from the formulas of popular rites of late antiquity to philosophical debate and meditation, their obscurity giving them an air of authority.[40] They are in fact *emblems* or emblematic conceits, their form influenced by the humanists' study of Egyptian hierogly-phics, thought of as hierophantic secrets, and informed by the con-viction that the universe itself is an emblem in which divine truth is hidden, or a "vast symphony of correspondences" of which such symbols, intuitively perceived by the inspired poet, constitute a revelation to the initiated.[41] Poetry is a "speaking picture," and in this context one sees the force of Chapman's use of the "perspective" analogy and of the device on the title-page of the *Ovids Banquet* quarto, a gnomon rising from the sea (the stick bent in water), which McKerrow conjectures is "an emblem of the author's and has nothing to do with the printer or publisher,"[42] with the motto *sibi conscia recti*. In this period, says Dieckmann, "hieroglyphics were ... the common ground on which art and poetry met." There is a further analogy with alchemical symbolism (noted, incidentally, by William Vaughan, who treasured up commonplaces of this kind in his *Golden Grove*), in which nature is treated as a great hieroglyph, and Jacquot has noted the recurrence of such images in Chapman's poem.[43]

Loaded thus with theory like a well-equipped but therefore clumsy diver, we totter on the brink of the poem, encouraged by the com-mendatory sonnets (by Richard Stapleton, Thomas Williams of the

---

The XV Bookes of ... Metamorphosis, ed. W. H. D. Rouse (London, 1904), "Preface to the Reader":
> [The poets] Did under covert names and termes theyr
>   doctrines so employe
> As that it is ryght dark and hard theyr meaning too espye ...

(cf. Reynolds on secret meanings in Ovid, "though perhaps hee understood not their depth," in Spingarn, I, 160). William Vaughan, *The Golden Grove* (1608), sig. Z3: "Poets do speak that which is most true, and by their mysticall fables do decipher profound matters."

[40]Wind, pp. 14–19.

[41]Frances A. Yates, "The Emblematic Conceit in Giordano Bruno's *De Gli Eroici Furori* and in the Elizabethan Sonnet Sequences," *JWCI* VI (1943), 108; E. H. Gombrich, "*Icones Symbolicae*: The Visual Image in Neo-Platonic Thought," *JWCI* XI (1948), 167, 171; Wind, p. 24 (for Pico's definition of "hieroglyphic" imagery and his citation of the Orphic hymns).

[42]R. B. McKerrow, *Printers' and Publishers' Devices* (London, 1913), p. 162.

[43]L. Dieckmann, "Renaissance Hieroglyphics," *Comparative Literature* IX, no. 4 (1957), 314; *Golden Grove*, sig. Z4; Jacquot, p. 64.

Inner Temple, and Sir John Davies) which promise "the soule of brightnes" in this darkness, the utterance of a "bright Saturnian Muse," a "spright-fild darknes," a "sacred vierse" too "misticall and deepe" for such as are not "true lovers," and in effect "deeper misteries," encouraged too in general by a modern authority who assures us that "this universal delight in the cryptic statement must be taken most seriously, for it was on the image level of the mind (if one may speak thus) that the Renaissance man achieved his unified outlook."[44] But there are unsettling voices, from critics who have looked at the poem around the corner of all this palisade of cross-reference, and, observing how it seems to record an elaborate fore-play to sexual intercourse, from hearing the beloved's voice to seeing her in her nakedness to touching her, and their moral sensibilities being roused, have uttered a series of troubled ejaculations, which, though sometimes memorable pieces of rhetoric, are hardly helpful to what Chapman would call the "understander." Yet three such different readers as Swinburne, M. Schoell and Professor Bush issue judgments which must be heeded. For Swinburne, the "sensual metaphysics" of the *Banquet* are served up "by the awkward and unwashed hands of an amorous pedant"; Schoell dismisses the poem as "une mélange de pedantisme grave et de subtile lascivité"; and Bush notes that it presents "a series of pictures marked by a voluptuousness at once lavish and dry."[45] Is it possible that the "philosophic conceits" are no more than window-dressing, and that the "sacred Poesie" is after all, as Davies (who in the first of his two prefatory sonnets calls it "this sacred vierse") puts it in his second sonnet, inspired by "Ovids easie supple Muse," who calls Chapman "second Maister of her love?"

The poem is, of course, ostensibly in the Ovidian erotic mode of *Venus and Adonis*, though Chapman obviously intended it as a "correction" to the "Muses that sing loves sensuall Emperie." As the "Argument" states, it tells the story of how Ovid, "newly enamoured of *Julia* (daughter to *Octavius Augustus Caesar*, after by him called *Corynna*),[46] secretly convaid himselfe into a Garden of the Emperors Court: in an Arbor whereof, *Corynna* was bathing; playing upon her Lute, and singing." His hearing is first satisfied by the sweetness of her voice, then his sense of smell by the odours of her bath, then his

[44]Frances A. Yates, *The French Academies of the Sixteenth Century* (London, 1947), p. 132.

[45]A. C. Swinburne, *George Chapman* (London, 1875), p. 159; Schoell, p. 38; Douglas Bush, *Mythology and the Renaissance Tradition* (Minneapolis, 1932), p. 204.

[46]For "Corinna," see L. P. Wilkinson, *Ovid Recalled* (Cambridge, 1955), pp. 46, 52, 152.

sight by the splendour of her nakedness, then he persuades her to a kiss for his taste, "then proceedes he to entreaty for the fift sence and there is interrupted." The "narratio" proceeds in the conventional way by description of the luxuriant setting, analysis of the lover's feelings, *débat*, sophistical or learned, between the lover and his mistress.

Among sources for what one might call the "accidents" of the poem, there is a considerable choice. M. Jacquot suggests plausibly a chapter of Jean Lemaire de Belges's *Illustrations de Gaule* (1509–12) of which "l'esprit est semblable, ainsi que le plan général," and tentatively a poem from the *Rymes* of Pernette du Guillet, but he wisely does not claim much for these.[47] I suspect that Chapman may have read Boccaccio's *Ameto*, but I would not claim much for that either, though a little more for the *Hypnerotomachia* (partly translated by "R.D." in 1592 as *The Strife of Love in a Dream*), which, Linda Fierz-David argues,[48] conceals the alchemical principle of transformation, and in which (chapter 7) Poliphilo meets five maidens representing the five senses, who incite him to lust and then appease it. The elaborate description of Niobe's fountain in the *Banquet* may possibly owe something to this strange production, which in one of its aspects is an essay on architecture. The description of the act of seeing in stanza 64 may have come from Aristotle's *De Anima* through the *Margarita Philosophica* (1583),[49] and the conventional setting of the "jardin d'amours" may be studied with profit in the great collection of Van Marle, including many "conversations galantes."[50] The garden is also, be it noted, an alchemical symbol, "le vase qui contient la matière du grand oeuvre."[51] Finally, nearer home, we should note Barnabe Barnes's *Parthenophil and Parthenope* (1593), in which the senses triumph in eagles/eyes, barbarian spices/taste, rich Arabian odours/smell, music/sound, "sacred hands"/touch, but above all in Parthenope.[52]

[47]Jacquot, pp. 66–7. But see Frank Kermode, "The Banquet of Sense," *Bulletin of the John Rylands Library* XLVIII (1961), 87–8.

[48]*The Dream of Poliphilo, Related and Interpreted*, Bollingen Series XXV (1950).

[49]. . . *corporalem & pyramidalem, cuius basis in re visa, & conus in oculo videte est* (*Margarita*, p. 790).

[50]R. van Marle, *Iconographie de l'art profane au moyen-âge et à la renaissance* (The Hague, 1931–32), I, 451 ff., especially 468; II, 425 ff., and figs. 457, 459.

[51]See Pernety, *Dictionnaire Mytho-hermétique* (Paris, 1787), s. v. "jardin."

[52]Other contemporary appearances of the "banquet of sense" topos are noted by Kermode (e.g. Shakespeare's sonnet 141, Harington's marginal note to the Rogero-Alcina espisode in *Orlando Furioso*, VII, &c.). See also his "Milton's Hero," *RES*, n.s. IV (1953), 524–5, citing *Timon of Athens*, I, ii, 129 ff., and Jonson, *The New Inn*, III, ii. To these we may add Drayton, *Idea*, xxix; Constable, *Diana*, first decade, 5 and 6; Jonson, *Poetaster*, IV, v, 198 ff., and *Mortimer His Fall* (*Ben Jonson*, VII, 62).

When it comes to the substance, the "philosophy," we can be more precise. The title suggests that Chapman had the *Symposium* in mind, and inevitably, as Professor Bush long ago pointed out, Ficino's *Commentarium* on it.[53] And Professor Kermode has described the tradition of the "banquet of the senses" and its relation to the other tradition of the "choice of Hercules" from Xenophon and S. Paul to *Paradise Regained*. But the hierarchy of the senses in the *Banquet* goes against (or on the face of it seems to go against) Ficino's *ideal* progression:

... no value whatever can be attached to mere lust which sinks from the sphere of vision to that of touch and should not be given the name of love by self-respecting Platonists. Only he whose visual experience is but the first step, however unavoidable, towards the intelligible and universal beauty reaches the stage of the "divine love" which makes him an equal of Saints and Prophets.[54]

The poem seems in honour of Aphrodite Pandemos rather than Aphrodite Ourania; Ovid (in the poem) is a "counter-Plato." But one can find anything one wants in Ficino, and if Chapman read his *De voluptate* or his *Epistola de felicitate* (which I very much doubt) he could have found that "pleasure and joy, in a philosophic lover, are superior to inquiry and vision."[55] There was a "spiritual cult of the senses" in neoplatonism, explained thus by Sperone Speroni:

The senses are a ladder and path to the reason: whence whoever is so foolish in love that he takes no care of their respective appetites, but like a pure intelligence with no body tries simply to satisfy the mind alone, may be said to resemble the person who, gulping down some food without touching it or chewing it, grows weaker rather than gains nourishment.[56]

The pathway to perfection in love set out in the *Banquet*, then, is outwardly opposed to the way of rejection of the senses in *The Shadow of Night*—the opposition being at places verbal and explicit, as in "Eyes should guide bodies, and our soules our eyes" vs. "soule are ruled by eyes"—but inwardly complementary in its end or purpose, "teaching by passion what perfection is," as the "Coronet" puts it.

[53]*Mythology and the Renaissance Tradition*, p. 204n.

[54]Panofsky, *Studies in Iconology*, p. 143. Cf. the views of Leone Ebreo and Bembo, quoted in John Charles Nelson, *Renaissance Theory of Love* (New York, 1958), pp. 98, 107.

[55]Wind, pp. 54–9; cf. Jacquot, p. 227.

[56]In Nelson, p. 128. See also John Buxton's illuminating suggestion that Chapman was indebted to Donatus' commentary on a passage in Terence's *Eunuchus*: Quinque lineae perfectae sunt ad amorem: prima visus; secunda loqui; tertia tactus; quarta osculari; quinta coitus. *Elizabethan Taste* (New York, 1965), p. 302.

Chapman insists throughout on the spiritualizing and aspiring quality of sense experience, but it must be admitted that Ovid's progress through the senses has a dangerously close resemblance to that imaged by Lorenzo de Medici in his sonnets and justified on frankly sensual grounds in the commentary.[57] This is where the accusation of prurience comes in. Kermode counters it by observing that surely Chapman cannot be writing here the kind of poem he elsewhere deplores, and that accordingly we should read this as an ironical poem, with Ovid's transports apparently glorified and his amorous pleas thoroughly argued, but both to be taken as reprehensible. This reading correlates nicely with the interpretation of the pageant of the amorous hunt in "Hymnus in Cynthiam" which I have suggested above, and the strongest argument for it is the presence of the "digression" in stanzas 51–55, where the poet drops his narrative, and turns to celebrate the heavenly beauty, "the feast of soules" beside which the other beauty is "natures witchcraft," "of vertuous light/A feeble Image," and then significantly proceeds:

> With this digression, wee will now returne
> To *Ovids* prospect in his fancies storme.

My own view is that the whole poem is an extended exercise in paradox, in theme and figures, and that the paradoxes are intended covertly to undermine the Ovidian "philosophy" of the senses. This is the "judiciall perspective" which Chapman asks of his readers. It may be that he asks too much. Certainly the paradox is asymmetrical enough to raise speculation (however illegitimate) on how far Chapman's own uncertainty is involved in his narration.

The poem is emblematic, and the setting is portrayed as a "device," Corinna's spring being the "eye" of the arbour, as the marginal note to stanza 2 explains:

By *Prosopopaeia*, he makes ye fountaine ye eye of the round Arbor, as a Diamant seems to be the eye of a Ring: and therefore sayes, the Arbor sees with the Fountaine.

And in the fountain stands a statue of Niobe with her fourteen children (their names from Comes), a figure of the conflict of earthly and divine. The "eye" of the arbour, then, looks toward the "heavenly light" of the sun; it weeps, with Niobe, toward earth; Earth and Sun meet (st. 1) in the vaporous fertility of this alchemical "still."

---

[57]Nelson, p. 52. Cf. Mario Equicola, cited in Kermode.

But Niobe is also, of course, an emblem of presumption,

> And that her story might be still observed,
> *Octavius* caus'd in curious imagrie,
> Her fourteen children should at large be carved.

And every schoolboy knew some version of the story of Ovid and Julia (Corinna).

Then at once appears "this Romaine Phoebe" (another paradox, for Corinna was no Phoebe), "Natures naked Jem":

> In a loose robe of Tynsell foorth she came,
> Nothing but it betwixt her nakednes
> And envious light. The downward-burning flame
> Of her rich hayre did threaten new accesse,
> Of ventrous *Phaeton* to scorch the fields. . . .
> Then cast she off her robe, and stood upright,
> As lightning breaks out of a laboring cloude;
> Or as the Morning heaven casts off the Night.
>
> (st. 7–8)

She bathes in the fountain, and then upon a Spenserian flowerbank she dries herself and sings,

> all naked as she sat,
> Laying the happy Lute upon her thigh,
> Not thinking any near to wonder at
> The blisse of her sweet brests divinitie.

She sings a song of "beauties sorcerie," and Ovid, hearing her, begins to celebrate "the purifying rapture" of his "eares sence," the "first service" to his banquet (st. 16–29). His hearing, he says, is "sette on fire" by her voice, which rears his spirits to "theyr highest function," his "soule in *Cupids* Furnace blazeth," and his flesh fades "and into spyrit turns." Although he attributes to her voice the power of Amphion's lyre and the skill to make the world all music (st. 19–20), "Cupid's Furnace" is no place for the aspiring soul to be. He explains, with marginal references, how the sound is transmitted from "her soules discursive fire" to his own "intellectual life, or soule," so that in the listening

> My life, that in my flesh a Chaos is
> Should to a Golden worlde be thus dygested,

and in "her voyces stillerie" earth is transmuted into air,[58] flesh into spirit, and Nature and Art are confined in trance (st. 28–29).

[58]Cf. the correspondences in Ficino, *Comm. in Conviv.*, V, ii: visus igni, aeri auditus, vaporum odori olfactus, aqua gustus, tactus terrae, and *OBS*, st. 49, 28, 34, 99, 102.

As he draws nearer, her "Odors," the "fiery ayre" of this phoenix, assault him, "in these liberall fumes" he burns in the flames of his "disease"; but the fire also refines:

> And as the ayre is rareified with heate
> But thick and grosse with Summer-killing colde,
> So men in love aspire perfections seate,
> When others, slaves to base desire are sold. . . .
>
> Gentle and noble are theyr tempers framde,
> That can be quickned with perfumes and sounds. . . .
>
> Odors feede love, and love cleare heaven discovers.
>
> (st. 33, 35, 36)

The effects of sounds and odours "imitate the eternitie of vertue," says the gloss.

> O soveraigne Odors; not of force to give
> Foode to a thing that lives nor let it die,
> But to ad life to that did never live;
> Nor to ad life, but immortallitie.
> Since they pertake her heate that like the fire
> Stolne from the wheeles of *Phoebus* waggonrie
> To lumpes of earth, can manly lyfe inspire.
>
> (st. 38)

We note how the association of Corinna with the sphere of fire ("where reason moves"), with the sun, is continued, but Cupid's furnace is still supplying heat to this "still" of amorous desire. Ovid insists that the senses have power to "in-forme" lumpish natures, but when it comes to his desire to gaze upon his mistress, to satisfy that sense which is above all the initiator of desire,[59] "vulture love on his encreasing liver" begins to feed, he fears to show his "rudenes," and wavering between desire and trepidation he prays to Juno to speed his suit since she assists "such as in Cyprian sports theyr pleasures fix."

> This sayde, he charg'd the Arbor with his eye,
> Which pierst it through, and at her breasts reflected,
> Striking him to the hart with exstasie:
> As doe the sun-beames gainst the earth prorected,
> With their reverberate vigor mount in flames,
> And burne much more then where they were directed,
> He saw th' extraction of all fayrest Dames:

---

[59]See Varchi, *Sopra sette d'amore*; Tasso, *Conclusioni amorose*, quoted in Nelson, pp. 142, 154. Cf. "Hymnus in Noctem," 11. 364–5.

> The fayre of Beauty, as whole Countries come
> And shew theyr riches in a little Roome.
>
> (st. 49)

Here, dramatically placed after this Marlovian extravagance, is the digression already noted, which explicitly denies the immortality claimed by Ovid at stanza 38, but also titillates the "fancy" of the reader by postponing the apparition of what Ovid sees. As Corinna lies "attirde in nakednes,"

> His eye did carve him on that feast of feasts:
> Sweet fields of life which Deaths foote dare not presse. . . .
> Her body doth present those fields of peace
> Where soules are feasted with the soule of ease.
>
> (st. 59)

(The gloss adds: "He calls her body [as it were divided with her breasts,] ye fields of Paradise, and her arms & legs the famous Rivers in it.") Ovid concludes:

> *Elisium* must with vertue gotten bee,
> With labors of the soule and continence,
> And these can yeeld no joy with such as she,
> Shee is a sweet *Elisium* for the sence
> And Nature dooth not sensual gifts infuse
> But that with sence, shee still intends their use.
> The sence is given us to excite the minde,
> And that can never be by sence excited
> But first the sence must her contentment finde,
> We therefore must procure the sence delighted,
> That so the soule may use her facultie.
>
> (st. 62–63)

This is the paradoxical heart of the poem expressed in its central "philosophical conceit": the "Diamant" (quintessence) set in flesh, that flesh an earthly paradise which enables the soul to "use her facultie." The poem is not so eloquent again; the association of Corinna with fire-sun-heat continues, but gets smothered in sophistry and perplexing *quaestiones amoris*.

Corinna begins to braid her hair, in one of Chapman's most magnificent macrocosmic images:

> Shee lifts her lightning arms above her head,
> And stretcheth a Meridian from her blood,
>
> (st. 69)

gracing her hair with "Jewels of devise," three esoteric emblems within "the figure of a swelling hart." These "empreses" are indeed dark but they all represent some kind of warning: the first (*decrescente nobilitate, crescunt obscuri*) of the waning of true nobility; the second (*Medio caret*) "to showe not eyes, but meanes must truth display"; the third, of a world within a dial and the posy *Teipsum et orbem*, of the order within the microcosm(?).[60] If these are warnings, Ovid does not heed them; he decides that he "must through hell adventure to displease." Revealed to Corinna and accused by her of impurity, he reads her a long lesson of mixed optics and ethics, in which he claims to reject "Vulgar Opinion" and argue by "autentique Reason," insisting that in the function of seeing it is he, not the object, that is harmed; she is moved enough by his lecture to let her sun of beauty shine forth again from the clouds in which it has been hidden, and he proceeds to plead for the satisfaction of his other senses. The heart of their debate (st. 92–93) is highly technical: she argues that pure love does not act by contact of lips or bodies but by "bodies vertues," analogous to the "powers" of the stars; Ovid replies that her "vertuall presence" cannot "effuse/The true and solid parts" of her essence but only its "forme," and for *his* longing he needs "substance." This piece of sophistry, which runs against much of what he has said before, persuades Corinna, and he receives a "perpetual-motion-making kisse," making his breast "an endless Fount of blisse."

The aspiration which informed the earlier part of the love-ritual has apparently been reversed: the kiss works high joy in his *heart* (seat of the passions), and he pleads at once for touch, arguing that "Love is a wanton famine, rich in foode," controlled by appetite which works against reason "with a senceless will." We seem to have left the realm of reason for the other power of will and desire. Yet a recovery is attempted. Ovid asks that his "sences ground-worke, which is, Feeling" be contented too—"Dames may be felt, as well as heard or seene," a ludicrous note—but continues:

> The minde then cleere, the body may be usde,
> Which perfectly your touch can spiritualize;
> As by the great elixer is trans-fusde
> Copper to Golde.
>
> (st. 104)

He addresses an apostrophe to his hand, conjuring it to "Use with pietie that sacred place," and in a fine bit of impropriety likens the

---

[60] Kermode, 70.

sense of touch to "that power the world did guise." Somewhere in
Chapman's mind is the figure of the world created by Amor, but he
spoils the effect, for when Corinna "startles" at the touch upon her
side she is proved "sharpe, unduld with handling yet,/Which keener
edge on *Ovids* longings set." This is the language one uses of a filly, not
a neoplatonic symbol. There follows, however, a highly characteristic
passage:

> And feeling still, he sighed out this effect:
> Alas why lent not heaven the soule a tongue?
> Nor language, nor peculier dialect,
> To make her high conceits as highly sung,
> But that a fleshy engine must unfold
> A spirituall notion. . . .
>
> O nature how doost thou defame in this
> Our humane honors? yoking men with beasts
> And noblest mindes with slaves? thus beauties blisse,
> Love and all vertues that quick spirit feasts
> Surfet on flesh; and thou that banquets mindes,
> Most bounteous Mistresse, of thy dull-tongu'd guests
> Reapst not due thanks; thus rude frailtie bindes
> What thou giv'st wings.
>
> (st. 111–112)

I take this to be an apologia for the poem, or at least for those parts
of it which, as I have noted, seem not to be directed toward the sphere
of fire. This inference is supported by the fact that the rest of the poem
is in effect an introduction to a poetics. For the sake of "sweet touch,
the engine that loves bow doth bend," Ovid says that he will write
"the Art of love," and write it against those "who hate societie/And
such as self-love makes his slaverie."

> In these dog-dayes how this contagion smoothers
> The purest bloods with vertues diet fined
> Nothing theyr owne, unlesse they be some others
> Spite of themselves, are in themselves confined
> And live so poore they are of all despised,
> Theyre gifts, held down with scorne should be divined,
> And they like Mummers mask, unknowne, unprised:
> A thousand mervailes mourne in some such brest
> Would make a kinde and worthy Patrone blest.
>
> (st. 114)

The poet is now speaking in his own person, voicing his usual complaint against the "outward" world of gold-seekers—and incidentally fishing for a noble patron.

After this, the last two stanzas, which return to the narration, are anticlimactic: "other Dames" enter the garden, Ovid "shrowds" himself again, grieving that "there were no more worlds to subdue," but consoling himself that "there was much more intended"—that is, one supposes, sexual consummation. The simile used is that of painting: as we do not blame a painter for not showing all the monarch's fingers around the sceptre, but infer their presence in the model, so here we may infer a conclusion to which what has been enacted must lead. The poem ends, as we should expect, with a paradox, and paradox of image and "sentence" has sustained it throughout. If we listen to one side of the witty contention between the two Venuses, we may find the poem more salacious than others of its genre outwardly intended to be so; if we listen to the other, we shall find, with Hallett Smith, that the banquet is in reality "an education for the soul" and that Corinna with her lute is "the philosophical nude."[61]

One may suppose that the "his" of "A Coronet for his Mistresse *Philosophie*" should be italicized, and in that case we may take it as a palinode to the Corinna-Ovid relation—for surely Corinna is *not* the philosophical nude! It is an "answer" also to the amatory sequences then at the height of their vogue. But the "Coronet" is very interestingly placed: between the *Banquet* and two amatory poems not Chapman's; the first ("The amorous Zodiak") a translation from Gilles Durant, a blazon of the beauty of the poet's mistress with correspondences of the parts of her body to the zodiac; the second ("The amorous contention of Phillis and Flora") a translation by R.S. of a medieval Latin *débat* on the question whether a soldier or a clerk is "fitst for venerie"—Cupid decides for the clerk. Chapman's mistress is Sapience ("Learning"), who dwells in the sphere of fire where reason moves:

> Her minde (the beame of God) drawes in the fires
> Of her chast eyes, from all earths tempting fewell. . . .
> And in th'untainted Temple of her hart
> Doth the divorceles nuptials celebrate
> Twixt God and her; where loves prophaned dart
> Feedes the chast flames of *Hymens* firmament.
>
> (nos. 3, 4)

In "th' inversed world that goes upon her head," among those who "dwell in darknes" (in that other Night of the "Hymnus in Noctem")

[61]Hallett Smith, *Elizabethan Poetry* (Cambridge, Mass., 1952), pp. 96–7.

the fires are "Cupids bonfires burning in the eye" which "eate the entrailes out with exstasies." But his love, he affirms,

> is the cordiall of soules
> Teaching by passion what perfection is,
> In whose fixt beauties shine the sacred scroules,
> And long-lost records of your humane blisse
> Spirit to flesh, and soule to spirit giving,
> Love flowes not from my lyver, but her living.
>
> (no. 2)

She is the patroness of the "inward" life:

> Nor riches, to the vertues of my love,
> Nor Empire, to her mighty government;
> Which fayre analisde in her beauties grove,
> Showes Lawes for care, and Canons for content:
> And as a purple tincture given to Glasse
> By cleare transmission of the Sunne doth taint
> Opposed subjects: so my Mistresse face
> Doth reverence in her viewers browes depaint,
> And like the Pansye, with a little vaile
> She gives her inward worke the greater grace.
>
> (no. 8)

(We may note in passing that this sonnet illustrates Chapman's figurative powers at their full stretch: the first simile is laboured and accurate, oratorical; the second a happy invention, delicate and grave.) And as Philosophie presides over society, anticipating the figure of "Ceremony" in the continuation of *Hero and Leander* in her rejection of "thoughts cupidinine" and her "right line" turning deadly vices to living virtues, so in the contemplative life she is the poet's Muse "that well will knowe/Her proper inspirations," and the poet's "friendlesse verse" will never envy "Muses that Fames loose feathers beautifie." Accordingly in the last sonnet of the ring Chapman asserts by inference his intention to "tread the Theater," which in Athens and Rome was the place of "noblest wits," and "men of highest doome," and condemns both those who contemn the stage and those servile writers who pervert it to "base empayre."

"Philosophie," then, has a religious, a literary, and a social significance—and the first two are really one. In his completion of Marlowe's *Hero and Leander* Chapman for the first time sought to expound his ideas of "form" and virtue in a social setting.

"It was scarcely a happy thought," remarked Havelock Ellis, "as though Browning undertook to complete Keats's *Hyperion*—yet the close contact of Marlowe seems to save Chapman from his besetting sins of obscurity and infelicity." Ellis, like others since, sees Chapman as needing to be saved from himself always. It is true that even Homer could not save him from obscurity and infelicity, true that Marlowe's unfinished poem provided the form he needed, but also true that *Hero and Leander* needed the kind of conclusion he could give it. By the end of the second sestiad there was hardly any *story* to tell, but there was much of an "unfinished Tragedy," which is not the same thing. "At the very moment when a graver voice is needed," observes C. S. Lewis, "a graver voice succeeds."[62]

Chapman apologizes, in what is perhaps the least attractive of his dedications (to Lady Walsingham), for employing his serious time "in so trifeling a subject,"[63] but in the same place he says he was "drawne by strange instigation" to complete the poem. This of course does not mean that Marlowe, on some dramatic moment like the morning before his fatal assignation, happened to meet Chapman and say, "If I should die. . . ." Nor does it mean (at least I hope not) that after his death in 1593 Marlowe became one of Chapman's "heavenly familiars." What it probably means is that Chapman thought he knew what Marlowe, that "free soule" (III, 189), was up to in his apparently unfinished poem, and he saw a way to turn and round it.

Reading Marlowe's poem, Chapman could hardly have failed to notice two essential elements in that lovely artefact: first, that the loves of Hero and Leander are accomplished within a purely mythological frame, richly decorated, that the tone is never soft and luscious but hard as jewels, and that, overruled by Fate, the lovers are moved, like jewelled pieces, to their destiny; second, that not only the ironical *sententiae* and epithets ("*Venus* Nun") but also the association of love with gold and greed suggest that Marlowe was not merely celebrating but judging the lovers, albeit with amusement, and that consequently it would not be wholly contrary to his "late desires" to make the tragedy of Hero and Leander a mirror for lovers and in doing so to "censure" their delights. But I think he noticed, too, that Marlowe had celebrated "the triumph of Nature over Ceremony, erecting a Bower of Bliss upon a basis of truant learning," as Miss Bradbrook puts it. He resolved to correct this, and, in doing so, to substitute for

---

[62]Havelock Ellis, *Chapman* (London, 1934), p. 14; C. S. Lewis, "*Hero and Leander*," *Proceedings of the British Academy* XXXVIII (1952), 30.

[63]*Poems*, p. 132.

the mocking reduction of the gods in Marlowe an elevating mythological pantheon of his own.[64]

The poem, then, taken as a whole, becomes an Elizabethan synopsis
of love, and by the way a compendium of figures of rhetoric and mine
of High Renaissance metaphor. The analogy with the *Roman de la Rose*
is not the less suggestive for being obvious and is the more interesting
because intricate. Each is a synthesis of ode and palinode, of innocence
and experience. The long-winded didacticism of Jean de Meun
parallels the encyclopedic sententiousness of Chapman, but the
dialectic of reason and sensuality which informs both poems has its
parts reversed. Where Jean exposed the natural world beneath
Guillaume's lovely protocol of courtship, Chapman, to use Katherine
Mansfield's accusing phrase, put Marlowe's "divine poem into a
blouse and skirt." But this is exactly what had to be done before the
tragedy was complete, for love is not only the private (and elegantly
remote) banquet of sense which Marlowe sang, but a social act; Eros
reigns over the first two sestiads, but Ceremony over Chapman's,
and Ceremony, as D. J. Gordon has brilliantly demonstrated,[65] is
Law, Order, Degree, Form (εἶδος), she who presides over "civill forms,"
in whom "all the sweetes of our society/[Are] Spherde" (III, 143–4).
Like the goddess of *Hymnus in Cynthiam* she wears a "Pentacle,"[66]
like her she freezes "the lawlesse flames of Cupids Godhead"; she is
Queen Elizabeth "moralized" in fact. Appearing as Leander "shakes
with passionate desire" (III, 105), her awful manifestation portends
the tragedy of lovers whose secret delights "being enjoyd aske judgement" (III, 9). The poem accordingly turns, as Chapman begins, in a
relentless "new direction," marked by the pun on *guilt*: the "guilt"
of Leander's morning-sun-kissed limbs (so luxuriously caressed by
Neptune before) and the "guilt" of his incontinence. The "golden
bubble" breaks, and not all Hero's "Cupid-prompted" sophistry
(III, 341–96), which ironically balances Leander's "bold sharpe"
argument against virginity before (I, 198–294), can resist the fate of
those who have no covenant with Time but only with passion. Hero's
religion turns into idolatry, her reverence into dissimulation; her
unsanctified state is set against the ordered nuptials of Hymen and

[64]M. C. Bradbrook, *Shakespeare and Elizabethan Poetry* (Peregrine Books, 1964),
p. 57. See also Clifford Leech, "Venus and her Nun: Portraits of Women in Love by
Shakespeare and Marlowe," *SEL* v(1965), 247–68.

[65]"Chapman's 'Hero and Leander'," *English Miscellany* (Rome) V (1964), 41–94.
My discussion of the poem owes much to this essential study.

[66]Cf. Jonson's *Hymenaei, Ben Jonson*, VII, 213.

Eucharis (V), postponing the catastrophe, which follows, surrounded by all the panoply of terror and pathos.

The architecture of the work, then, is nothing less than grand, so that it is no mere eulogy to call it an epic metamorphosis, or mirror for lovers. Marlowe's glittering fountain overflows into the deep contemplative pool of Chapman's mind; its iridescent bubbles explode one by one, and we gaze upon twisted reflections and enigmatical depths. For there is no clean break, no antipathy of feeling: Chapman does not disdain the images of passion. The action of his part begins with a glimpse of Leander's "*Hero*-handled bodie," a more intimate epithet than any of Marlowe's shining descriptions; in Hero's reverie, Leander "came in swimming painted all with joyes,/Such as might sweeten hell," her inner dialogue is resolved by the dangerous "logick of *Leanders* beautie," and the "Epithalamion Teratos," though sung within the hymeneal circle of sanctified loves, is sufficient to kill the legend of the dismal pedant who "fell short of the spirit and Invention" of the "dead shepherd":[67]

> Come, come deare night, Loves Mart of kisses,
> Sweet close of his ambitious line,
> The fruitfull summer of his blisses,
> Loves glorie doth in darknes shine.
> O come soft rest of Cares, come night,
> Come naked vertues only tire,
> The reaped harvest of the light,
> Bound up in sheaves of sacred fire.
>
>   (V, 426–34)

The counterplay of these and other recollections of consummated passion with the stately masques of society, each phase in the ominous dialogue punctuated by *sententiae*, marks the progress of Chapman's poem. In substance the four sestiads may be defined as a series of emblems: the picture drawn, the *sententia* holding its meaning in a couplet, and the explanatory commentary relating it to art (the form and colour of the picture) and to nature (the psychology of love). Witness, for example, the apparition of Ceremony (III, 108–54), the description of Hero's "conceited skarf" (IV, 76–121), of the creation of Eronusis (IV, 286–314), or of Hero's torch (VI, 50–61). These emblems, set moving in sequence, make up a mask or triumph of tragedy, which is guided not only by its processional weight but by a line of meditation, by the poet's preoccupation with "form"

---

[67]Edward Phillips, *Theatrum Poetarum* (1675), p. 24.

itself, which may be said to constitute the "moral sense" of the poem, a sense certainly less conspicuous in Marlowe's beginning.

Chapman's use of the term "form" is obsessive rather than philosophically definitive—a fair enough practice for a poet.[68] He applies it indifferently to the worlds of art, politics, physiology and ethics. The complex idea for which the word is a shorthand sign appears in *Hero and Leander* as a kind of *temperance*, not abstinence but an ordering of sensuous enjoyment by which something is saved for tomorrow and Time becomes the ally of desire and not its enemy (III, 48–64). Next as Ceremony, who, as I have already noted, is the goddess of "civill formes," without whom true joys are impossible to taste; where her dignity is not recognized, "Feare fils the chamber, darknes decks the Bride" (III, 154). This order, then, is really the ally of desire, for desire must have an element of composure or else it is not complete, it is "close and flat," "loose and secret." "Uncourtly" Hero is shown divided against herself, her breast "ransacked" by contrary passions, afraid of giving away her secret at her eyes, for the "in-forme" of the soul is shown in the "animate glasse" of the eye (III, 235–52). If the soul's form is out of harmony with the forms of society, the result is a divided soul, "one for the face, one for the heart" (III, 271–72), and Hero in sorrowful meditation on her fault sits "wrapt in unshapefull foulds" (III, 298), an outward image of her inner condition. Form in the Pythagorean symbolism is number; Hero's sophistical and self-deceiving play with love's "vertue . . . to make one of two" is answered in the exposition of the odd number five in the Tale of Teras (V, 323–40), which is generally a hymn to the "sweete concord" of the ceremonious rites of marriage, presided over by "forme-giving Cyprias," which Chapman had already celebrated in his *De Guiana* as part of his vision of a new golden age on the banks of the Orinoco. The "number" of society must be added to the two of passion or there is no perfection, only the pathetic fall of beauty and worth which the poet ruthfully describes in the Sixth Sestiad. Leander swimming in his "high thought," full of the *hubris* of passion, is significantly (and apologetically) compared to "an emptie gallant full of forme," one of the rash and empty gentlemen who populate the satires of the '90's, each tacking about in his "swelling ship of vacantrie."

Taken on its own terms, accepting the force of its special, almost private vocabulary, the argument of these sestiads is remarkably

---

[68]Aristotle's *De Anima* is the fundamental source for the nexus of ontological and psychological ideas of "form" in the poem. See Gordon, 70 and 81 (for Ficino's influence).

tough and consistent, its theme the triumph of *civility*, or *Romeo and Juliet* seen from the point of view of a younger and less hasty Capulet, one for whom the dance rather than the plunge is the right figure for fruitful loves. But there is so much of it; here we face 1558 lines of verse, a small if pregnant theme flourished out of all measure, it seems, in an accumulative style which at the same time strives for "point" and is distributed in discursive allegorical pictures. The mode, as I have said, is weightily processional and so appropriate to the argument, but this "outward" majesty is complemented by an "inward" line of meditation which swells the poem too, through simile and sentence, and gets us close to the working mind of the poet. For example, as he images Hero wondering how she can conceal her passion, the poet reflects:

> For yet the worlds stale cunning she resisted
> To beare foule thoughts, yet forge what lookes she listed,
> And held it for a very sillie sleight,
> To make a perfect mettall counterfeit:
> Glad to disclaime her selfe, proud of an Art,
> That makes the face a Pandar to the hart.
> Those be the painted Moones, whose lights prophane
> Beauties true Heaven, at full still in their wane.
> Those be the lapwing faces that still crie,
> Here tis, when that they vow is nothing nie.
> Base fooles, when every moorish fowle can teach
> That which men thinke the height of human reach.
> But custom that the Apoplexie is
> Of beddred nature, and lives led amis,
> And takes away all feeling of offence,
> Yet brazde not *Heros* brow with impudence.
>
> (III, 253–68)

This is moralizing comment, and there is much more of it. There is some curious "science": Hero, finding Leander's "picture" in her bosom, is renewed by love's joy:

> *Leanders* forme left no ill object there.
> Such was his beauty that the force of light,
> Whose knowledge teacheth wonders infinite,
> The strength of number and proportion,
> Nature had plaste in it to make it knowne
> Art was her daughter, and what humane wits
> For studie lost, entombed in drossie spirits.
>
> (IV, 139–45)

There are reflections of painful observation—

> And as when funerall dames watch a dead corse,
> Weeping about it, telling with remorse
> What paines he felt, how long in paine he lay,
> How little food he eate, what he would say;
> And then mix mournfull tales of others deaths,
> Smothering themselves in clowds of their owne breaths;
> At length, one cheering other, call for wine—
>
> (V, 187–93)

of hard reading—

> Since an even number you may disunite
> In two parts equall, nought in middle left,
> To reunite each part from other reft:
> And five they hold in most especiall prise,
> Since tis the first od number that doth rise
> From the two formost numbers unitie
> That od and even are; which are two, and three,
> For one no number is—
>
> (V, 332–39)

and moments, too few perhaps, of gnomic wisdom:

> What man does good, but he consumes thereby?

Looking at the composition more intimately, we can follow the poet working out the logic of his comparisons and searching the hearts of his metaphors.

> His most kinde sister all his secrets knew
> And to her singing like a shower he flew

is very good; but Chapman continues:

> Sprinkling the earth, that to their tombs took in
> Streames dead for love, to leave his ivorie skin,
> Which yet a snowie fome did leave above,
> As soule to the dead water that did love:
> And from thence did the first white Roses spring.
>
> (III, 73–79)

This is conceited ornament; in Hero's passionate speech at the close of the Third Sestiad, where a paronomasia is assisted by touches of anadiplosis and epanalepsis, the effect is dramatic:

> His motion is like heavens Orbiculer:
> For where he once is, he is ever there.

> This place was mine: *Leander* now t'is thine;
> Thou being my selfe, then it is double mine:
> Mine, and *Leanders* mine, *Leanders* mine.
> O see what wealth it yeelds me, &c.

This suits the decorum of the pathetic occasion, but inevitably the actions and speeches of the characters in the narration are developed rhetorically toward the poet's central obsessions, expressed in a limited set of repeated key-words. Thus when Hymen gives Eucharis a lily (in the "tale of Teras"), we have:

> As two cleere Tapers mix in one their light,
> So did the Lillie and the hand their white:
> She viewd it, and her view the forme bestowes
> Amongst her spirits: for as colour flowes
> From superficies of each thing we see,
> Even so with colours formes emitted bee:
> And where Loves forme is, love is, love is forme.
>   (V, 221–27)

"Form" here obtrudes; in another place, where Hero meditates on the torch which is to show the way to her lover, the "free soule" (which we shall meet again) is teased from the image:

> When Bees makes waxe, Nature doth not intend
> It shall be made a Torch: but we that know
> The proper vertue of it make it so,
> And when t'is made we light it: nor did Nature
> Propose one life to maids, but each such creature
> Makes by her soule the best of her free state,
> Which without love is rude, disconsolate,
> And wants loves fire to make it milde and bright,
> Till when, maids are but Torches wanting light.
>   (VI, 67–75)

The continuation of *Hero and Leander*, for all its pomp, remains a private poem; its figures are as public and openly expressive as those of a masque, yet coloured and informed by the poet's rhetoric, they move centripetally toward the furious dark intelligence which gave them birth. Yet the interplay of outward panoply and inward signification is a step out of the shadow of night.

Whether it was the experience of writing this poem, or of writing for the stage, or, more likely, of beginning to saturate himself in Homer, "this Artizan, this God of rationall loves," by 1598 and thereafter Chapman tries less to create the arcane emblem, is more discursive (and indeed windy) in style, and is more the moralist and religious poet, the unacknowledged legislator. In the epistle to Thomas Harriott accompanying *Achilles Shield* (1598), for example, he recognizes that his friend's powers are different from his own, though both work to the same end, to show "what true man is." He would still sit at the feet of this Gamaliel—

> Skill and the love of skil do ever kisse—

but he acknowledges his own insufficiency, his "hid soule," his "spirits oppression," his "prest soule." This poem records something like a religious crisis:

> O that my strange muse
> Without this bodies nourishment could use,
> Her zealous faculties, onely t'aspire,
> Instructive light from your whole Sphere of fire:
> But woe is me, what zeale or power soever
> My free soule hath, my body will be never
> Able t'attend: never shal I enjoy,
> Th'end of my happles birth: never employ
> That smothered fervour that in lothed embers
> Lyes swept from light, and no cleare howre remembers.[69]

His difficulty in composition is a symptom of his imperfection, of his inability to reach some unworldly state in which the Word will be revealed to him, in which "Philosophie," the "beame of God," will shine upon his darkness. He is in search of what Northrop Frye has called "a visionary and theosophical *via media*," such as that professed alike by the cabbalists, Ficino, Bruno and the alchemists—and in less sophisticated terms by the Anabaptists.[70] This condition, or power, he describes variously in this poem as the "whole Sphere of fire," the "genuine formes" of his soul, "true learning" which "hath a body absolute," "true wisedome," "Heavens inward brightnes shewing cleare," "soules strength," "the worth of all the Graces,/Due to the mindes giftes"—and all this he attributes to Harriott, who has found

---

[69] *Poems*, p. 381.

[70] Northrop Frye, *Fearful Symmetry* (Princeton, 1947), p. 151. See also Paul Shorey, *Platonism Ancient and Modern* (Berkeley, 1938), p. 122; Ernest Cassirer, *The Platonic Renaissance in England* (London, 1953), pp. 14–23; Frances A. Yates, "The Religious Policy of Giordano Bruno," *JWCI* III (1939–40), 191. For the poet as priest of his own religion, see R. W. Battenhouse, *Marlowe's Tamburlaine* (Nashville, 1941), p. 36.

it by *his* learning, which makes Nature "all transparent," while affirming that it can be achieved by poetry too,

> From whose reflections flow eternall lines;
> *Philosophy* retirde to darkest caves
> She can discover.[71]

The mind so elevated and transfigured is "free and royall," despising
the "skornefull, this despisde, inverted world," and all the "formall
Clearkes/Blowne for profession," who "spend their soules in sparkes"
instead of the true fire.

The image of the poet conveyed in this poem is Promethean[72] rather
than Orphean, with the world set to peck at his liver, seat of his earth-
adhering passions, and the powers attributed to poetry prophetic of the
claims made in the dedication to *Andromeda Liberata*:

> For as the Bodies pulse (in Phisique) is
> A little thing; yet therein th'Arteries
> Bewray their motion, and disclose, to Art
> The strength, or weaknesse, of the vitall part;
> Perpetually mooving, like a watch
> Put in our Bodies: So this three mens catch,
> This little Soules Pulse, *Poesie*, panting still
> Like to a dancing pease upon a Quill,
> Made with a childes breath, up and downe to fly,
> (Is no more manly thought); And yet thereby
> Even in the corps of all the world we can
> Discover all the good and bad of man,
> Anatomise his nakednesse, and be
> To his chiefe Ornament, a Majestie:
> Erect him past his human Period
> And heighten his transition into God.[73]

The uncertainty he feels—though this may be only formal humility—
about the poet's functions and powers is to be resolved by Homer,
who will, he hopes, not only find him a patron in the "outward" world
(in the person of Essex) but lead him to a revelation: "Homer being
my roote I cannot die." In *The Tears of Peace* this is what Homer does.

[71]Cf. William Vaughan, *Golden Grove*, sig. Ziv: "Poets were the first that observed
the sacred operations of nature, and especially the celestial courses. . . . They lived
chast, and by their exceeding continence came to receyve visions & prophesies."
[72]Cf. "Hymnus in Noctem," ll. 131 ff. For the emblem of the artist as Prometheus
see Olga Raggio, "The Myth of Prometheus: its Survival and Metamorphoses up to
the Eighteenth Century," *JWCI* XXI (1958), 59.
[73]*Poems*, pp. 305–6.

In *Euthymiae Raptus* (the alternative title), a verse-letter to Prince Henry following the presentation of the *Iliads* (1609), Chapman's centripetal imagination returns to the figure of Euthimya introduced in the "Hymnus in Cynthiam." There she was pursued by daylight passions, here met in vigil and contemplation. *The Tears of Peace* is the first of Chapman's two vigil poems—the second being *Eugenia*; in both he anticipates, more conspicuously than in *The Shadow of Night*, the nocturnal aspect of the Romantic temperament. But in both also—and his profession of Christian faith in "A Hymne to our Saviour" comes between them—he appears as a lay preacher of a Stoic-Protestant cast.

M. Jacquot judges that the idea for this poem and the sources for some passages in it come from Erasmus' *Querela pacis*, and he finds in the apparition of Homer to the brooding poet a reminiscence of that book of the *Hermetica* named in the sixteenth-century editions "Pimander."[74] Another very likely source is Petrarch's *Secretum*, which Chapman used elsewhere;[75] like this poem, it is an *apologia pro vita sua*, in which St. Augustine is introduced to Petrarch by Truth, and the opinions of the crowd are abjured in favour of self-reverence, self-knowledge, self-control—as in Chapman.

The argument of *The Tears of Peace* is tedious and repetitive, but must be considered at length, for it is the centre of Chapman's thought and the clue to his inner life. The poem may deserve the maledictions upon its style which M. Jacquot (who at least has read it) heaps up, but though prolix and confused it is also full of rich and diverse matter, and not without an occasional felicity. Nor is it sufficient to toss up the terms neoplatonism, stoicism, Christianity over the poem and watch where they settle, or simply to use this poem as a rich collection of proof-texts to make a general decision about a theoretical unified Chapman.[76] With Chapman, the process is usually more interesting than the conclusion.

First of all, the poem hangs upon the by now familiar paradigm of "outward–inward": the King, Chapman begins, has "cleard . . . warres outward ill," and has turned to "cast learn'd ynke upon those

---

[74]Jacquot, pp. 73–6. I think that Chapman had been reading Pierre Charron's *De la Sagesse* (1601); his "Learning" is close to Charron's idea of wisdom. See Eugene F. Rice, Jr., *The Renaissance Idea of Wisdom* (Cambridge, Mass., 1958), ch. 7.

[75]In *Monsieur d'Olive*, III, i.

[76]As with R. W. Battenhouse, "Chapman and the Nature of Man," *ELH* XII (1945), 87–107; or Ennis Rees, *The Tragedies of George Chapman* (Cambridge, Mass., 1954), ch. 1.

inward fires/That kindle worse Warre, in the mindes of men";[77] meanwhile the poet, mourning the triumph of self-love and sensuality, shuns the "jarring preace" and seeks the "least trodden fields, and fre'est shades." To him, in this path of contemplation, walking solitary in the waste wood of a fallen world from which inward peace seems to have departed, appears "a comfortable light,"

> and, after it, the sight
> Of a most grave, and goodly person shinde;
> With eye turnd upwards, & was outward, blind;
> But, inward; past, and future things, he sawe;
> And was to both, and present times, their lawe.
> His sacred bosome was so full of fire,
> That t'was transparent; and made him expire
> His breath in flames, that did instruct (me thought)
> And (as my soule were then at full) they wrought.
>
> (11. 34–42)

Not Vergil (as to Dante), but Homer, the seer, the heavenly familiar, the affable familiar ghost, instructs and comforts him, announcing himself as

> that spirit *Elysian*,
> That (in thy native ayre; and on the hill
> Next *Hitchins* left hand) did thy bosome fill,
> With such a flood of soule; that thou wert faine
> (With acclamations of her Rapture then)
> To vent it, to the Echoes of the vale.
>
> (11. 75–80)

He is the poet's "Angell . . . Starre, and Fate"; promises a "free and harmelesse life" in old age, and at this time commends what he "onely studiest," the nature of man, what he unhappily is, and what he should be, in other words the "exalted and problematic" nature (so in Pico) of the being who can be both beast ("horrid") and god ("divine").

The seer then "rent a Cloude down," and shows him a pageant, a *pompe funèbre*; a "Lady, like a Deitie indew'd" bearing a coffin, and following her "in funerall forme" a procession of beasts, male and female, two by two. This figure of an ark, being interpreted, is an emblem of the hidden truth of "that maine defect" that makes men

---

[77]For the various ways in which James's devotion to peace was symbolically represented by the poets and masque-makers, see A. H. Gilbert, *The Symbolic Persons in the Masques of Ben Jonson* (Durham, S.C., 1948), pp. 132–42.

reject "inward Peace," for this is Peace herself, banished into the wilderness by man, mourning the death of Love. The poet now beholds a Fall:

> And now fell all things from their naturall Birth:
> Passion in Heaven; Stupiditie, in Earth,
> Inverted all; the Muses, Vertues, Graces,
> Now suffered rude, and miserable chaces
> From mens societies, to that desert heath;
> And after them, Religion (chac't by death)
> Came weeping, bleeding to the Funerall:
> Sought her deare Mother Peace; and downe did fall,
> Before her, fainting. . . .
> Thus the poore broode of Peace: driven, & distrest,
> Lay brooded all beneath their mothers breast;
> Who fell upon them weeping, as they fell:
> All were so pinde, that she containde them well.
> And in this Chaos, the digestion
> And beautie of the world, lay thrust and throwne.
>
> (11. 200–8, 220–5)

The images, reminiscent of *The Shadow of Night*, have a strange power, derived from their extension of paradox to the edge of the grotesque—appropriate enough, for this is a nightmare vision, terrifying and pitiful. Then Peace, leaning on Religion's bosom, "first shed teares of anger" and so begins the main colloquy with the visionary, the complaint of Peace, 814 lines of it. When the "unworldly conference" is over, Peace rises up, and before her fly all the sins and afflictions of man, leaving such a silence that the poet hears "the musique of the Spheres,/And all the Angels, singing, out of heaven." She passes into the "horrid wood" of Murther,

> A heape of panting Harts, supported him;
> On which, he sate, gnawing a reeking lymme,
> Of some man newly murtherd. As he eate
> His grave-digg'd Browes, like stormy Eaves did sweat;
> Which, like incensed Fennes, with mists did smoke;
> His hyde was rugged, as an aged Oke
> With heathen Leprosies; that still hee fed
> With hote, raw lyms, of men late murthered.
> His Face was like a Meteor, flashing blood;
> His head all bristl'd, like a thornie wood;
> His necke cast wrinkles, like a Sea enrag'd;
> And, in his vast Armes, was the world engag'd,
>
> (11. 1139–50)

and there she rescues the body of "dead Human Love," buries it with Poesie's "speciall obsequie," from which he is "ravisht . . . to heaven," and with him "Peace, with all her heavenly seede."

Between these visions of fall, harrowing and resurrection, in this Holy Saturday of the inspired poet, this intersection time, during this colloquy in which both speak with one voice, the ideal of "Learning," darkly suggested from the beginning, is clearly set forth—and the world is condemned. I have ventured a phrase from *Little Gidding*, and indeed the opening of the colloquy discovers the lot of the religious poet in somewhat similar terms:

> Why haunt'st thou freely, these unhaunted places,
> Emptie of pleasures? empty of all Graces,
> Fashions, and Riches; by the best pursude
> With broken Sleepe, Toyle, Love, Zeale, Servitude;
> With fear and trembling, with whole lives, and Soules?
> While thou break'st sleepes, digst under Earth, like moules,
> To live, to seeke me out, whome all men fly:
> And think'st to finde, light in obscuritie,
> Eternitie, in this deepe vale of death:
> Look'st ever upwards, and liv'st still beneath;
> Fill'st all thy actions, with strife, what to thinke,
> Thy Braine with Ayre, and skatterst it in inke
> Of which thou mak'st weeds for thy soule to weare,
> As out of fashion, as the bodies are.

(11. 268–81)

One does not need to infer from this that Chapman wore a dark doublet and no French slops, but in his reply he certainly rejects the world of "news," of "ayrie" men, of riches, and the wrong kind of "formes," for the inward world of virtue.[78] In the outward world, Peace replies, distinction of the orders of society is broken, but "regular Learning" (like "Ceremony" in *Hero and Leander*) should "set difference/Twixt all mens worths, and make the meane, or great,/ As that is meane or great."[79] In the inward life, Learning is

> (the soules actuall frame;
> Without which, tis a blanke; a smoke-hid flame)

---

[78]Cf. *Poems*, pp. 19 (". . . their Idolatrous platts for riches" [an interesting choice of words: playwriting?]), 82 ("Riches may from a poor verse be deduced"); cf. the emblem (riches vs. virtue) in Achilles Bocchi Bonon., *Symbolicarum Quaestionum &c.* (1574), symb. xli.

[79]For this view, and the comments expressed in the lines following (337–45), see *Nennio, or a Treatise of Nobility* (1595), and Chapman's commendatory sonnet, *Poems*, p. 353.

> Should sit great Arbitresse, of all things donne,
> And in your soules, (like Gnomons in the Sunne)
> Give rules to all the circles of your lives;
> I prove it, by the Regiment God gives
> To man, of all things; to the soule of man;
> To learning, of the Soule.
>
> (11. 352–59)

Learning is an Art which works upon Nature, as a "Statuarie" upon a lump of alabaster:

> So when the Soule is to the body given;
> (Being substance of Gods Image, sent from heaven)
> It is not his true Image, till it take
> Into the Substance, those fit formes that make
> His perfect Image; which are then imprest
> By Learning and impulsion; that invest
> Man with Gods forme in living Holinesse,
> But cutting from his Body the excesse
> Of Humors, perturbations and Affects;
> Which Nature (without Art) no more ejects,
> Then without tooles, a naked Artizan
> Can, in rude stone, cut th'Image of a man.
>
> (11. 373–384)

This definition is repeated, in essentials, twice:

> But this is Learning; To have skill to throwe
> Reignes on your bodies powres, that nothing knowe;
> And fill the soules powers, so with act, and art,
> That she can curbe the bodies angrie part;
> All perturbations; all affects that stray
> From their one object; which is to obay
> Her Soveraigne Empire . . .
>   to make her substance still contend
> To be Gods Image.
>
> (11. 504–514)

> . . . th'effect
> Proper to perfect Learning [is] to direct
> Reason in such an Art, as that it can
> Turne blood to soule, and make both, one calme man.
>
> (11. 556–559)

And again in an epigram in the *Petrarchs Seven Penitentiall Psalms* volume:

> Learning, the Art is of good life; they then
> That leade not good lives, are not learned men.

Learning is soul-craft, self-making, not an infusion of grace; as the re-statement of the definition in "To young imaginaries in knowledge" (in the same collection) shows, the inspiration is Epictetus. What Chapman adds to the Stoic *gravitas* and the equation of virtue and knowledge is, first, a colouring of the neoplatonic way of "purification,"[80] and to the sense of the supernatural which that affords a further Christian *pietas*. The tone of *The Tears of Peace* is not by any means sacramental, but it is close to that of *Paradise Regained*.

But to note these definitions is not, as I have already argued, to get at the real "form" of Chapman's thought; he is eclectic but he is also passionate. The Stoic ideal can appeal to personalities as diverse as Calvin and Montaigne—and can be rejected by both. This poem undoubtedly marks the transition from Chapman's admiration of the Achillean virtues to his glorification of the inward powers in Odysseus, or from Bussy and Byron to Clermont, or from wisdom as the initiation into *mysteria* to wisdom as the *habit* of self-discipline and virtue:

> ... wisedome is nought else, then learning fin'd
> And with the understanding Powre combin'd;
> That is, a habite of both habits standing;
> The Bloods vaine humours, ever countermanding.[81]
>
> (11. 483–6)

But it is a transition, not a mere log-book; a treatise *de contemptu mundi* written out of some agony of spirit by one who had been struck by "greatness," fascinated by wit and tempted by study.

Who are the enemies of Learning? The vulgar and ignorant bestial men certainly; but chiefly the "Active men," who "consume their whole life's fire" in mounting after power, the tragic heroes; the "Passive men," who are "in meates, and cuppes laborious," and "bangle in the Ayre,/To stoope at scraps," the comic gulls and perhaps even their tormentors the intriguers; and the "Intellective men," who pursue the shadow of knowledge only. The active men are slaves of passion, the passive men victims of the "frantique humour of ridiculous blood," the intellective men live by their jarring controversial pens, mere scholars, "walking dictionaries," "Clearkes that goe with God & man to warre" against Peace. Greatness is vain:

> For great men; though such ample stuffe they have
> To shape contentment; yet, since (like a wave)

---

[80]Cf. Kristeller, *Ficino*, p. 302.

[81]He confessed to Henry Reynolds that "for more then matter of morality" he had discovered little in the "meanings" of Homer, no "hidden wayes & workings" of Nature enigmatically set out. See *Mythomystes*, in *Critical Essays of the Seventeenth Century*, I, 165, and chapter 5, below.

> It flittes, and takes all formes, retayning none;
> (Not fitted to their patterne, which is one)
> They may content themselves; God hath not given,
> To men mere earthly, the true Joyes of heaven;
> And so their wilde ambitions either stay;
> Or turne their headstrong course, the better way.
>
> (ll. 640–7)

Not such the "tun'd body" of the disciplined learned man, which
turns away from "unquiet, wicked thoughts . . . howrely fluctuations,"
tuned by "proportion," which

> must traverse her accesse
> Betwixt his powre, and will; his Sense and Soule;
> And evermore th'exorbitance controule
> Of all forms, passing through the bodies Powre,
> Till in the soule they rest, as in their Towre.
>
> (ll. 867–71)

To this of Peace the poet replies, in a strongly confessional passage,
marked as always by the image of fire:

> But; as Earths grosse and elementall fire,
> Cannot maintaine it selfe; but doth require
> Fresh matter still, to give it heate, and light;
> And, when it is enflam'd; mounts not upright;
> But struggles in his lame impure ascent;
> Now this waie works, and then is that waie bent,
> Not able, straight, t'aspire to his true Sphere
> Where burns the fire, eternall, and sincere;
> So, best soules here; with heartiest zeales enflam'd
> In their high flight for heaven; earth-broos'd and lam'd)
> Make many faint approches; and are faine,
> With much unworthy matter, to sustaine
> Their holiest fire.
>
> (ll. 872–84)

Born under one law, to another bound: Chapman's version of the
Fall (into matter from spirit) may be neoplatonic rather than Christian
in its formulation, but in the ethical context the result is the same.
Peace's response, couched in strongly Scriptural language (ll. 886–924)
is uncompromising: take His yoke upon you, reject the world. To
which the poet still pleads the *unfairness* of life, his "poore, and abject
life," his "desert fortunes," and while asserting his love to God and his
submission to the divine will, confesses his sometime despair in his

"Birth-accurst life," and how his soul wrestles with angels, resolves to forsake the world:

> To which end, I will cast this Serpents skale;
> This load of life, in life; this fleshie stone;
> This bond, and bundle of corruption;
> This breathing Sepulcher; this spundge of griefe;
> This smiling Enemie; this household-thiefe;
> This glass of ayre; broken with less then breath;
> This Slave, bound face to face, to death, till death;
> And consecrate my life to you, and yours.
>
> (11. 1014–20)

Peace replies that she sees his "friendlesse life converted" to God— and promises him (perhaps) the favour of the Prince.

The mildest inquisition would find Chapman full of heresies: he is a Catharist and a Pelagian at once; but the idea of heresy seems wholly absurd, applied in this context. The contention of James Smith, that Chapman is neither thinker nor scholar,[82] has some relevance here, for in the later religious poems, as in *The Tears of Peace*, while the poet seems to be formulating a creed he is actually giving a portentous form to an obsession, seeking by exhortation and ejaculation to reconcile two warring halves of his being: the self-sufficient and the penitential, the soldier and the quietist. The "mortall Monarchie" of the soul, surveying "th' admired Fabricke of her world," so proudly (and, as some would have it) bumptiously proclaimed, in the manner of Bussy or Byron, in the epistle dedicatory to *Andromeda Liberata*, had been, as we have seen, hard enough won from the claws of the foul panther earth. But its end is pious contemplation, whereas Christian humility (figured in the Redeemer) harrows hell and scourges the chapmen of the temple. Hence Chapman's Christ is Promethean or Herculean and his "good" or wise man would pass for a Christian in the light of this world.

One may suppose (with Schoell)[83] that it is some such reconciliation of opposites which prompted the citation of the motto from Wolfius' translation of Epictetus on the title-page of *Petrarchs Seven Penitentiall Psalms* (1612): *Progressus sum in medium, & pacem/Omnibus hominibus proclamo*. But this slender volume (too slender or too harsh in matter for the Prince, Chapman says), the whole end of which is "good life, and the true feeling of our humane birth and Being," is more a collection out of his commonplace books than a formed work. It is perhaps

---

[82]"George Chapman," *Scrutiny* III (1934–35), 343.

[83]Schoell, p. 104.

oversophistication in the reader to see the self-abasement and sense of sin in the translations of Petrarch's Psalms balancing the self-conscious "art" of good life and precepts of Stoic integrity variously inculcated in the group of translations and adaptations from the Vergilian epigrams, Plutarch's *Moralia* and especially from the *Discourses* and *Enchiridion* of Epictetus which close the volume, with the "Hymne to our Saviour on the Crosse," the only original work in the group, as the thematic fulcrum of the whole. Some of the short adaptations are notes for *The Revenge of Bussy d'Ambois*, and indeed almost all of them could be arranged as footnotes to that work and to *The Tears of Peace*; in the centre of the group is "Virgils Epigram of this letter Y," the Pythagorean emblem, opposing "vertues hard way" to the outward sensual way of "shadows" and "braverie," with which we may place the third verse of Psalm V:

> No outward light, my life hath graced,
> My mind hath ever bene my onely Sunne:
> And that so far hath envie chaced,
> That all in clouds her hated head is runne.
>   And while she hides, immortall cares
>   Consume the soule, that sense inspires:
>   Since outward she sets eyes and eares,
>   And other joyes spend her desires.[84]

The "Hymne" is Chapman's profession of faith; it is also, appropriately, a digest of his non-dramatic poetry, in matter and manner. Its central image is, of course, biblical; but that is extrapolated out of Ficino and completed by sentences from Epictetus. The Passion of Christ demands that paradox be taken as an article of faith; and Chapman had faith in paradox as a tool of rhetoric and as salve for the soul. "Height in humilitie," fire out of darkness, creation out of suffering, falling to rise, the inward triumph in the outward defeat—all these and more cluster about the Word made flesh. For part of the poem (11. 60–137), it is true, the poet turns his gaze outward upon the visible church, asserts the primacy of Scripture over "antiquities," deplores controversies in a tone which anticipates the position of Rev. John Hales, condemns corruption and sensuality in the church, and touches darkly on antinomianism and hypocritical professions. But the main argument, after a fervent invocation to "our Champion Olympian," from a world in which simple piety suffers as much as Christ did on the cross, sees the Redeemer's "abject plight" as an

[84]*Poems*, p. 212.

emblem of "true pietie [wearing] her pearles within," and his atonement as a relief from the "smothering" clogs of the flesh, as a stripping off of the "formes of earth" to reveal the image of God in us. The Fall is defined (from Ficino) as the soul's rapture with her "shadow" or "base corporeall forme," in which state she is like Narcissus enamoured of "this vile bodies use." The light which shines in this darkness is only truly available, it seems, to the elect who incline to heaven, who are "inward," to "those few" (as the marginal note puts it) "whom God hath inspired with the soules true use." While "ascribing still/All to [Christ's] merits: both our power and will./ To every thought of goodnesse," Chapman obviously thinks of his Saviour as a kind of first cause or "enabling" agent to set at work the art of Learning. Hence his final prayer, with its pronounced Stoic overtones:

> Order these last steps of my abject state,
> Straite on the marke a man should levell at:
> And grant that while I strive to forme in me,
> Thy sacred image, no adversitie
> May make me draw one limme, or line amisse:
> Let no vile fashion wrest my faculties
> From what becomes that Image. Quiet so
> My bodies powres, that neither weale nor wo,
> May stirre one thought up, gainst thy freest will.
> Grant, that in me, my mindes waves may be still:
> The world for no extreme may use her voice;
> Nor Fortune treading reeds, make any noise.[85]

"Chapman's Christ," says Battenhouse, "is a Promethean poet,"[86] "heightening" man's transition into God out of the Epimethean or "corporeall part" of him. It is not surprising to find that this Redeemer is a despised and rejected artist, or that Learning is *imitatio Christi*.

With *Eugenia* (1614) we return to the shadow of night, an obsequy for William, Lord Russell, whom Chapman professed to find one of those whom nobility made sacred, like himself a Netherlands veteran and man of action, but his life "grounded" in Religion, and apparently the very thought of him a reminiscence of the "crowne of ould Humanitie" which conservatives like Chapman associated with the days of Elizabeth.

This, intended to be the first of a set of "anniversaries,"[87] must be the most cluttered poem in English literature. "Eugenia or true

---

[85] *Poems*, pp. 226–7.
[86] "Chapman and the Nature of Man," 95.
[87] Dedication to Francis, Lord Russell, *Poems*, p. 271.

Noblesse," seeing "nought noble now, but servile *Avarice*," flies for comfort to the house of Fame,[88] where she finds "the *Russelides*" registered; to her from "the base world" fly the Muses and Graces, and before them Religion, "Roote to all acts, noble and renown'd." Then springs up a terrible tempest, presaged by the ominous actions of birds, beasts and fish (a curious bestiary, which has found a place in John Hayward's *Penguin Book of English Verse*),[89] but not even this— a nice hyperbole—is worthy to announce the death of "this rare religious Lord." Eugenia bleeds—here the allegory is scarcely dark— and is comforted by Religion, who (in one of Chapman's most grotesque emblems)

> . . . halfe intraunc'd her selfe was; all the part
> She had of humaines pinde even to her heart:
> And made her forme, as if transformd she were,
> Into a leane, and lisping Grashopper:
> As small and faintly spake she; her strength's losse,
> Made her goe lame, and leaning on the crosse,
> Stooping, and crooked, and her joints did cracke,
> As all the weight of earth were on her backe:
> Her lookes were like the pictures that are made,
> To th'opticke reason; one way like a shade,
> Another monster like, and every way
> To passers by, and such as made no stay,
> To view her in a right line, face to face,
> She seem'd a serious trifle; all her grace,
> Show'd in her fixt inspection; and then
> She was the onely grace of dames and men:
> All hid in cobwebbs came she forth, like these
> Poore country churches, chappels cald of ease
> For so of worldly ends, men zealous were. . . .
> All full of spiders was her homespun weede,
> Where soules like flies hung, of which, some would strive
> To breake the net, their bodies yet alive,
> Some (all their bodies eate) the spiders thighes
> Left hanging like the onely wings of flies.
>
> (11. 165–191)

Eugenia is roused and in her vigil sings the praises of the deceased, reviews his accomplishments, and invites Fame to sound his praise. The morning interrupts, burning up "all things sacred," and the "Night-birds of the day" begin to gibber; all is tumult in a hellish

---

[88]Adapted from Ovid, *Metamorphoses* XII, 39–52; see Jacquot, p. 78.

[89]The passage is plagiarized from Angelo Poliziano's *Rusticus*; see S. K. Heninger, Jr., "Chapman's Plagiarism of Poliziano's *Rusticus*," *MLN* LXXIII (1958), 6–8.

transmutation; when Night and Silence, which "best fit Contemplation," come again, Fame introduces Lord Russell, who, like Addison,
teaches us how to die, with a long lecture, mainly out of Plutarch,
against the fear of death. Another day of "the clamorous game-given
world" intervenes, after which "the world-scar'd broode of Peace,"

> The despisde of day,
> (The Muses, Graces, Vertues, Poesie
> But then arriv'd there) on the Pavement by
> Sate round: Religion (as of that rich Ring
> The precious stone) did th'ends together bring
> Of their Celestiall circle,

and they listen while Fame, with a great deal of assistance from Rev.
William Walker's funeral sermon on the late lord, gives an account of
his religious end. The scornful Morn, introducing the "inverted"
daylight world, turns all this exemplary and elevating exhortation to
nothing, but evening comes again, and with her alchemy turns the
"Iron world into the goulden age," while "poore Poesie" sings a
funeral hymn. Eugenia rises from her trance, resolves to return to earth
to dwell with the noble lord's son—and the day returns, described in
lines which have something of the effect of the close of *Little Dorrit*:

> To these, the Night, thus short sem'd, and thus bare
> Was every clamorous worldling, at his care,
> Care cried in Cities, and in Countries ror'd:
> Now was the soule, a Toie; Her gifts abhor'd,
> All Ornament, but bravery, was a staine:
> Nought now akinne to wit, but Cosening Gaine. . . .
> Now bellies deafned eares, in every streete,
> And backs bore more then heads, heads more then feete.

In the midst of all this hyperbolic clutter and pomp, appropriate
to the genre and in this case recapitulating some of the images of his
first production, we hear a familiar voice, now melancholy, now
strident, now ecstatic, now sententious, *learned* always, expounding
the familiar lesson. The world is given over to "outward" men,

> Not knowledge, but opinion, being their Guide;[90]

Religion and "good life" are the grounds of all good action.

[90]On Reason (inward, of the soul) or Opinion (outward, of the body), see [Justus
Lipsius], *Two Bookes of Constancie . . . Englished by John Stradling* (1595), I, 5; John
Day, *The Parliament of Bees* (1641), sigs D3v-EZ, on "worldlings" contempt for poets
and scholars "come undone" by Opinion. On Opinion as the offspring of the "fan-
tasy," and its evil effects, Pierre Charron, *Of Wisdom*, trans. Samson Lennard (1609),
pp. 67-8. On "Opinion" in Chapman generally, Peter Ure's valuable article "A Note
on 'Opinion' in Daniel, Greville and Chapman," *MLR* XLVI (1957), 331-8.

> A man, all Center is, all stay, all minde,
> The bodie onely, made her instrument:
> And to her ends, in all acts must consent,
> Without which order, all this life hath none,
> But breeds the other lifes confusion.
> Respect to things without us, hinder this
> Inward consent of our soules faculties.
> Things outward therefore, thinke no further yours
> Then they yeeld homage, to your inward powers,
> In their obedience to your reasons use,
> Which for their order, deitie did infuse.
>
> (11. 633–43)

"Good life takes her light/From her owne flame": "the gawdie light" of "this Pied world" is to be cast off; sense interposes delays to Reason's comforts; when once we are assured that God "to every sound beliefe convaith/A Regular knowledge," our "generall peace [is] so circulare/ That Faith and Hope at either end shall pull/And make it come: Round as the Moone at full."

It is ironic that this climactic image should on inspection turn out to be a figure of mutability. Indeed there is a significant contradiction between the ideal of completeness and calm, symbolized by these benign feminine deities (Cynthia, Euthimya, Eugenia) and the images and epithets continuously and perhaps unconsciously applied to the seeker or seer, who alternates between melancholy and rage, watery earth and aery fire, drowning or consuming, and in both obscured. There is no *stillness* in Chapman. The landscape is a waste place, either a craggy wilderness of savage thickets and roaming beasts, or a teeming city of vainglorious shows, Vanity Fair, an antipodes, an inverted world of gibberers walking on their empty heads—Circe's realm. Even the grave goddesses cry out in anguish, and Ceremony appears in offended majesty. Chapman commended pastoral,[91] but he has left us none, no greensward, no *otium*, only a mocking echo of Marlowe in an apprentice play.[92] A stranger alike to Drayton's historical streams and Marvell's entranced garden, Chapman's imagination creates a world as surrealistic as the sterile vistas of the emblem-makers. For him Nature was a paradigm and Art a pulse.

These are general observations, the result of meditation over these dark poems which punctuate the most productive period of his life, like bands in the spectrum of his really impressive range of talents. I shall have to qualify them as I proceed, but not reject them.

[91] In a commendatory poem to *The Faithful Shepherdess, Poems*, p. 363.
[92] *The Blind Beggar of Alexandria*, ix, 24–33.

III · COMEDY

L. BEDDOES, who should have found Chapman in some ways a kindred spirit, observed that he had the least dramatic talent of any of the Elizabethans, and critics have not generally been kind in their assessment of his powers as a playwright. His tragedies have been taken seriously, as documents if not as play-books, but the comedies are lightly regarded. "Chapman's a sad dul Rogue at Comedy," said an anonymous satirist of the Restoration, starting it off; "exercises in art rather than animate theatre," pronounces Miss Bradbrook, ambiguously; works of secondary importance, according to M. Jacquot; purely conventional, asserts Paul Kreider, who codified the conventions of Elizabethan comedy in terms of Chapman's plays. On the other hand, Swinburne, while finding Chapman "by temperament and inclination . . . rather an epic or tragic than a comic poet," praised the easy and graceful style of the comedies, where Chapman "felt himself no longer bound to talk big or to stalk stiffly," and Parrott, who makes great claims for his poet as an innovator and technician in comedy, also commends Chapman's achievement in the blank verse of comedy as a model for Middleton, Fletcher and others.[1]

Shakespeare and Jonson cast long shadows in this genre, but Chapman is not obscured, for he had a line, or lines of his own, either in the adaptation of the comedy of the schools, or in mixed "romantic"

[1]"The Tory-Poets, a Satyr" [1682], in G. E. Bentley, *Shakespeare and Jonson: Their Reputations in the Seventeenth Century Compared* (Chicago, 1945), II, 281; M. C. Bradbrook, *Growth and Structure of Elizabethan Comedy*, p. 172; Jacquot, p. III; Paul Kreider, *Elizabethan Comic Character Conventions as revealed in the Comedies of George Chapman* (Ann Arbor, 1935), p. 4; Swinburne, *Chapman*, p. 167; *Comedies*, p. 676.

comedy. His development of the character of the *dolosus servus*, the intriguer of Roman comedy, into a Hermes-figure of commanding proportions, has been noted by Parrott, Bradbrook and others. Chapman, like other pious and unsocial contemplatives before and since, was fascinated by *power*, whether in the grandiose tragic hero or in the masters of ceremony at a comic feast of fools. Is power, he wondered, the gift of Fortune or Virtue? This question, on which Plutarch sums up the thought of the ancient world, troubles the comedies a little and the tragedies much. Not so much noticed is his fascination with the themes of melancholy and entombment (from *An Humorous Day's Mirth* to *The Widow's Tears*), with comedy as the breaking-up of mourning into saturnalia (conventional if you will, but that is not a bad word). He is, as we should expect, Jonsonian in his affiliation: not only in the delineation of humours and his gallery of gulls and boobies (LaBesha, Sir Giles Goosecap, Poggio) but in his generally unsympathetic portrayal of female characters, and the easy savagery of his comments on the cankers of a society of parvenus; he can occasionally rival Jonson in an allusive and athletic piece of prose (e.g. *Widow's Tears*, II, i, 20ff.). Seeming to go ahead without theory— if we except the remarks in the Prologue to *All Fools* and a late humanist profession of contempt for the "puppetry, and pied ridiculous antics" of the popular stage[2]—he created, not a comic "world," neither the crowded parish where Jonson's hungry and obsessed time-servers choke on each other's hyperboles, nor the formal garden where Shakespeare's ladies and gentlemen dance their witty galliards and pavanes, but certainly a set of very interesting divertissements.

Even with such modest expectations, the reader who begins with *The Blind Beggar of Alexandria* will be baffled and irritated, and, if he has learned that Henslowe recorded 22 performances of this piece in 1596–97, and that it was revived in 1601,[3] he will have cause to reflect grimly (as every reader of minor Elizabethan drama must) on the curious tastes of our ancestors—or, if he stops to think further, he may notice in these ridiculous antics a strong resemblance to the quality and in some cases the substance of the fare provided on commercial television. Granted that William Jones's quarto does not represent the play as produced, the romantic plot being almost entirely lost, the title page shows that it was the "variable humours" of the blind beggar, here rescued from oblivion, which were popular. And it is easy to see why, for the piece was obviously designed to remind the

[2] *The Revenge of Bussy D'Ambois*, I, i, 324 ff.

[3] Here, as elsewhere in accounts of performances and publication, I follow Parrott unless otherwise noted.

spectators continually of Marlowe and especially of Tamburlaine. The central figure, a megalomaniac quick-change artist, appearing as Irus (*Odyssey*, xviii), Count Hermes (note the name) a swaggering ruffian, Leon a usurer and Duke Cleanthes, is "a shepherd's son"; there are echoes like "Why, what is dalliance, says my servant then?"; there is a pompous entrance of barbarous kings "with soldiers and drum and ensign," and so forth. The language is frequently a travesty of Marlowe's style:

> My sweet Acates and Acanthes slain!
> Grief to my heart and sorrow to my soul!
> Then arouse thyself, Cleanthes, and revenge
> Their guiltless blood on these base miscreants.
> Oh, let the canker'd trumpet of the deep
> Be rattled out and ring into their ears
> The dire revenge Cleanthes will inflict
> On these four kings and all their complices.
>
> (sc. ix)

There are other allusions too. In fact this fragment is a kind of index to the catch-words and conventional phrases, the little literary jokes and the general idiom of the popular theatre of the nineties. Every student (or parodist) of the Elizabethan drama will recognize these— and many others:

> Leave me awhile, my lords, and wait for me
> At the black fountain. . . .

> And offering stain to Egypt's royal bed. . . .

> Come, gird this pistol closely to my side,
> By which I make men fear my humour still,
> And have slain two or three, as 'twere my mood. . . .

> I am Signor Bragadino, the martial Spaniardo. . . .

Sweet nymph, I love few words; you know my intent, my humour is insophistical and plain. I am a Spaniard born, my birth speaks for my nature, my nature for your grace . . . .

> Die, thou vile wretch, and live, Aspasia. . . .

> Who calls out murther? Lady, was it you?

Did Chapman really think such leaden nuggets as these could be transmuted into the gold of dramatic rhetoric? It is impossible to say, but I suspect a certain cynicism. Parrott's hypothesis, that the printed play represents "a stage version which was in many respects a perversion of the original," certainly helps us out of the difficulty, but not altogether, for though the action may be mangled the words are there and presumably they have some fairly close relation to what the dramatist wrote down in the first place. There are hints, too, of the poet's serious preoccupations and even of some kind of allegory. The master trickster and seducer, who turns his society upside-down, is by turns a "reverent" seer or "skilled" man, a "wild and frantic" soldier of fortune and swaggerer, a usurer or master of avarice, and a nobleman; his "transformations" or "humours" thus constitute a microcosm of the social order. A certain seriousness keeps creeping in: Irus has skill "to tell the drifts of fate,/Our fortunes, and things hid from sensual eyes"; he compares himself to Homer, who, blind, could "best discern/The shapes of everything"; the irony sharpens his enjoyment of his roles, and he delights in the game as well as in its rewards. His wooing of Elimine (in the character of Leon) is not without merit, being sophistical, ironic, and full of rhetorical bravura:

> And therefore, beauteous lady, make not strange
> To take a friend and add unto the joys
> Of happy wedlock; the end of every act
> Is to increase contentment and renown,
> Both which my love shall amply joy in you.
>
> ELI.   How can renown ensue an act of shame?
> No act hath any shame within itself,
> But in the knowledge and ascription
> Of the base world, from whom this shall be kept,
> As in a labyrinth or brazen tower.
>
> LEON.   But virtue's sole regard must hold me back.
> The virtue of each thing is in the praise,
> And I will rear thy praises to the skies.
> Out of my treasury choose thy choice of gold,
> Till thou find some matching thy hair in brightness;
> But that will never be, so choose thou ever.
> Out of my jewelry choose thy choice of diamonds,
> Till thou find some as brightsome as thine eyes;
> But that will never be, so choose thou ever.
> Choose rubies out until thou match thy lips,
> Pearl till thy teeth, and ivory till thy skin
> Be match'd in whiteness, but that will never be;
> Nor ever shall my treasury have end,
> Till on their beauties ladies loathe to spend;
> But that will never be, so choose thou ever.
>
> (v, 91–115)

It appears that, in terms of Chapman's private ethical principles, this comic "lord of the ascendant" (Bradbrook's word) professes

"Opinion" to be the world's commander and makes hay while that sun shines. At all events, the comic world is certainly "outward."

But *The Blind Beggar* is a fragment; *An Humourous Day's Mirth* (1599), though a bad text, is a whole play. Whether Chapman in this play "initiated the whole Jonsonian comedy of humours,"[4] is an open question; at least here we find an informing idea and symbol: liberation by the "word," for the intriguer who reverses everything, and turns prison into festival, is named Lemot:

> . . . my name signifies word.
> —Well hit, Monsieur *Verbum!*
> —What, are you good at Latin, lady?
> —No, sir, but I know what *verbum* is.
> —Why, 'tis green bum: *ver* is green, and you know
> what bum is, I am sure of that.
> —No, sir, 'tis a verb.
>
> (v. 67–74)

Lemot *is* for the green world: for youth against age, for crowds against solitude, for cakes and ale against sobriety, for free love against jealousy. He is an active verb too, for he, as the tale-teller, sets all in motion and dissolves all secrecy.

At the opening of the action, jealousy rules: old Count Labervale jealously guards his young Puritan wife Florilla, since "pure religion being but mental stuff" she may "yield unto the motion of her blood"; old Countess Moren is jealous of her young husband; old Count Foyes jealously guards his daughter Martia, whom he intends to marry to the "very fine gull" Labesha, "one that's heir to a great living." By a series of misinformations and crossing plots, by spreading the word, Lemot shifts the action from the shut-up homes to the open tavern; at the end, amid general festival, and pardon for misunderstandings, the fair Martia is betrothed to Dowsecer, Labervale's son by a former marriage.

The portrait of Florilla is not, *pace* Parrott, of any great interest, being pieced together from the most obvious commonplaces, condemnation of the superstitions of the "times of ignorance," of the vanity of fine clothes (sc. iv), of "idols" (sc. xiv); she has a spiced conscience and is a hypocrite. So much for her, except that her entrance line is very funny indeed:

What have I done? Put on too many clothes.

Rather, to come to the "rare humours" of the play, we must concentrate upon the triad Dowsecer–Lemot–Labesha: Dowsecer the

[4]Bradbrook, *Growth and Structure*, p. 144; cf. *Comedies*, pp. 687–8.

melancholic scholar whose humour is purged by love; Labesha the "outward" fool who plays at the fashion of being melancholy ("I will in silence live a man forlorn,/Mad, and melancholy as a cat"); and Lemot, "the very imp of desolation," who danced at his parents' funeral, does all his trickery with complete detachment, and remains unmoved by the passions. Lemot is the airy agent of freedom whose activities expose the true soul of Dowsecer and the false front of Labesha. Scholar and fool, inward and outward man, are contrasted formally, even in this loose and confusing action: as Dowsecer is confronted by hose, sword and picture to remind him in his dumps of the active life (sc. vii), so Labesha, having "taken on him the humour of the young Lord Dowsecer," is tempted by "a mess of cream, a spice-cake and a spoon" to purge his humour (sc. xii).

As Lemot's essence is movement, as he is the pipe to make all dance, the ducdame to call all fools into a ring, so Dowsecer's element is stillness; he contemplates, and is contemplated, he sees the true object of his soul's desire, and obtains his reward. He is consequently, except for one scene at the centre of the play (sc. vii), in the background, but not, as Parrott had it, "crowded" into the background; that is where he belongs, for he is Chapman's "shadow."

Premonitions of *Hamlet* abound in this scene, which, in a modern production, would come just before the interval. Trumpets sound, not telling (the King says) "what I am, but what I seem," for he is full of imagined love and is "a king of clouts, a scarecrow, full of cobwebs"; the court comes to observe "the young Lord Dowsecer," who is "rarely learned, and nothing lunatic/As men suppose,/But hateth company and worldly trash." In his way, standing "close," the courtly Lavel places a picture, "a pair of large hose" with a codpiece, and a sword, "to put him by the sight of them in mind of their brave states that use them," for, as the King remarks, "the sense doth still stir up the soul." The melancholic enters, quoting Cicero's *Tusculan Disputations*, marvelling that Cicero could sell for glory "the sweet peace of life," and praising the age of Saturn. The King remarks that "this is no humour, but perfit judgment." Dowsecer, seeing the sword, condemns the "art of murder" of which it is the symbol; his eye falling upon the hose and codpiece, he condemns pomposity in apparel; when he sees the picture of the fair maiden, he speaks sharply of women's painting; confronted by his father, he affects to despise the joys of fatherhood. But Martia's appearance launches him into a neoplatonic (and un-Ovidian) passion:

> What have I seen? How am I burnt to dust
> With a new sun, and made a novel phoenix.

Is she a woman that objects this sight,
Able to work the chaos of the world
Into digestion? Oh, divine aspect!
The excellent disposer of the mind
Shines in thy beauty, and thou hast not changed
My soul to sense, but sense unto my soul;
And I desire thy pure society,
But even as angels do to angels fly.

(vii, 207–16)

At the close of the play, when a maid dressed as "Queen Fortune" draws the posies for all the assembled guests in the tavern, Dowsecer is given a caduceus (Q. "a cats eyes") "or Mercury's rod, of gold set with jacinths and emeralds," and Martia "the two serpents' heads set with diamonds." The hermetic rod of wisdom and healing is appropriate, for Dowsecer is a "holy" figure, inspiring reverence. Chapman seems to attribute to Learning something of the magic with which Shakespeare endows innocence, in his late plays. This impression is sustained when we turn to the portrait of the scholar Clarence in *Sir Giles Goosecap*, which M. Jacquot calls "une image embellie de Chapman lui-meme."[5] Clarence, the hero of a little romance based on *Troilus and Creseide*, and surely the strangest and most unfashionable of all Troilus's avatars, is praised by his friend Momford (Pandarus) for his "dove-like innocence," for "a soul/Where all man's sea of gall and bitterness/Is quite evaporate with her holy flames"; and both his condition and his studies, with his neoplatonic love for Eugenia ("Noblesse"), remind us of the *persona* created in the non-dramatic verse.

His first appearance (I, iv) may be some sort of recollection of Orsino's love-melancholy in *Twelfth Night*, for he enters to music (as does Byron), and later, composing a letter to Eugenia, he invokes the more soulful harmonies of *Ovids Banquet*, and anticipates some of the musical effects in *The Tempest*:

Sing, good Horatio, while I sigh and write.
According to my master Plato's mind
The soul is music, and doth therefore joy
In accents musical, which he that hates
With points of discord is together tied,
And barks at Reason consonant in sense.
Divine Eugenia bears the ocular form
Of music and of Reason, and presents
The soul exempt from flesh in flesh inflam'd.

(III, ii, 1–9)

---

[5]Jacquot, p. 89.

In fact this "musical Clarence" (as Momford calls him) works a counterpoint of "sense" and "soul" throughout the piece. Most musical, most melancholy, he begins by choosing love to salve his distressed estate:

> Work on, sweet love; I am not yet resolv'd
> T'exhaust this troubled spring of vanities
> And nurse of perturbations, my poor life;
> And therefore, since in every man that holds
> This being dear, there must be some desire,
> Whose power t'enjoy his object may so mask
> The judging part, that in her radiant eyes
> His estimation of the world may seem
> Upright and worthy, I have chosen love
> To blind my reason with his misty hands
> And make my estimative power believe
> I have a project worthy to employ
> What worth so ever my whole man affords:
> Then sit at rest my soul, thou now hast found
> The end of thy infusion; in the eyes
> Of thy divine Eugenia look for Heaven.
>
> (I, iv, 1–16)

("Troubled spring of vanities" is a good phrase.) His estate is "mean," a "waspish and petulant" star frowns upon him; he is "a thing created for a wilderness," and he is "all liver, and turned lover," loves *passionately* the worthy Eugenia. In this sad state, afflicted with a double melancholy—of the intellectual and of the lover—Momford recommends "confidence":

I tell thee, friend, the eminent confidence of strong spirits is the only witchcraft of this world; spirits wrastling with spirits, as bodies with bodies.

In the triangle of Clarence–Momford–Eugenia, then, will mediates between passion and reason, until sense is turned to soul, reason touched by sense ("Her sensual powers are up, i'faith!"), and in the conclusion Eugenia sees her lover's heart, and they are united in the "knot of [their] eternity."

This is almost technical; the language of these scenes is generally informed with terms from "natural philosophy," of "the strange affections of enchanted number," and what we should now call psychology. For example, we hear a lecture from Momford, in answer to Clarence's assertion that to love a woman is to turn the mind from its proper objects to unsubstantial shadows, to the effect that women's "souls" add fair "forms" to man: "but for women, who could care for forms?" (III, ii, 62 ff.) Clarence's supposed sickness is discussed in terms of the passions, the body and the mind, by the patient and his doctor (V, ii), and here Clarence affirms that the only true "mixture" of souls is in "reason and freedom." The doctor, persuaded finally that Clarence's "passion" is a "high perfection" of his mind, decides that his patient's mind has "so incorporate itself with flesh/And therein rarefied that flesh to spirit" that he has no need of a physician.

Clarence's "field" (as we should say) is astronomy, akin to music, though his studies have a religious end; he broods upon

> ... what Eternesse is,
> The world, and time, and generation;
> What soul the world's soul is, what the black springs
> And unreveal'd original of things,
> What their perseverance, what is life and death,
> And what our certain restauration.
> (II, i, 9–14)

A large order, but undertaken not by way of accumulation of knowledge, but of purification. Eugenia, though she is said to be "the best scholar of any woman, but one [i.e. the Queen], in England ... wise and virtuous," is not exhibited in such a holy light as the melancholy young sage. It is not easy to represent learning (in the ordinary sense) on the stage without the danger of caricature, and though Chapman allows her to misquote Horace once, he does not present a bluestocking. She is simply "Noblesse" (εὐγένεια), at first turned "outward" when she respects, as a widow, "the judgment of the world" (II, i, 169). Accepting graciously Momford's trickery in changing the sense of her letter to Clarence in the dictation (IV, i), she suddenly perceives Clarence's "inward wealth and nobleness" and pledges herself to him, since

> knowledge is the bond,
> The seal, and crown of [their] united minds.
> (V, ii, 215–6)

This serious, pedantic, neoplatonic allegory of the Troilus–Cressida story is set down in the midst of a farcical action of gulled knights and witty pages, or rather little or no action and much straining at wit, with a lady of a "drinking humour" for broad effects, apparently, though this scene did not get printed.[6] Yet if the play was composed before 1603, as the reference to Queen Elizabeth suggests, it marks a

[6]*Comedies*, p. 892.

fairly early experiment in the mixing of romantic and farcical plots and a delight in the set piece of paradox, in this case Clarence's defence of women's painting (IV, iii, 42–72), and prepares us for the same effects in *The Gentleman Usher* and *Monsieur D'Olive*—nothing quite prepares us for *The Widow's Tears*. Before considering these characteristic productions, however, we must glance at Chapman's achievements in the comedy of manners.

All Fools, Chapman's contamination of the *Heautontimoroumenos* and *Adelphi* of Terence, with many original touches, is certainly the best made of his comedies, and the most suavely written, so polished as to be almost impersonal. The sources provided a firmly complicated plot structure, and the humours device a basis for sketching character; to these elements is added another unifying element, the motif of Fortune. The magnificent intriguer Rinaldo, no *servus* but a scholar (I, ii, 85) with a humour of meddling, is a follower of Fortune, "the great commandress of the world" (V, i, 1), hence an opportunist or "occasional" artist, who triumphs over the stern father Gostanzo, a "wretched Machiavellian" as Rinaldo calls him (I, i, 148), a Polonius-like "politician" (also Rinaldo's word) who believes that affairs can be arranged by taking the lowest view of human nature (II, i, 69–85). Fortune is the theme of the "Prologus," and the play opens with a discussion of the different fortunes of the young men: Valerio (son of Gostanzo), who is secretly married to Gratiana, and Fortunio (elder son of Marc. Antonio), who, loving Valerio's sister Bellanora, is denied sight of her by her father. Rinaldo "takes hold on [each] occasion" that will serve to settle their "fortunes"; "blind Chance," the "ape of counsel and advice," brings forth a "rude plot," which his "learning" brings to a "perfect shape" (I, ii, 122–4). (This sounds like a parody of the *forming* power of Learning to make all "circulare," in Chapman's high philosophy.) Rinaldo's "wit" puts "blind Fortune in a string" into Valerio's hand (II, i, 209–10), and Fortune "shifts the chances" of the final scene of recognition, so that Gostanzo, accepting the fact that he has been deceived, as the comic "amnesia" (Frye's word) demands, caps the conclusion with "Marriage is ever made by destiny" (V, ii, 157).

The sub-plot of the jealous husband Cornelio (i.e. he who believes he is a *cornuto*) is deliberately planned as a "rest" or diversion from the main action: to contemplate it serves, Rinaldo says, "to vary/ The pleasures of our wits" (II, i, 213), and it is introduced by his "Well, now let's note...," or "Now we must expect...," or "Now in what taking poor Cornelio is ... I long to see." Rinaldo stands, as it were, between the main intrigue in which he assists Fortune and the secondary entertainment for which he draws the curtain and which he contemplates with delight. In each action the humour of the victim is his downfall: Gostanzo thinks himself very deep indeed and is an unwitting agent of the device to deceive him (IV, i); Cornelio is the victim of his own jealous suspicions. All who suppose "their wits entire" are "laid flat on earth for gulls."

This is all very neat, nor does the design lack the ornament of eloquence. Not to speak of Gostanzo's superb recollection of his youthful gallantry (II, i, 148–78)—

> I had my congé—plant myself of one leg,
> Draw back the tother with a deep-fetch'd honour,
> Then with a bel-regard advant mine eye
> With boldness on her very visnomy—

which is in character, and easily the best chance for an actor in a play rich in such chances, the traditional debate on the nature of woman appears as a flourish on the theme of "all fools," with a paradoxical conclusion set to it. It is introduced in the first scene, where Rinaldo, who has loved and been beloved, scorns womankind as "unconstant shuttlecocks" or proud and wayward sluts; to this Valerio (out of character, for he is a rake and swaggerer) replies with an elevated praise of Love,

> Nature's second sun,
> Causing a spring of virtues where he shines. . . .
> So Love, fair shining in the inward man,
> Brings forth in him the honourable fruits
> Of valour, wit, virtue, and haughty thoughts,
> Brave resolution, and divine discourse.
> (I, i, 97–8, 107–10)

Love makes the "absolute" man. Set against this we have the page's homily to Cornelio (III, i) on the nature of women, "the light sex," "unfinished creatures," with a large portion of will and a small of wit, and Gostanzo's comical consolation to Cornelio:

As for your mother, she was wise, a most flippant tongue she had . . . and she was honest enough too. But yet, by your leave, she would tickle Dob now and then, as well as the best on 'em . . . your father knew it well enough, and would he do as you do—think you?—set rascals to undermine her, or look to her water, as they say? No, when he saw 'twas but her humour . . . he . . . would stand talking to his next neighbour to prolong time, that all things might be rid cleanly out of the way before he came, for the credit of his wife. This was wisdom now for a man's own quiet. [V, ii, 187–202]

Since the women in the play are mere puppets, the hymn to love must carry all one side of the argument, to which is set as epilogue Valerio's long oration in "praise and honour of the most fashionable and autentical HORN" (at the end of the play). This set piece could be and probably was cut; there is an easy transition from V, ii, 230 (Cornelio's "And now shall the world see I am as wise as my father") to 1. 330 (Gostanzo's "Very well done; now take your several wives"), but if "all the world is but a gull,/One man gull to another in all kinds" (II, i, 360-1), then the speech is appropriate enough in a play in which all are fools because all blaspheme "Love's most unmatched ceremonies." Chapman may be covertly insinuating his own high ethics—but this is doubtful, as doubtful as to find Valerio's encounter with "a sort of corporals" sent to arrest him for debt (II, i, 304-35) inspired by Chapman's own troubles.

May Day, a clever adaptation to the English stage of Alessandro Piccolomini's commedia erudita *Alessandro* (from which Chapman also borrowed the names of Gostanzo, Cornelio and Fortunio for *All Fools*) has the very complicated plot of its genre, and its language is rich in parody, allusion and double entendre; the action is boisterous, the pranks of adults seen down the perspective of the Blackfriars as mad children. Apart from such imitations of Jonson, Marston and Shakespeare, and parodies of single lines from popular plays and ballads as have been noted by Parrott, the piece might serve as a source-book for the clichés of Elizabethan comic dialogue. It sounds like parts of "So That's The Way You Like It" in *Beyond the Fringe*; it has all the strenuous anonymity of revue. I cannot follow Parrott in his emphasis upon the character of Lodovico, whom he sees as another of Chapman's "confident" and reckless intriguers; he has one big self-explanatory speech (III, iii, 118-49), in which he boasts of taking Occasion by the forelock, like Rinaldo, and contemns Idleness, being himself "begot in a stirring season," but he does not dominate the play, in which the most conspicuous elements are the practical jokes played on the senile lecher Lorenzo disguised as a chimney-sweep, and the humours of the swaggering captain Quintiliano (a grammarian?), who is modelled on Jonson's Tucca (*Poetaster*) and sounds sometimes also like Falstaff played on a cracked recorder.

Of Chapman's part in *Eastward Ho*, a venture in which Marston was probably the leading spirit, there is little to say. Chapman's contribution seems to have been concentrated in II, iii, in III, and in IV, i: he was concerned, then, with the sub-plot of Sir Petronel

Flash and the usurer Security.[7] One would like to think for the sake of his reputation as a comic dramatist that he wrote III, ii (Gertrude taking her coach); the talent which framed *The Old Joiner* would certainly be capable of those effects. But if he could manage the comic delineation of London types, he certainly could not approach Jonson in creating a solid, anti-romantic world which maintains the decorum of comical or savage absurdity, nor, perhaps surprisingly, did he diagram his comic action in morality terms, so that his comedies are not fundamentally *serious*—or rather the seriousness is elevated and "inward," and the laughter is directed outward. He has only one fool who makes us think, and no noble creature who makes us laugh. In consequence, his most interesting comedies are unsophisticated tragicomedies, weak in structure, uncertain of their level, but sometimes striking in their diverse effects. I cannot subscribe to the view that these productions with which we must next be concerned are to be compared with Shakespeare's last plays, even by suppressed implication.[8] There is more indigestion than digestion into a "golden worlde" in these plays. No writer is as consistent as his critics; he hasn't time.

The first of these, *The Gentleman Usher*, is on the face of it an absurd play, a real gallimaufry, weak in construction and faltering in illusion. At the beginning we see a corrupt social order: the old duke Alphonso, abetted by his sinister and illiterate favorite Medice, seeks in marriage the virtuous Margaret, who is loved purely and passionately by his son Vincentio. The latter, who has as friend the noble Strozza, uses the silly gentleman usher Bassiolo as go-between and secretly makes Margaret his betrothed. Strozza, wounded on a boar hunt by a henchman of Medice, becomes suddenly a figure of Christian piety and fortitude,[9] the bearer of magical powers and of a "spirit prophetic"; miraculously recovered, he unmasks Medice, who is really Mendice, once king of the Gypsies. Meanwhile Margaret, who has disfigured her face to foil the amorous pursuit of the old Duke, is miraculously cured by the doctor Benevemus (this from *Arcadia*, the Parthenia story) and all is forgotten and forgiven. The first two acts are largely taken up with the "shows" arranged by the Duke in his wooing of Margaret; the

---

[7] *Comedies*, pp. 842–6.

[8] See Henry M. Weidner, "The Dramatic Uses of Homeric Idealism: The Significance of Theme and Design in George Chapman's *The Gentleman Usher*," *ELH* XXVIII (1961), 123. My reading of *The Gentleman Usher* is considerably less elaborate than Weidner's.

[9] See Ennis Rees, *Tragedies of George Chapman*, pp. 146–7.

centre of the play with the ridiculous humour of Bassiolo, gulled by Vincentio and Margaret; and the closing scenes with the elevated sentiments of Strozza. As accidents we have the ludicrous Poggio, the foolish nephew of Strozza; Sarpego a pedant; and a drunken old lady, Cortezza, aunt to Margaret. These last flourishes seem to have been left over from *Sir Giles Goosecap*; they serve here merely to disfigure the romance elements, since they do not constitute a genuine sub-plot, but only a series of coarse diversions. Critics in search of Chapman's characteristic sentiments have naturally concentrated on Strozza, who has been compared to Clermont and Cato, in the tragedies.

There is, however, a theme, if we look hard for it, and a theme highly appropriate to romance too: it is the theme of *noblesse*, of the gentle soul and mind, its evidence in virtuous and gracious behaviour, its absence in the base born, and its parody in the apes of gentility. As a character in a play, Medice is a total failure; but he is Strozza's opposite in the matter of noblesse. In the first scene, Strozza, already defined as of a "virtuous spirit" and "hardy mind," describes Medice as a "fustian lord, who in his buckram face/Bewrays a map of base-ness," and Vincentio echoes that he is an "unknown minion rais'd to honour's height/Without the help of virtue, or of art," a creature of "base-bred ignorance"; he cannot read or write besides (I, i, 107–27), and he picks his teeth in public. We think that jokes at the expense of the illiterate may be enjoyed only by the semi-literate; Vincentio's and Strozza's scoffs at Medice's uncourtly ignorance may jar upon sentimental ears (Medice seems to have needed a good foster-home, as it is now called). But eloquence is a main mark of noblesse, and the point is made again, at the end, when the Duke, now enlightened, speaks of his favorite's "pretended noblesse," and Strozza underlines this with the authority of his occult powers:

> Set by your princely favour,
> That gave the lustre to his painted state,
> Who ever view'd him but with deep contempt,
> As reading vileness in his very looks?
> And if he prove not son of some base drudge,
> Trimm'd up by Fortune. . . . then that good angel
> That by divine relation spake in me . . .
> now fails my tongue.
>
> (V, iv, 194–204)

In the end, Medice confesses the "wrong [he] did to noblesse" and is banished to "live a monster, loath'd of all the world."

So much for this impossible but instructive villain. Poggio inverts noblesse quite literally: a gentleman by connection, he abuses the rhetoric of gentility by his vulgar and mistaken language—Strozza calls him "cousin Hysteron Proteron," the one who gets things backwards, and he is a messenger of fear. Cortezza should be a great lady; she is a drunken, deceived (by Medice) and tattle-tale old bitch. Bassiolo, whose "humours" of correctness (II, ii, 5 ff.) and susceptibility to flattery carry the comic tenor of the play, has pretensions to noblesse: he knows the alphabet of love-letters (III, ii, 392–460), has read the lighter classics and courtesy books (Ovid and Guevara), but he is a hollow man who only reverberates to others' phrases. True noblesse is in Vincentio and Margaret, and, with a difference, in Strozza.

In what Parrott tenderly calls "the highest flight of pure poetry in Chapman's comedies," Vincentio and Margaret "marry before heaven" (IV, ii, 132 ff.), Margaret affirming:

> Are not the laws of God and Nature more
> Than formal laws of men? Are outward rites
> More virtuous then the very substance is
> Of holy nuptials solemnized within
> Or shall laws made to curb the common world,
> That would not be contain'd in form without them,
> Hurt them that are a law unto themselves?

The familiar terms of Chapman's hieratic vocabulary sanctify this match, "far remov'd from custom's popular sects," "sacred," what is called in *All Fools* one of "Love's most unmatched ceremonies." It is not only evidence of noblesse, as with Sidneian overtones the lovers, after Margaret's disfigurement, contend with each other in noble self-abnegation (V, iv, 95–121), but in its proclamation of the "free soul" above law, raised to the lower levels at least of Strozza's transformation. Strozza, wounded, rages against his torment, and threatens suicide, saying that "manliest reason" commands him to take his life into his own power rather than submit to "the torturing delays of slavish Nature" (IV, i, 35 ff.), but from this pagan position he is converted by his wife Cynanche, who "salves with Christian patience pagan sin," reminds him of his "religious noblesse," and counsels patience—turns him in other words from raging Hercules ("I'll break away, and leap into the sea") to suffering Christ.

He accordingly becomes a seer and God's minister and prophet; he is "naught else but soul" since his mind has spread "her impassive powers" through all his suffering body, and expelled its frailty (IV, iii, 45–52). This sounds technical, and M. Jacquot has found passages in Ficino's *Theologica platonica* which might have served as inspiration for the idea,[10] but Cynanche's explanation is clear enough:

> . . . 'tis said afflictions bring to God
> Because they make us like him, drinking up
> Joys that deform us with the lusts of sense,
> And turn our general being into soul.
>
> (IV, i, 63–6)

At any rate, Strozza is raised "to the stars" by his "humility," his "free submission to the hand of Heaven," and sees "things hid from human sight"; he predicts that the arrow-head will fall out of his side on the seventh day, and by his "good angel" (or heavenly familiar) foresees harm to Vincentio (who is wounded by Medice). Against the tyrannous Duke he invokes the doctrine of the free soul:

> And what's a prince? Had all been virtuous men,
> There never had been prince upon the earth,
> And so no subject; all men had been princes:
> A virtuous man is subject to no prince,
> But to his soul and honour, which are laws
> That carry fire and sword within themselves,
> Never corrupted, never out of rule.
>
> (IV, iv, 56–62)

(One is reminded of Achmat in Greville's *Mustapha*: "I first am Natures subject, then my Princes.") It is a perfect human realm, a golden age restored, which is miraculously created in the peripeteia of this play in the triumph of innocence and piety. When Bussy D'Ambois—who is Herculean—utters a similar sentiment,

> Who to himself is law, no law doth need,
> Offends no law, and is a king indeed,

the commonplace book sentence has a different and more complex significance, political and tragic.

Monsieur D'Olive is shorter, somewhat better integrated, and in every way more interesting than *The Gentleman Usher*, though its chief claim to our attention is D'Olive himself, a superb comic creation. Without a scaffolding provided by someone else, Chapman never attempts much of a plot, and the romantic action in this play hardly deserves the name of plot at all. Vandome, returning after three years

---

[10]Jacquot, pp. 94–5.

absence, finds that his mistress Marcellina (mistress in terms of courtly love), injured by the jealousy of her husband Vaumont, has retired from "the common pandress light" and wakes only by night, muffling her beauties in darkness, while Vandome's brother-in-law, St. Anne, watches over the embalmed body of his dead wife and refuses to let her be buried. The hero by persuasion and policy liberates St. Anne from his obsession and attaches his affections to Marcellina's sister Eurione, and tricks Marcellina into the world again. Vandome, then, is the deliverer, by the enchantments of his "divine wit"; "our quick Hermes, our Alcides," Vaumont calls him (IV, i, 95). He speaks himself of his rousing of Marcellina as a "Herculean labour." But as he is at the beginning a noble and innocent soul, a veritable angel to St Anne, when he tricks Marcellina by convincing her that her husband is unfaithful and mocks her (V, i), he becomes another kind of Hermes, a cheap trickster; the whole tone changes, symbolized by the shift from the elevated language of Vandome's opening tribute to "circular" love and the eloquence of Petrarch's *Secretum* (III, i) to slangy prose and a reference to "Petrarch in Italian" as a means of "entertaining time" in private courtship with a gallant (V, i, 190–200). This indecorum would be more glaring if Chapman were really interested in delineating character, but he is not. He had two climaxes to arrange: St. Anne is liberated and in love with Eurione by the end of IV, i, and D'Olive, whose preparation for an embassy to the French king, requesting him to command the burial of his niece, wife to St. Anne, makes up the sub-plot, has no further *raison d'être* after the lady is buried. So having to start over again, Chapman borrows the letter-trick from *Twelfth Night* (the cloistered Olivia must have been in his mind anyway) to keep D'Olive in the play, lest "all our audience will forsake us" (IV, ii, 171), and descends to the most obvious intrigue to manage a total denouement, since he has already exhausted the meaning of the romantic action.

As for that meaning, Chapman obviously intended *Monsieur D'Olive* to be in one aspect a little treatise on melancholy and its cure, with two case histories.[11] Both Marcellina and St. Anne are victims of melancholy. Marcellina has allowed "opinion," which is "a vaine, light, crude and imperfect judgement of things drawn from the outward senses, and common report, setling and holding it selfe to be good in the imagination," lodged in the "sensible soul," to overcome her "judgment," that is the exercise of her "rational soul." Before

[11]See the references to this play in Lawrence Babb, *The Elizabethan Malady* (East Lansing, Mich., 1951).

Vandome learns of her "entombment" in melancholy, he praises her "eminent judgment," and, confronting her, exclaims:

> Oh shall it e'er be said
> Such perfect judgment should be drown'd in humour?
> (II, i, 75–6)

That she is cured by arousing her *passions*, by a "shoeing-horn," as Vandome calls it, to bring her back into the world of opinion—since she says she aims to prevent her husband's shame in his supposedly unworthy courses (V, i, 246–7)—is surely ironic, especially when we remember Chapman's opinion of "Opinion." "Policy" cynically applied is good enough for a woman; for St. Anne's nobler nature nobler methods are employed. He is "passionate," "feeds his passion" upon his grief, is the victim of "hurtful passions," and, since he is a creature of "blood,"

> fram'd for every shade of virtue
> To ravish into true inamorate fire,
> (IV, i, 89–90)

he can be cured not only by the example of Vandome's judgment "suppressing" *his* passion of grief for his deceased sister (III, i, 3–6), but by the "diffusion" or diversion of his passions to another object—in this case Eurione. The authority for this remedy is a series of metaphors from the *Secretum*.[12]

Where Bassiolo's "humour," in *The Gentleman Usher*, is connected with the romance only at the level of action, D'Olive participates in the central theme of this play, for when the gulled courtier is presented to the Duke by the exploiters Rodrigue and Mugeron (II, ii) it appears that he has assumed the pose of the contemplative recluse, and his condition is a parody of the "entombment" of his betters. He has lived "conceal'd," "his mind in his kingdom," and the Duke, entering into the joke, reproaches him:

> ... what makes wise Nature
> Fashion in men these excellent perfections
> Of haughty courage, great wit, wisdom incredible ...
> But that she aims therein at public good;
> And you in duty thereto, of yourself,
> Ought to have made us tender of your parts,
> And not entomb them, tyrant-like, alive.
> (II, ii, 52–9)

---

[12]See *Comedies*, pp. 781–8.

If we remember Chapman's own pose of withdrawal to the inward life, and wonder too if that greater melancholic Robert Burton sitting in his window in Christ Church read this play, we will enjoy the more D'Olive's reply. He murmurs gracefully that "the times before" were not so favourable as they are now, under so sweet and wise a prince (James I, with irony?), for "wits of hope" such as himself, and in those days he accordingly "shrunk [his] despised head in [his] poor shell":

> Faith, sir, I had a poor roof or a pent-house
> To shade me from the sun, and three or four tiles
> To shroud me from the rain . . .
>   yet saw all
> That pass'd our State's rough sea, both near and far . . .
>   our great men
> Like to a mass of clouds that now seem like
> An elephant, and straightways like an ox,
> And then a mouse, or like those changeable creatures
> That live in the burdello, now in satin,
> Tomorrow next in stammel;
> When I sat all this while in my poor cell,
> Secure of lightning or the sudden thunder,
> Convers'd with the poor Muses, gave a scholar
> Forty or fifty crowns a year to teach me,
> And prate to me about the predicables,
> When, indeed, my thoughts flew a higher pitch
> Than genus and species.
>
>   (II, ii, 83–103)

This is the mad offhanded eloquence of a Lord of Misrule, a "Christmas Lord," as Mugeron calls him later; in this he is Falstaffian (though diluted by the antics of fashion in which he first appears), as also in his description of the "followers" who seek to attach themselves to his embassy, three hundred "goldfinches" whom he is "ashamed to train abroad" (III, ii, 149–200). His account of his powers of eloquence, in a discussion on the lawful use of tobacco in a commonwealth (II, ii, 164–280), is easily the finest piece of rhetoric in Chapman's comedy, particularly in its narrative part (in verse) where D'Olive describes how a Puritan weaver (here another smile in the direction of the author of the *Counterblast to Tobacco*?) condemned "the gentleman's saint and the soldier's idol," calling it "a rag of popery." The tone and syntax of this speech are modelled on Hotspur's description of the perfumed gentleman who came to demand the prisoners, but it suffers not at all for that, and there are even touches of that happy simplicity which we call Shakespearean, and which it is not easy to imitate, even in a comic context:

> A little fellow, and yet great in spirit,
> I never shall forget him....
>
> ... the colour of his beard
> I scarce remember; but purblind he was
> With the Geneva print....
>
> ... but I myself...
> Brake phlegm some twice or thrice, then shook my ears ...
> Thus I replied....

D'Olive's supposed reply, in prose, is a panegyric in little, complete with hyperbolic exordium, *narratio* confirmed by reason, example, and authority (Giovanni Savonarola's *Practica Canonica de Febribus*), and ironic peroration. He carries this off well, so well that he begins to think himself a model of presence before the great; "'tis boldness, boldness does the deed in the Court," he counsels (III, 2, 23), thus anticipating in the Phrygian mode the theme of confidence which Tharsalio, in *The Widow's Tears*, varies in the Doric, and his catechism of the little pages in "court accidence" (IV, ii) must have been especially delightful as acted by the Revels boys.

The golden thread which runs through all D'Olive's immensely fluent discourse is money: he lives in the world of those who live by their wits, "few trades but live by wit," he says. Younger brothers turned poets (like Chapman himself), pandars, soldiers, lawyers—he is himself "the compound of a poet and lawyer"—all the world lives by wit, which he of all things admires, being also "prodigal in wasteful expense," and at the end he repents, a fool's repentance. Tricked into appearing in his "careless cloak," he proclaims that he will no longer be a block for his tormenters to whet their dull wits on, accuses them of presenting him with a set of "threadbare, unbuttoned fellows," to be his followers. "A plague on that phrase, raising of fortunes," he cries. The Duke rescues him, and the last word of the play is "Good Monsieur D'Olive!"

D'Olive asks for justice, without really expecting it; such justice as the amused favour of his lord can provide, he receives, with the suggestion that he "reserve [himself] till fitter times." The lord of misrule has had his splendid—and uncomfortable—hour. Through his absurdity appears for a moment a genuine protest; as with Malvolio the joke has gone too far. "There's as much trust in a common whore as in one of you" has a broader application than the attack upon those "good wits" Rodrigue and Mugeron, and D'Olive is more humane, in the end, than Vandome.

But Chapman's romantic comedy oscillates usually between lofty religiosity and amoral intrigue. Unlike Jonson, he has no vision of a total social harmony disordered by folly and vice, and one looks in vain for a spokesman for the social norm. His last and most powerful comedy, *The Widow's Tears*, is not the production of a grave moralist viewing the "swift decadence of his age" (Parrott), but an "amorality," un-measure for un-measure. The source for the main plot is the story of the Ephesian matron in the *Satyricon*, which has attracted more than one dramatist,[13] and which certainly offers scope for cynicism, particularly when, as in this version, the soldier who tries the entombed widow's virtue is her supposedly dead husband in disguise. But the intrigue of jealousy and far-from-impregnable chastity is contained, so to speak, within the adventure of Tharsalio, the husband Lysander's younger brother, in wooing and winning the "late governor's admired widow" the Countess Eudora, by an exercise of "Confidence." It is Tharsalio who opens and closes the play, and his spirit infuses it throughout.

The scene is not Ephesus (sacred to Diana), but Cyprus, the island of Venus; the inhabitants swear by Venus, and Tharsalio professes himself her "true servant." The Governor is of mean condition, but raised by bribery of courtiers and "Fortune's injudicious hand" to his "high seat of honour" (V, i, 143–6), while the noble house of Lysander and Tharsalio, the "ancient and most virtue-fam'd" Lysandri, is decayed. In the purely comic milieu of *All Fools*, Rinaldo attaches himself to Fortune; entering the tragic scene, Bussy professes Virtue in a world inverted by Fortune; but Tharsalio (θάρσος–boldness, confidence) in his opening soliloquy, mirror in hand to put a face on his enterprises, renounces Fortune in favour of Confidence:

> Thou blind imperfect goddess, that delights
> (Like a deep-reaching statesman) to converse
> Only with fools, jealous of knowing spirits,
> For fear their piercing judgments might discover
> Thy inward weakness and despise thy power,
> Contemn thee for a goddess; thou that lad'st

---

[13]In "The Widow of Ephesus," *Durham University Journal*, n.s. XVIII, no. 1 (1956), 1–9, Peter Ure describes the variations on the folk-lore theme in Petronius from the *Satyricon* to Christopher Fry, observing by the way that the English seventeenth-century treatments of the motif (including Chapman's, "the first known dramatization of the subject") are "original and even eccentric" in their treatment.

> Th'unworthy ass with gold, while worth and merit
> Serve thee for naught, weak Fortune, I renounce
> Thy vain dependence, and convert my duty
> And sacrifices of my sweetest thoughts
> To a more noble deity, sole friend to worth,
> And patroness of all good spirits, Confidence;
> She be my guide, and hers the praise of these
> My worthy undertakings.
>
>   (I, i, 1–14)

"Confidence" (really a personification of his own *virtù*, "spirit" he calls it, virility) is his guide at all times; Love and Fortune are, he believes, her servant deities (I, ii, 178), and she certainly protects him, though in no glorious conflict, since her only opponent is the vowed chastity of widows. Where he is sanguine, his brother is of a melancholy temperament (II, iii, 43), hence subject to jealousy, and *his* "confidence," grievously misplaced, is in his wife's fidelity, in which, as Tharsalio savagely notes,

> he hath invested her in all his state, the ancient inheritance of our family . . .
> so as he dead, and she matching (as I am resolved she will) with some young
> prodigal, what must ensue, but her post-issue beggared, and our house, already
> sinking, buried quick in ruin. [II, iii, 81-6]

His planting the seed of non-confidence in Lysander is not, then, motiveless malignity, the fruit of a free mischief, but grounded upon hard ambition, like all his actions. He is, says M. Jacquot, "un ambitieux sans rêves et sans foi, et par conséquent sans grandeur."[14] Too much of that "Italian air" drunk in his travels, his sister-in-law Cynthia thinks, has poisoned the very essence of his soul and infected his whole nature; not so, he replies, rather "it hath refined my senses, and made me see with clear eyes, and to judge of objects as they truly are, not as they seem" (I, i, 132–43). A Machiavel too—and also a mean little boy, for when he is turned back in his first onslaught on the countess, and Lysander mocks him, he takes that moment to revenge his wounded self-esteem by undermining his brother's "confidence" in his Cynthia, thought by her husband heir of the moon-goddess's "bright purity" and "all soul." "That's veney for veney," he exults (I, iii, 132).

[14]Jacquot, p. 102. It has been suggested that Tharsalio, standing for everything Chapman denounces elsewhere, exemplary of the "heroism" of an iron age, makes *WT* "Chapman's satiric commentary on the fallen world and on its chief disciples." H. M. Weidner, "Homer and the Fallen World; Focus of Satire in George Chapman's *The Widow's Tears*," *JEGP* LXII (1963), 518–32.

When we see Tharsalio "with his glass in his hand" and Lysander entering in turn with *his* glass, and the dialogue begins,

—Morrow, brother! Not ready yet?
—No, I have somewhat of the brother in me. I dare say your wife is many times ready, and you not up,

We might almost imagine we were witnessing the first scene of a Restoration comedy of the second class, with two elegant gentlemen exchanging a morning bawdy, but Tharsalio is too savage, too *committed*, for that elegant atmosphere, and he takes his first repulse in a more turbulent fashion:

> Hell and the Furies take this vile encounter!
> Who would imagine this Saturnian peacock
> Could be so barbarous to use a spirit
> Of my erection with such low respect?
> 'Fore heaven, it cuts my gall; but I'll dissemble it.
>
> (I, iii, 9-13)

He succeeds the second time, after braving Eudora's silly Spartan suitor, by a device which the shocked Parrott calls an example of "physical grossness almost unparalleled in Elizabethan comedy," bribing the bawd Arsace (from ἀραρίσκω, to join together, hence the "joiner," though not of Aldgate this time) to tell Eudora (εὔδωρος = generous) that he can satisfy nine women in a night, at which news "her blood went and came of errands betwixt her face and her heart," and she murmurs to herself: "Contentment is the end of all worldly beings." ("Contentment is our heaven, and all our deedes/Bend in that circle," says the poet of the "Coronet.") "Here are your widow-vows, sister," he reports in triumph, being a kiss-and-tell man,

thus are ye all in your pure naturals; certain moral disguises of coyness, which the ignorant call modesty, ye borrow of art to cover your busk-points; which a blunt and resolute encounter, taken under a fortunate aspect [he is not altogether consistent] easily disarms you of; and then, alas, what are you? Poor naked sinners, God wot! Weak paper walls thrust down with a finger. This is the way on't, boil their appetites to a full height of lust; and then take them down in the nick. [III, i, 93-100]

Eudora, like the Player Queen in *Hamlet*, has made infinite protestations of fidelity to her late lord, has protested too much (II, iv, 23–35), and so has Cynthia (II, iii, 79–90), all for "the shadow of popular fame"—"The praise I have had, I would continue." The poison poured in Lysander's ear works, and he feigns death on a journey to test his wife; with Act III the Petronius plot begins, the fall of Eudora providing clinching evidence of female frailty. Since it is useless to demand range or subtlety in Chapman's characterizations of women, the tomb episode must be taken as fabliau, dressed though it is in the hyperbolic rhetoric of Lysander's apostrophe to his still-faithful wife as he contemplates the tomb (IV, ii, 1–4), but the tone changes, as it should, with Cynthia's acceptance of the drink, and the ironic reference to "Dido and Aeneas met in the cave" (IV, iii, 85) as the disguised Lysander enters the vault, underlines the burlesque.

A widow's chastity, then, is a mask for the world's "opinion," and "Opinion" is "the blind goddess of fools, foe to the virtuous," as Lysander ironically counsels Cynthia (V, i, 98–100). She, advised of the plot, determines to "sit out one brunt more," showing neither fear nor shame, evincing, in the end, a boldness worthy of Tharsalio. As in a fabliau, the husband is the victim, and Tharsalio, whose tongue leaves a slime upon everything, is gratified.

Now if the play was to prove a thesis, it might have been closed off just after V, iii, 147, when Cynthia leaves Lysander in the tomb, having revealed to him that she knows his deceit, for the betrothal of Lysander's son Hylus to Laodice, Eudora's daughter, made possible by Tharsalio's success and promised in the masque that attends his nuptials (III, ii, 82–114), and the hurried reconciliation of Cynthia and Lysander through the whispered good offices of Eudora, could have been easily joined on—and perhaps were. The text of the late scenes is often corrupt, and Parrott thinks that Chapman simply burked the conclusion, but the fact remains that with the presentation of the supposed culprits Lysander and his accomplice before the Governor, a final twist is given to the play which no conventional dialogue of reconciliation could possibly have produced.

Nothing in Chapman's earlier comedies encourages us to expect such a sophisticated handling of theme as this final scene seems to hint at. A "Vice," a "wooden dagger . . . gilded over with the title of Governor," presides over the comic resolution. A memory of Dogberry's voice went to his making, and perhaps of Angelo's situation: he accuses Lycus of "a most inconvenient murther" and adds, of the culprit, "I had ever a sympathy in my mind against him"; describing his judicial procedure, he says that he "know[s] no persons. . . . If a suitor . . . thrusts a bribe into my hand, I will pocket his bribe, and proceed"; he tells Eudora that her late husband, "no statesman," "left a foul city behind him," full of vices, and announces an era of reform. Drunkenness, lechery, *jealousy* will be whipped out; "fools shall have wealth, and the learned shall live by their wits." (Such, I take it, would be Chapman's view of conditions in his own time and place.) The Governor continues: "I'll have all young widows spaded for marrying again. . . . To conclude, I will cart pride out o' th'town." But in spite of his assumed role of cleanser of the commonwealth, he is put to a non-plus by the complications of a situation he does not understand, "state points" for which he is not yet trained, and he surrenders it to Tharsalio and Eudora. His role is played.

If we wish, we may find in the Governor's pronouncements a criticism of the pride (another name for "Confidence"), jealousy and lechery which animates the business of the play, with the added irony that this criticism comes from a fool who can preside only over days of mis-rule. Paradox rules here too. Comedy was then, as it is still, the genre of experiment, and in that solvent Chapman examined some of his most cherished opinions and found, finally, no golden precipitate. The requirements of comedy—and of tragedy too, as we shall see—revealed his capacity of seeing both sides of a case, and his incapacity in forming a synthesis of the elements in his divided imagination.

HAPMAN'S DEFINITION of tragedy is frequently quoted, with or without the reservation that it does not necessarily describe his own contributions to the genre:

> Poor envious souls they are that cavil at truth's want in these natural fictions; material instruction, elegant and sententious excitation to virtue, and deflection from her contrary, being the soul, limbs and limits of an autentical tragedy.

A highly characteristic utterance, complete with physiological analogy, moral energy, and contempt for such poor creatures as might take any other view, though it echoes pretty closely some Jonsonian phrases in the preface to *Sejanus*: "truth of Argument," "gravity and height of Elocution," "fulnesse and frequency of Sentence," with the end of "imitating justice and instructing to life." As two recent books on Jacobean tragedy[1] remind us, the post-Senecan and post-morality tragedy of the Jacobean age was bound to try good and evil by the assay of rhetoric in search of the vision of a moral order; and as two recent critics of Chapman[2] for their different purposes emphasize, such a trial is characteristic of Chapman's efforts in other genres as well. We know that while he was writing his plays he was reading Stoic ethics as preparatory to "good life," translating Homer as the *ground* or determinant by which human action is to be judged, and, apparently, looking out from his study through his cousin Grimeston's window[3] at recent French history as a fruitful garden of *exempla*.

---

[1]Robert Ornstein, *The Moral Vision of Jacobean Tragedy* (Madison, 1960); Irving Ribner, *Jacobean Tragedy: The Quest for Moral Order* (London, 1962).

[2]Ennis Rees, *Tragedies of George Chapman*; George de F. Lord, *Homeric Renaissance: The Odyssey of George Chapman* (London, 1956).

[3]Edward Grimeston, *A General Inventorie of the History of France* (1607), a trans-

But all Chapman's critical dicta are occasional, and this is no exception. It comes from the prefatory apology for *The Revenge of Bussy D'Ambois*. "Some maligners" at the "scenical representation" (note the implication that the play exists independent of the theatre, the performance being only one manifestation of the "absolute" play) must have complained that the play was, to say the least, hardly true to historical fact: there was no such person as Clermont, brother to Bussy, and Montsurry (Montsoreau), killed in the play, was very much alive when it was performed. Chapman quite properly rejects such cavillings at the true apprehension of a poem, whose subject is not truth but things like truth, and, besides, he was engaged to support his portrait of the Stoic hero, so making of this immediate exercise a general case. We should hardly be surprised to find his definition of tragedy falling short of explaining *King Lear*, say, or *The Duchess of Malfi*. Perhaps it falls short of explaining his own tragedies too. Also it is easy to misinterpret what his dictum actually does say: "natural fictions" are not formulas, and "excitation to virtue" is not mere instruction. Chapman's tragedies are not just political moralities, though they are (with one exception, *The Tragedy of Bussy D'Ambois*) political in subject, moral in intention, and heroically sententious in language.

Compassed about by the cloud of witnesses who have discussed these plays in terms of Rees's sub-title, "Renaissance Ethics in Action," I shall attempt a beginning with some obvious considerations which have been frequently ignored or at best under-emphasized in the learned commentaries. In the first place, as Chapman experimented with different kinds of comedy, so he also tried different kinds of tragedy. No two of these plays (counting the *Conspiracy* and *Tragedy* of Byron as one) are alike in structure and effect. Bussy and Byron are Achillean heroes, exemplifying wrath and "outward fortitude," but we see them in different perspective glasses, "cozening pictures"; Clermont and Cato are exemplars of "the Mind's inward, constant and unconquerd Empire,"[4] Ulysses' "Proposition" filling out the other face of Chapman's Janus-faced portrait of the *great* condition of man, but each of them has his own perspective image too, whereas *Chabot* is a dramatic exercise which blurs these contrasting images by a meditation on the glory and fault of "innocent" greatness. *Bussy D'Ambois* is, roughly speaking, a Marlovian extravagance, in which

---

lation and continuation of *L'Inventaire général de l'Histoire de France* of Jean de Serres.

[4]The contrasting qualities of the "Propositions" of the *Iliad* and *Odyssey* are set out in the epistle to Somerset, in *Whole Works of Homer* (Homer, II, 4).

an overreacher displays a "spirit" and potential in excess of the actions through which his *virtù* is exhibited; the Byron plays are massive secular oratorios set from commonplace-book texts, centripetal compositions in which the central figure revolves slowly while we listen to his own and others' choric comments upon his state, the effect being, as Pagnini has noted, *emblematic*; *Chabot* has this quality too, but the action moves with a certain firm incisiveness—perhaps owing to Shirley's work on it; *The Revenge* is an eccentrically developed revenge play; *Caesar and Pompey* is ostensibly a Roman "history," a new chronicle of an old subject.

Secondly, Chapman, unlike the closet dramatists Greville and Daniel, who also thought heavily about the tragic possibilities in political situations, chose for his subjects familiar history, familiar even to those who had not read Pasquier[5] or Grimeston. Even *Chabot* recalled the great figure of Francis I, sweet enemy of Henry VIII; Amyot and North had made Caesar and Pompey virtually contemporary; Bussy's fate was notorious, and the Duke of Guise appeared to the English imagination (helped by Marlowe) in the lurid colours of St. Bartholomew's night; as for Byron, he had visited England, and in any case some of the auditors must have seen him and even known him, while some had fought for Henry of Navarre and perhaps even had speech with him. It is well to be assured of Chapman's austere moral sensibility; it is well also to remember (and keeping in mind *The Old Joiner*) that he was perfectly capable of exploiting popular interest in his subjects, an interest evidenced by a number of other plays on recent French history.[6]

Rees has found in Chapman a Christian humanist, consistent in his "primary concern with doctrine," and reads the tragedies as deliberate essays promulgating the doctrines of order, *form* and inner peace. This will not work, but Chapman is consistent in another way. We have noticed (and will notice again in the *Homer*) how his course of self-dramatization in poems and prefaces and apologiae presents one recurring image: the lonely figure, assured by inward powers, drawing his inspiration from secret and noble essences, and surrounded by ignorants, backbiters, misunderstanders, savages, baying monsters. In the comedies, the lords of misrule especially endowed with "confidence," or the Hermes-figures filled with divinely directed virtue, succeed in transforming their societies into something they were not

[5]Estienne Pasquier, *Les Recherches de la France* (1607, 1611), the source for *Chabot*.
[6]See A. H. Smith, *Les Evénéments politiques de France dans le théâtre anglais du siècle d'Elizabeth* (Paris, 1906).

before; in the tragedies, the self-sufficient men of excessive *virtù* (or virtue) are destroyed by the world of "policy" about them. As Edwin Muir has put it,

Chapman is not interested in human nature, or in practical morality, or in evil, but in the man of excessive virtue or spirit or pride. His tragedies show us one great figure and a crowd of nobodies who succeed somehow in destroying him. . . . [We] seem to be watching the pursuit and destruction of "royal man" by an invisible hunter. . . . These heroes really exist in another dimension from the rest of the characters, and have a different reality from the action in which they are involved. They wander about, like Chapman himself, enclosed in a dream of greatness and breathing the air of that dream. . . . [They] really talk to themselves.[7]

This is very well said, though Muir was thinking primarily of Bussy and Byron, and there are other qualifications to be made. The excessive men, the great men, whether Achillean or Odyssean, are not simple and whole, any more than Chapman himself was. They are, finally, mysteries, not test cases exhibiting the problems of the individual versus society or the operation of certain laws of human behaviour.[8] Each of them is possessed (even Clermont) not by a theory but by a *daimon*, the author, so to speak, of a private play in which the protagonist, looking constantly in a mirror to see the world, sees all but himself out of focus. It is this image, the *persona* of heroic energy or Stoic calm or holy innocence which we contemplate "perspectively,"[9] in the context of an action barely sufficient in its momentum to shift the view from time to time. The method, which underlies all the superficial variations in technique, reminds Professor Ure, happily, of Henry James.

The "outward" world, however, *judges*, defines, analyzes this greatness in the only terms its inhabitants can know, and the heroes themselves, dwelling in divided and distinguished worlds, choruses to their fates, use the same vocabulary. Virtue confronts Fortune or is bound to her wheel; Nature is good, or indifferent to man's fate; the violence of "humour" and excess of "spirit" oppose order and the righteousness

---

[7]"Royal Man: Notes on the Tragedies of George Chapman," in *Essays on Literature and Society* (London, 1949), pp. 20–1.

[8]In this connection see L. L. Schücking, "The Baroque Character of the Elizabethan Tragic Hero," *Proceedings of the British Academy* XXIV (1938), 1–29; a useful corrective to discussions of Chapman as a dramatist of ideas.

[9]See Peter Ure, "Chapman's Tragedies," in *Jacobean Theatre* (Stratford-upon-Avon Studies I, London, 1960), p. 236. This whole essay is of the greatest interest and importance.

of law, "Ceremony"; the composed mind opposes "Opinion"; "Learning" is preferred to "policy"; "innocence" is destroyed by power. The commentary—and these plays are heavy with commentary, as the *Homer* is heavy with the glosses translated into it—proceeds dialectically, but is finally transcended, for Chapman knows that all this bravery of thought is fastened to a dying animal. Perhaps he learned this from *Iliad* XXIV.

In these plays, then, the ethical argument, the political parable, and the autumnal, elegiac *mythos* of the hero are not always integrated, so that one can get a sense of discrete and separable layers of expression, something that it is tempting to call allegory. The hero is not all in the play, but has in the poet's imagination another life the shadow of which falls, often very undramatically, into the business of the action. In the first Bussy play, for example, the literal level offers the spectacle of a confident swaggerer and seducer, bound to rise, victorious in a duel and caught in an amorous intrigue, himself the unreliable instrument of the political Monsieur; in the moral realm, he is held up as an example of man's "native noblesse," a product of Nature "in her prime"; finally, anagogically if you will, he is the dying Hercules. And we shall see something like this pattern repeated in the Byron plays, in the *Revenge*, and even in *Chabot* and *Caesar and Pompey*. Chapman's tragedies cannot be adequately interpreted solely in terms of ethical and political discussion; in that light they are "problem plays" in more ways than one. Rees is thus forced to interpret some key speeches of Bussy and Byron as ironic; Madeleine Doran finds the moral comment inconsistent with the "imaginative direction of his plays"; K. M. Burton notes that Chapman, like Jonson, is "concerned with the tragic flaw within the social order, not within the individual"; Michael Higgins is led by the affirmation, so often repeated, that the just man is a law unto himself, to see in Chapman a "classical republican," a precursor of Milton and Locke, repudiating the "medieval and Catholic reverence for the sacred name of king"; Hardin Craig sees in these plays a "psychological determinism," so that Byron, for example, is not to be blamed for his excesses, but rather "the fervour of his blood"; R. H. Perkinson, observing correctly that there is a shift in the concept of Nature from *Bussy* to the *Revenge*, is forced finally by the logic of his argument to state that underlying both Bussy plays is a failure to grasp the traditional idea of Christian providence; and R. W. Battenhouse finds Chapman exploring the paradox that in a fallen world a display of evil forwards good, that the endings of *Bussy* and *Byron* should be taken as "an apology for violence in the name of piety."[10]

None of these observations, except perhaps Rees's and Higgins', is wholly inconsistent with the development of Chapman's speculation, such as it was; all of them create more problems than they solve. I certainly admit that the *Revenge* is a retractation of *Bussy*, indeed I shall prove it, that the "moral structure" (Ure's phrase) of the later plays is more consistent with the fable than it is in *Bussy*, that every one of the tragedies exemplifies the opposition between an inward world of "Confidence" or "Learning" and an outward world of "Ceremony" or "Opinion," that, finally, it would be absurd to minimize or try to ignore Chapman's intense moral seriousness; but I still think that it is possible to read these plays as something different from attempts to "dramatize through hackneyed theatrical devices the essential political and moral issues of the time" (e.g. in *Bussy*) and to dissent from the characterization of the later plays as "upright Moralities . . . but only incidentally or coincidentally dramatic in conception."[11]

Louis de Clermont d'Amboise, Seigneur de Bussy, was not, historically, a "great" man, but he was certainly colourful, a reckless duellist and gallant, a fiery, murderous and independent spirit, active in the bloody skirmishes of the wars of religion and in other men's beds. In *The Tragedy of Bussy d'Ambois*,[12] Chapman, as Jacquot observes,[13] suppresses (if indeed he knew about them) the more despicable episodes in his violent career, such as his reign of terror as governor of Anjou,

[10]Rees, *Tragedies of George Chapman*, pp. 33, 38, 60, &c.; Madeleine Doran, *Endeavors of Art* (Madison, 1954), p. 122; K. M. Burton, "The Political Tragedies of Chapman and Ben Jonson," *EC* II (1952), 397; Michael Higgins, "Chapman's 'Senecal Man': A Study in Jacobean Psychology," *RES* XXI (1954), 184–6; Hardin Craig, "Ethics in the Jacobean Drama; The Case of Chapman," in *Essays in Dramatic Literature: The Parrott Presentation Volume* (Princeton, 1935), pp. 34–5; R. H. Perkinson, "Nature and the Tragic Hero in Chapman's Bussy Plays," *MLQ* III (1942), 278–80; R. W. Battenhouse, "Chapman and the Nature of Man," *ELH* XII (1945), 100.

[11]Ornstein, *Moral Vision*, pp. 47–8.

[12]The most recent (and best) discussion of the date and texts of *Bussy* is in Nicholas Brooke's introduction to his edition of the play in the Revels Plays (London, 1964).

[13]Jacquot, p. 133. See also his edition, with introduction, translation and notes, *Bussy d'Amboise* (Paris, 1960), particularly valuable in relating the play to the historical facts, and in collecting contemporary judgments of Bussy (his "grand esprit," "Le mignon de Vénus, le favori de Mars," "un amant exemplaire," &c.) which may have contributed to the ambiguities of Chapman's portrait.

in fact passes over his public life—if one can make such a distinction in the case of a sixteenth-century courtier—to concentrate upon two notorious episodes, the duel in triplicate from which D'Ambois emerges the sole survivor, and his intrigue with the wife of Montsoreau (Montsurry); the first announced with the Senecan dignity of a Nuntius, the second staged with all the trappings of popular tragedy, nocturnal assignations, diabolic ministers, passionate mistress, corrupt friar, and ranting jealous husband. The political theme, introduced with considerable emphasis at the beginning, where Monsieur (Queen Elizabeth's monkey) seeks to make Bussy his creature for 1000 crowns, is for the most part (except for the flyting between Monsieur and Bussy in III, ii) lost in this lurid atmosphere, from which the hero finally emerges magnificently to his dying stance. Bussy's heroic energy, *spirit*—the play is full of references to his spirit—finds no worthy matter to work upon, and ends

> like a falling star
> Silently glanc'd, that like a thunderbolt
> Look'd to have stuck and shook the firmament.
> (V, iv, 144–6)

This is Bussy's tragic recognition of his fate. In tragedy, the full meaning of the hero's fate being revealed in his agony, he is transformed by that knowledge, becomes as it were completed. Bussy, at the opening of the play, is as far from this apotheosis as possible. He enters in a "green retreat," in retired contemplation not heroic action, condemning an inverted world: the malcontent-type of the unemployed man-at-arms,[14] melancholy, "turn'd to earth," *procumbit*. (The audience would recognize the condition at once.) He dies *standing*, like an emperor—

> Here like a Roman statue I will stand
> Till death hath made me marble—

and his fame will be "spread to a world of fire." But as Monsieur enters to him in his dejection another motif is introduced, as Brooke has brilliantly observed:[15] Bussy is a morality-figure of Poverty and Monsieur with his two pages of Wealth, "gold and grace"; just before his fall, in the premonitory thunder (V, iii), Bussy enters "with two pages"—he is in Monsieur's clothing now. Bussy stands at the critical fork which separates the way of heroic and virtuous achievement from

---

[14]See Lawrence Babb, *The Elizabethan Malady*, p. 87.
[15]Brooke, p. xxviii. On the Hercules motif, see E. M. Waith, *The Herculean Hero in Marlowe, Chapman, Shakespeare and Dryden* (New York, 1962).

the way of policy and the "greatness" of the "glorious ruffian" (as he is later called) in *his* choice of Hercules, when he decides to accept the *fortune* of Monsieur's crowns (I, i, 119–43). Upon this decision the whole play turns, and it is not a simple choice of Hercules either. But it is spoken in his own person, as I take it, whereas his opening speech is choric prologue as well as a displaced person's outcry upon a corrupt world.

The state of things described in this opening soliloquy is inverted, under Fortune, which stands "Honour on his head." This is at once a description of the outward world which Chapman continually despised and rejected, a short characterization of the "well-head" to which Monsieur is about to invite the hero—"Fortune's banquet [of sense]"; "brave barks and outward gloss"—and the complaint of the poor soldier. Bussy goes on through three remarkable similes.

> As cedars beaten with continual storms,
> So great men flourish:

this sounds like a tribute to "great men," suggests strength and stability, or, suggests that one might prefer the calm, however stagnant, at the bottom of Fortune's wheel. But he continues: men "merely great" in Fortune's gifts, self-made, are like "unskilful statuaries" who think their work is good if they make a strutting colossus; by transition they are themselves like statues,

> Which, with heroic forms without o'erspread,
> Within are nought but mortar, flint, and lead.

(This, by the way, would not spoil the statues, but Chapman is busy with his outward-inward antithesis, as usual. Did he look back to this passage when he wrote "Till death hath made me marble," i.e. heroic and "complete" clear through, at the end?) Man is a very nothing, Pindar's σκιᾶς ὄναρ ἄνθρωπος—an elegant aside. Then the great are compared to seamen in tall ships putting a girdle about the world in their pride—a magnificent figure—who when they come to harbour must be piloted in by "a poor staid fisherman": so

> We must to virtue for her guide resort
> Or we shall shipwrack in our safest port.

The whole speech asserts the primacy of Virtue, not *virtù* (yet it is hard not to read Pagnini's *virtuoso* [p. 179] for Bussy in anything but its seventeenth-century sense) but moral goodness, simple, "mild" (the King's word), and essential like that fisherman, over Fortune and outward "bravery," what the actors' Prologue (in the 1641 edition), preserving for us the contemporary stage tradition, refers to as "the height and pride/Of D'AMBOIS' youth and bravery." It is thus a proper chorus to the action which follows; but the implied tribute (the cedars, the great ships) to magnificence must not be forgotten either, not only because it is appropriate to the demonic power so soon to be released in the hero, but because it indicates the ambivalence of Chapman's attitude toward him. As it is warning of what is to be, in his own words, Bussy's "worthless fall," so also its assertion that man is "a dream/But of a shadow" announces the hero's final recognition (V, iv, 87) that life is "a dream but of a shade."

The action is set in motion at once: no long exposition and discussion by onlookers as in *The Conspiracy* or *The Revenge*. Monsieur appears and contemplates his intended instrument, sees in him a "resolved spirit," young and haughty, "apt to take Fire at advancement." The tempter offers Bussy light out of darkness, adduces the Plutarchan examples of Themistocles, Camillus and Epaminondas. When Bussy replies scornfully with a savage attack on the hollow practices of courtiers, and remarks that one cannot play the "great man's part" in poverty, Monsieur offers "t'enchase in all show [his] long smother'd spirit"; Fortune's winged hands[16] give gifts suddenly. Bussy, left to argue with himself, first compares Monsieur to a "disparking husbandman" who will sow crowns upon his spirit, plow him up—but in "learning-hating policy" ("Learning" in Chapman's special sense), and concludes,

> I am for honest actions, not for great.

The hero, it would appear, has made Hercules' choice of the hard road of Virtue. But without pause he continues:

> If I may bring up a new fashion,
> And rise in Court for [Q1 *with*] virtue, speed his plow!
>   (I, i, 129–30)

Then seeming to remember what Monsieur had said about Fortune's swift gifts which must be taken at once or lost for ever, he determines to seize the day—

> So no man riseth by his real merit,
> But when it cries clink in his raiser's spirit—

and to venture to rise, though

> Man's first hour's rise is first step to his fall.

----

[16]A. H. Gilbert has a note on this figure in *MLN* LII (1937), 190–2.

Bussy has made his fatal mistake, but it is not simply a fall from virtue for which we are supposed to condemn him and regard all that he does thereafter as subject to its evil. The decision has daring in it, and a kind of youthful innocence; it commits him, above all, to serving his own "spirit" alone. These qualities shine above his fortune, and the observers, the King, Monsieur and Guise, withdraw from time to time from the action to contemplate them.

After this high argument of Virtue and Fortune, the descent into the outward world of the French court is abrupt, though there are cautionary signs on the steep decline. The first is Monsieur's silly overbearing steward, who judges by outsides and is beaten by the angry Bussy so that the "crowns are set in blood." When the court assembles after this prologue, the King himself (as chorus) observes that his court is "a mere mirror of confusion" to the stately court of Queen Elizabeth. (So was the court of James I, to whose new knights a slighting allusion has already been made: I, i, 198.) The atmosphere is indeed "unformed," casual, domestic, one might almost say suburban. D'Ambois, "entered" upon this scene, savages it with his bluntness and bravado, and makes a challenge out of the scoffs of the courtiers. In the midst of the gallimaufry of insults, Monsieur interprets for the audience the true Bussy, of whom this "saucy companion" seems but a distorted "cozening" picture. The simile is one of Chapman's finest:

> His great heart will not down, 'tis like the sea,
> That partly by his own internal heat,
> Partly the stars' daily and nightly motion,
> Their heat and light, and partly of the place
> The divers frames, but chiefly by the moon,
> Bristled with surges, never will be won,
> (No, not when th'hearts of all those powers are burst)
> To make retreat into his settled home,
> Till he be crown'd with his own quiet foam.
>
> (I, ii, 157–65)

The duel, three to a side, with the envious courtiers, ends the first stage of Bussy's court adventure, and is raised from the blood of a courtiers' quarrel, sign of a disordered court, to a heroic level by the elevated narrative of the Nuntius (II, i). He begins with a kind of bombast invocation, wishing he might cry his "tale so worthy" from Atlas or Olympus; in his account the "perfumed musk-cats" of the previous scene appear as "the famous soldiers"—Barrisor had "stood the shocks/Of ten set battles" against "the sole soldier of the world,

Navarre," and in this encounter, brooded over by the angry spirits of Fury and Revenge, D'Ambois like an angry unicorn triumphs and stands alone untouched. Monsieur's plea for his pardon before the King is on the face of it a piece of sophistry in defence of wild justice, but he does invoke "a free man's eminence," and this theme is developed by Bussy himself in his justification:

> When I am wrong'd, and that law fails to right me,
> Let me be king myself (as man was made),
> And do a justice that exceeds the law;
> If my wrong pass the power of single valour
> To right and expiate, then be you my king,
> And do a right, exceeding law and nature:
> Who to himself is law, no law doth need,
> Offends no law, and is a king indeed.
>
> (II, i, 197–204)

We have heard this before (*GU*, V, iv, 56–60) and shall hear it again; it is a Chapman commonplace. In this context it speaks not for Bussy's fiery individualism but the theme of his primal "noblesse." Yet, left to himself at the end of the scene, confiding in the audience that he has long loved the Countess of Montsurry secretly, he proclaims:

> And now through blood and vengeance, deeds of height,
> And hard to be achiev'd, 'tis fit I make
> Attempt of her perfections,

a curious technique of seduction. Again the striking disproportion between the "overreaching" claims of his spirit and that upon which it works.

Teased by this problem, we tend to overlook Chapman's expert dramaturgy in this tragedy. If the first scene is prologue (and contrast) to Bussy's entrance upon the court and his first deed of bravery (in both senses of that word), then all that's past is prologue to the love-intrigue with Tamyra and its fatal outcome. The hero, more and more enmeshed in the toils of passion, escapes only in death. But more subtle than this is the interplay of Bussy and his patron in the fatal plot. We have already noticed how Bussy in effect puts on Monsieur's suit, and with it policy (IV, ii, 175ff.) and subjugation to Fortune. He also takes the place of Monsieur as suitor to Tamyra (II, ii), and as he was entered by Monsieur he is betrayed by him. And as he is "enlarged and elevated" (Ure's phrase) by the choric speeches of his enemies, so Tamyra, creature of passion that she is, is endowed with a double glamour by involvement in "urgent destiny" and by proving

PERFETTIONE

Di Pier Lione Casella.

"Perfettione," from Cesare Ripa, *Iconologia*, 1611 (Warburg Institute Library). See pp. 41, 60.

Ouids Banquet of
SENCE.

A Coronet for his Miſtreſſe Phi-
loſophie, and his amorous
Zodiacke.

VVith a tranſlation of a Latine coppie, written
by a Fryer, Anno Dom. 1400.

Quis leget hæc? Nemo Hercule Nemo,
vel duo vel nemo : Perſius.

AT a *LONDON,*
Printed by I. R. for Richard Smith.
Anno Dom. 1595.

Title-page of *Ovids Banquet of Sense* (Bodleian Library). See p. 49.

the
CROWNE of all HOMERS WORKES·
Batrachomyomachia
Or the Battaile of Frogs and Mise·
His Hymn's——and——Epigrams
Translated according   to y.ᵉ Originall
By George   Chapman.

London, Printed by Iohn Bill, his MAIESTIES Printer·

Title-page of *The Crowne of All Homers Workes* (Bodleian Library). See p. 204.

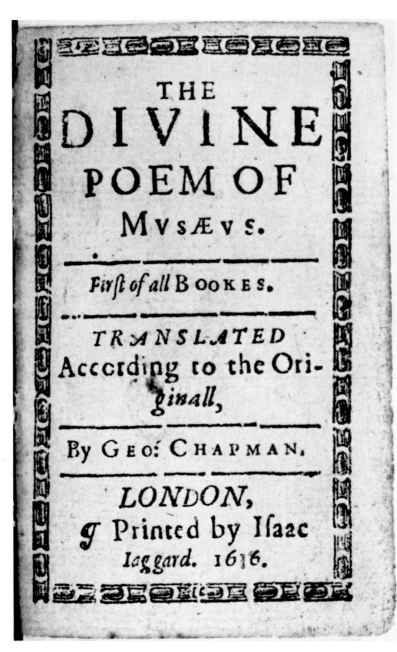

THE DIVINE POEM OF MVSÆVS.

First of all BOOKES.

TRANSLATED According to the Originall,

By GEO: CHAPMAN.

LONDON, *g* Printed by Isaac Iaggard. 1616.

Title-page of *The Divine Poem of Musaeus* (Bodleian Library). See p. 211.

a heroic heart, as contrasted with her brutal and cowardly husband.
It may be that 11. 1–49 of II, ii (cancelled in the revision) were omitted
to this end, for there she first plumes herself as more discreet and chaste
than the Duchess of Guise, and then confesses in soliloquy:

> ... of a sudden, my licentious fancy
> Riots within me: not my name and house,
> Nor my religion to this hour observ'd,
> Can stand above it; I must utter that
> That will in parting break more strings in me,
> Than death when life parts, and that holy man
> That, from my cradle, counsell'd for my soul,
> I now must make an agent for my blood.[17]

"I must" repeated. Chapman has no great opinion of female capacity
to reason, to be calm or innocent, and his Tamyra, full of heat, sheds
no light at all—a nocturnal creature. Her repudiation of Monsieur's
politic overtures and her asseverations of wifely fidelity are outward
only, since her "own dark love and light [is] bent to another," to
Bussy. Expecting his arrival with the holy pander, flying her "sex,
[her] virtue, [her] renown," she invokes darkness:

> Now all ye peaceful regents of the night,
> Silently-gliding exhalations,
> Languishing winds, and murmuring falls of waters,
> Sadness of heart and ominous secureness,
> Enchantments, dead sleeps, all the friends of rest,
> That ever wrought upon the life of man,
> Extend your utmost strengths, and this charm'd hour
> Fix like the Centre!
>
> (II, ii, 108–15)

Darkness and cunning are her ministers, and the Friar's inverted
rhetoric makes it clear that Bussy in this amour is turning *his* world
upside down too. Here "the direct is crooked," the "affections'
storm" is proof against reason (II, ii, 140–1, 174), the night of female
"humours" enshrouds the hero. Tamyra's sanctimoniousness—the only
tribute she can pay to virtue—galls him in his absolute self, and he
cries for light. She worries about the "One/That wakes above," who
"sees through doors, and darkness, and our thoughts," the old bugaboo
of those whose "conscience is too nice,/And bites too hotly of the
Puritan spice," as Bussy says (III, i, 1–2); she cringes from the
"dangerous siege/Sin lays about us." For Bussy, "sin is a coward,"

---

[17] *Tragedies*, p. 564.

made of shadow into a monster by "the witch Policy," and he promises
that her fame will fly "in golden vapours and with awful wings." Her
lover gone, she visits her offence upon destiny once more (she is
certainly no theologian)—

> What shall weak dames do, when th' whole work of nature
> Hath a strong finger in each one of us?

"Fortune's proud mushroom shot up in a night," as Montsurry calls
him, the Hercules who stands "like an Atlas underneath the King"
(III, i, 118; Q1 reading), is now at the top of the wheel. The long
second scene of Act III, set firmly in the middle of the play, is the point
of peripeteia. Here the envious Monsieur, hoping to "set snares for his
ranging greatness" in a "loose downfall" with a woman, learns from
Tamyra's handmaid, by "the happiest shot that ever flew," i.e. by
Fortune, of the secret love-affair. The coarse exchange between
Monsieur and Pero is set like a blot between two shining manifestations
of Bussy's fiery virtue, a betrayal between two testimonies of honesty.
At the opening of the scene, the King commends Bussy as his "eagle"
for speaking truth and no flattery, and Bussy "speaks home" in a
satiric review of the estates, promising to "hawk at" the "great man
(by the people's voice,/Which is the voice of God)", at worldly clergy
and predatory lawyers. He "hawks at" Guise, in a bitter course of
insults, and the King, averting another duel, holds up before the court
the perfect image of D'Ambois:

> A man so good, that only would uphold
> Man in his native noblesse, from whose fall
> All our dissensions rise; that in himself
> (Without the outward patches of our frailty,
> Riches and honour) knows he comprehends
> Worth with the greatest: kings had never borne
> Such boundless empire over other men,
> Had all maintained the spirit and state of D'Ambois. . . .
> No envy, no disjunction had dissolv'd
> Or pluck'd one stick out of the golden faggot
> In which the world of Saturn bound our lives,
> Had all been held together with the nerves,
> The genius, and th' ingenuous soul of D'Ambois.
> (III, ii, 90–7, 103–7)

The hero sticks fiery off in a degenerate world. Surely there is no irony
here, inviting the judicious to murmur, "O, very fine, but of course
we're not to believe it." If there is irony it is of a more complex order

than that: the King (or Chapman in his high dream speaking through the King, who, after all, has no *character* of his own) contemplates the perfection of the hero, of which only a distorted shadow is cast over the rough ground of the action. If there is "moral confusion" in the play,[18] then there is no tragedy: the tragedy is in the disproportion of substance and shadow, a disproportion which the hero creates in his free choice.

After the revelations of Pero, and Monsieur's determination to pull down the "advanced valour" of Bussy's spirit, which he has "rais'd without a circle," Monsieur and Bussy engage in the most savagely attractive colloquy in the play. It is Monsieur who is now, in that reversal of roles, engaged in "retir'd and sole discourse," brooding, Bussy insinuates, on "killing of the King"—that phrase rings like bronze throughout the scene. Asked by Monsieur to utter plainly what he thinks of him, Bussy asks the like favour for it: thereupon his patron tells him he is "as headstrong and as bloody" as a wild horse or a tiger, that he would

> quarrel with sheep,
> And run as mad as Ajax,

that he is ridiculous and vainglorious as a mountebank in his valour, that his "toad-pool" complexion is the sign of a "cold and earthy mixture," mother of putrefaction (i.e. he suffers from melancholy), and, of most interest,

> That in thy valour th' art like other naturals
> That have strange gifts in nature, but no soul
> Diffus'd quite through, to make these of a piece,
> But stop at humours.
>
> (IIII, ii, 435–8)

This significantly anticipates the Guise's estimate of Bussy in *The Revenge* (II, i, 80ff.), as it reminds us of the simile in *Hero and Leander* of the empty gallant, but it is spoken *in character* by Monsieur here, as his tribute to Bussy in V, ii, in his choric capacity, is not. Everything points to this scene as a clash of temperaments, in a formal *contentio veritatis* called ironically an assurance of love and trust on both sides. Bussy, in his turn, replies that Monsieur never did good but to do ill, and as he himself has been called soul-less, so in the climax of his condemnation, he says:

> [I think]
> That your political head is the curs'd fount

---

[18]On this crucial point see Ornstein, pp. 51–9.

> Of all the violence, rapine, cruelty,
> Tyranny, and atheism flowing through the realm. . . .
> That your foul body is a Lernean fen [Hercules again!]
> Of all the maladies breeding in all men;
> That you are utterly without a soul. . . .
> And lastly (which I must for gratitude
> Ever remember), that of all my height
> And dearest life you are the only spring,
> Only in royal hope to kill the King.
> (III, ii, 479-81, 487-9, 495-8)

This has been an interlude: the catastrophe is now at hand and the darkness deepens, complete with some of the most curious diabolic apparatus ever produced, even on the Elizabethan stage. The banquet scene (IV, i, 1–117) is ominous: the ladies have foul looks, as the King complains, and the sinister hints of Monsieur provoke an angry threat from Bussy, the King's "brave eagle" who hawks at all. "Such another spirit," says Monsieur, assuming for the moment his other glasses,

> Could not be still'd from all th' Armenian dragons.
> O my love's glory, heir to all I have
> (That's all I can say, and that all I swear)
> If thou outlive me, as I know thou must,
> Or else hath Nature no proportion'd end
> To her great labours; she hath breathed a mind [Q1: spirit]
> Into thy entrails, of desert to swell
> Into another great Augustus Caesar,
> Organs and faculties fitted to her greatness;
> And should that perish like a common spirit,
> Nature's a courtier and regards no merit.
> (IV, i, 97-108)

(If there is a fundamental incoherence in the play it is here—and later [V, ii] when Nature, allied to Fortune, is accused of Bussy's fall. The "disproportion," I have argued, arises from Bussy's choice; is the choice inevitable? Chapman insists on Bussy's *freedom*; it appears that he is free to put himself into servitude to Nature.)

Under a sky "hid in the dim ostents of tragedy" Tamyra defends herself against Monsieur's informations, protesting her innocence, but a "sudden night/Flows through [the] entrails" of Montsurry, and Bussy invites the Friar to summon up spirits to reveal Monsieur's mischief (IV, ii). The spirit Behemoth and Tamyra advise "policy," and Bussy agrees that "policy shall be flank'd with policy," announces

that he will "appear/Like calm security before a ruin." But Chapman
never shows his hero as a politician; and surely this is an outburst of
desperate naiveté from the despiser of "the witch Policy."[19]

The Friar's plea against Montsurry's revengeful blood (V, i, 5–41)
goes unheeded; Montsurry's abuse and torture of Tamyra (which
causes the death of the Friar, apparently from excess of horror) lays
the trap for the hero, as the revelation of his wife's crime virtually
turns Montsurry himself into a shrieking harbinger of the whole frame
of things in convulsion. The world has "her back-part upwards"; the
frame

> And shaken joints of the whole world should crack
> To see her parts so disproportionate.
>   (V, i, 178–80)

In this chaos, a man might well "die for thought." Bussy, visited and
warned by the "Umbra" of the Friar, invokes once more the "Prince
of Shades" and is warned of his death, but accepts the false summons,
brought by Montsurry in the guise of the Friar (V, iii).

The absurdities of this scene are, however, cancelled by the spirit
of Bussy which seeks light in this "terror of darkness," "instinctive
fire" in the drowsy and enchanted night, and makes him "apt t'
encounter Death and Hell." Having seen him in this admirable state,
the audience is provided a pause in which to consider his fate once
more, as it relates to the whole disorder in creation. Monsieur and
Guise engage in a reflective colloquy (V, ii)[20], during which Monsieur,
who has set the trap, does not gloat over his victim but praises him.
In fact he does not seem to be talking about one whose "blood is
multiplied . . . with spirit" (as in the last scene), but about a dream
of D'Ambois, or perhaps we should say with Cleopatra one "past the
size of dreaming." Nature, he says, "hath no end/ In her great works
responsive to their worths," for she is "stark blind herself," works by
"rote" or by "mere necessity of matter," so that she may make a man

---

[19]The name Behemoth would doubtless suggest "devil" to Chapman's audience
(v. Parrott's note, *Tragedies*, p. 558), but he does not really appear evil, rather, as
my colleague F. D. Hoeniger has reminded me, "like a spirit of Night who provides
the unusual man with insight"—a characteristic Chapman touch. Yet his activities
(supervising a burglary by the inferior spirit Cartophylax), and his advice ("curb
his valour with your policies") are either ludicrous or suspect. And Bussy's notion
of "policy" is to "make th' inspired thresholds of [Monsieur's] court/Sweat with
the weather of [his] horrid steps" (IV, ii, 184–5). The whole scene is full of contra-
dictions, on which see Jacquot, *Bussy*, pp. lxx–lxxxi.

[20]On the placing of this scene in the Qq see *Tragedies*, p. 568, and Brooke, pp.
xlix–1, lxix.

complete or incomplete, not knowing what she does. But usually when she gives a man merit that very quality proves his ruin. Guise replies, anticipating what he is to say in his transformed character in *The Revenge* (II, i, 80ff.), that Nature may "with as much proportion" make a "headless" man, as

> give a full man valour, virtue, learning,
> Without an end more excellent than those
> On whom she no such worthy part bestows.

But Monsieur (or Chapman rather)[21] will have none of this:

> Yet shall you see it here; here will be one
> Young, learned, valiant, virtuous, and full mann'd;
> One on whom Nature spent so rich a hand
> That with an ominous eye she wept to see
> So much consum'd her virtuous treasury.
> Yet as the winds sing through a hollow tree
> And (since it lets them pass through) let it stand;
> But a tree solid (since it gives no way
> To their wild rage) they rend up by the root:
> So this whole man
> (That will not wind with every crooked way,
> Trod by the servile world) shall reel and fall
> Before the frantic puffs of blind-born chance,
> That pipes through empty men, and makes them dance.
> (V, ii, 32–45)

Thus the final glory is prepared for the hero, who, appearing by the vault and warned by Tamyra, sounds at first like the "spirited" man, "buckled in [his] fate"—

> Foutre for Guise's shambles!—

then, nobly offering life to the beaten Montsurry and, dying, forgiving his murderers and bidding Montsurry and Tamyra to be reconciled, he evinces his "native noblesse." But, above all, he escapes his self, passes out of the "penetrable flesh" into the incorruptible realm of fame and fire, with Hercules:

> Oh, my fame,
> Live in despite of murther! Take thy wings
> And haste thee where the grey ey'd Morn perfumes
> Her rosy chariot with Sabaean spices!
> Fly, where the Evening from th' Iberian vales
> Takes on her swarthy shoulders Hecate,

---

[21]See Ure, in *Jacobean Theatre*, p. 234.

Crown'd with a grove of oaks: fly where men feel
The burning axletree, and those that suffer
Beneath the chariot of the snowy Bear:
And tell them all that D'Ambois now is hasting
To the eternal dwellers; that a thunder
Of all their sighs together (for their frailties
Beheld in me) may quit my worthless fall
With a fit volley for my funeral.[22]

(V, iv, 98–111)

But his prayer for reconcilement is not answered, and the play ends with Montsurry's "honour" turning him away from his love. The death of Bussy is superbly irrelevant to the world through which he has flashed; the kingdom is not cleansed, and a ghost pronounces his elegy:

Farewell, brave relics of a complete man,
Look up, and see thy spirit made a star;
Join flames with Hercules.

Bussy is not a demonstration but an experience. Chapman is not solving a problem, but finding one. What room is there for heroism in the world? The sibylline answer is: None, or some.

It seems safe to say that Chapman's wonder at the Herculean hero, imbued with "spirit" and outward fortitude, diminished as he read more Epictetus "the good Greek moralist" and began to meditate on Homer's "fashion of an absolute man" in the *Odyssey*. The process of disillusion is apparent in the Byron plays; how far it was suggested by the parallel of Byron and Essex I shall consider later. Certainly *The Revenge of Bussy D'Ambois*[23] is a retraction, by times almost formal, of *The Tragedy of Bussy*: Bussy is explicitly devalued in favour of his "learned" brother Clermont; the significances attached to "Nature" are in complete antithesis to those in the first play (i.e. Nature is assimilated to Virtue rather than to Fortune); Guise is (defying history) entirely reversed, being the "patron and disciple" (Parrott) of the Stoic hero. The action, like the hero, is invented to suit the thesis: the only episodes which have any basis in fact are the arrest of Clermont, transferred from Grimeston's account (in the *General Inventorie*, 1607) of the seizure of the Comte d'Auvergne, and the murder of Guise, which happened to fit Chapman's purposes.

[22]Adapted, as Boas was the first to note, from *Hercules Oetaeus*, ll. 1522–30.
[23]On date, text, sources, &c., see *Tragedies*, pp. 571 ff. See also Clifford Leech, "*The Atheist's Tragedy* as a Dramatic Comment on Chapman's *Bussy* Plays," *JEGP* LII (1953), 525–30.

Whereas in *The Tragedy* the action moves swiftly from prologue to crisis to catastrophe, following the flight of the "falling star," *The Revenge* is static, contemplative—indeed deliberately unfashionable, appearing the more so because it has the outward form of a tragedy of revenge, complete with instructing ghost, avenging fury (Charlotte), and motivated delay.

Yet these differences tend to conceal a fundamental continuity between the two plays. In each play the "absolute" man is set over against a world of policy and corrupted law in which the free man's individual act is justified. In each play, also, there are only three essential episodes: a prologue, in which the hero is introduced and his situation defined; an act of dauntless "spirit" (Bussy's duel; Clermont's struggle with his captors) as reported by a Nuntius; and a final engagement issuing in the hero's "translation." In each play there is a double vision of the hero.

Like *The Conspiracy of Byron* and unlike *The Tragedy of Bussy*, *The Revenge* introduces the hero obliquely and at some distance, and this, of course, is a clue to our apprehension of him. Bussy confronts us; we hear about Clermont. Baligny, a confessed "politician" (and Clermont's brother-in-law), and Renel, a "decayed" malcontent, starting from the "stupid permission of brave D'Ambois' murther . . . us'd/ To serve the kingdom" (a forced interpretation of that event, to fit this play), discuss how things have fallen from their first good estate, when "things most lawful/ Were once most royal." Now the realm suffers the vices of idleness, "good arts fail, crafts and deceits are us'd"; ignorant men aim all their study at getting money. This is Bussy's inverted society described over again—Chapman never gave up describing it all his life—as between them these two creatures of a fallen time praise by contrast the "first natures" of man's nobility, incidentally extolling the "greatest Guise" and the delayed revenge which Clermont has determined he will undertake only "in the noblest and most manly course." The horizon insensibly widens beyond the small compass of Bussy's tragedy: Guise is with his greatness the hope of those who desire a "new world" to replace Henry's court, and he is "in chief heat of his faction." At this point the court enters in tableau (a Tourneur touch?), and Baligny, observing Guise whispering with Clermont, wagers that they are not talking of state affairs,

> but of something
> Savouring of that which all men else despise,
> How to be truly noble, truly wise.
>
> (I, i, 149–51)

Clermont, it appears, is no politician; as another courtier observes, he is whispering "some doctrine of stability and freedom,/Contempt of outward greatness." If Bussy was imagined in the figure of hyperbole, Clermont was conceived as paradox—he is, when all is said, a figure of speech, the mouthpiece as hero. Whispering at court, the place of faction and policy, he whispers contempt of high place; counselling freedom, he is the "dear minion" of Guise, and "hangs upon his ear . . ./ Like to his jewel" (I, i, 152–3). If this be thought an envious sneer, it is further attested by Clermont himself, and, dying, he calls himself Guise's "creature." (He is the apex of a peculiar triangle of loves, as will appear.) To outsiders, Guise seems to cultivate him to be politic, being thought to "embrace his virtues," which are summed up in

> Holding all learning but an art to live well,
> And showing he hath learn'd it in his life.
>
> (I, i, 171–2)

Chapman is not apt in inventing dramatic episodes, least of all in this play, so it is no surprise to find him repeating the situation in *The Tragedy* (III, ii, 376–499), where Monsieur asks Bussy to speak plain truth to him; here (I, i, 180–297) he tries Clermont's "temper" in the same way, and the response points the contrast with the first hero. "Be a true glass to me," Monsieur says, your brother "let me hear/My grossest faults." But Clermont remains unmoved under repeated insults, finally saying calmly:

> You did no princely deeds
> Ere you're born . . .
> Nor did you any since that I have heard;
> Nor will do ever any, as all think.
>
> (I, i, 284–7)

Monsieur leaving on this in wrath, Clermont improves the occasion by commenting on the "huge heaps of outside in these mighty men," and reading his patron a "virtuous digression" from Epictetus (misquoted) and Democritus on the "maskeries" of the world's vanity. His unimpassioned decorum is set in sharp contrast to the passions of Tamyra and Montsurry (I, ii), the former crying revenge for Bussy's spirit, now in the "sphere of fire," the latter violent in "unmanly rages," haunted by the Furies, shut up cowardly in his house. By "policy" Renel and Baligny serve Clermont's challenge upon him—like a subpoena, but by policy too the revenge is delayed. In fact, except for one important moment, placed, like a different and "outward" crisis in *The Tragedy*, in the centre of the play, the revenge theme is virtually withdrawn, while the audience is invited to concentrate for three acts upon the virtues of the hero. At the beginning of Act II plans are made to apprehend him, at the end of Act IV he is freed to accomplish his revenge. Act II begins with a definition of "policy"; Act IV ends with Clermont's composed self-sufficiency, lectured on and demonstrated.

Baligny, commending to the King his policy in arresting Clermont as "capital" in Guise's faction, advances what a Jacobean would call a Machiavellian theory of private vices, public benefits (II, i, 30–56). Men should not

> Grudge at their particular wrong, if so it seem,
> For th' universal right of your estate.

(This view is explicitly repudiated by Clermont later, IV, i, 68–76.) But Baligny plays on both sides, as he puts it. With Guise, who praises Clermont for his "rare learning."

> Which Bussy, for his valour's season, lack'd;
> And so was rapt with outrage oftentimes
> Beyond decorum; where this absolute Clermont . . .
>   can contain that fire, as hid in embers,
>   (II, i, 88–90, 94)

comparing him to Brutus, he quotes *Antigone* to support the argument that God's laws are above king's. With Clermont, he murmurs appropriate interjections while that worthy descants upon the softness of the French nobility, on the vices of "these painted men,/ All set on out-side," and provokes him to a paradoxical defence of Guise's part in the St. Bartholomew massacre (II, i, 210–34). Guise's strange aims are to cross the "common custom/ Of servile nobles," Clermont continues, while his own function is to teach

> Guise to heighten, and make sweet
> With life's dear odours, a good mind and name;
> For which he only loves me, and deserves
> My love and life, which through all deaths I vow:
> Resolving this, whatever change can be,
> Thou hast created, thou hast ruin'd me.
>   (II, i, 272–7)

Here we return to this curious relation between the patron who is being "sweetened" by his "creature," who in turn is commended by his patron as "the crown of man," true as a star in his motion.

In his arrest Clermont is to be the victim of policy, of ambition and faction, as the unwilling lords set to trap him confess (III, i); by contrast his speech and behaviour in his sister's house at Cambrai (III, ii) are noble to the point of fatuity. He gives little lectures on "noblest knowledge" rising above "vile and vulgar admirations," i.e. he is not interested in the latest news, and he refuses to heed an anonymous warning. To his "brave virago" sister he seems to have a "defect of spirit and valour," as he regrets that he ever engaged to revenge his brother:

> Nor can we call it virtue that proceeds
> From vicious fury. I repent that ever
> (By an instigation in the appearance
> My brother's spirit made, as I imagin'd)
> That e'er I yielded to revenge his murther.
> All worthy men should ever bring their blood
> To bear all ill, not to be wreak'd with good:
> Do ill for no ill; never private cause
> Should take on it the part of public laws.
>   (III, ii, 108–16)

This is an exact retraction of Bussy's justification of his action in the duel (*Tragedy*, II, i, 197–204), but not easy to reconcile with Clermont's doctrine of the inner "decrees" he has set down to guide his life, the "native power" (*his* daemon), which makes him see Homer's Achilles as an example of the destruction that comes when men are "wrathful, revengeful, and insatiate/ In their affections" (III, iv, 10–25). Yet he proves himself a Hercules when the soldiers try to catch him, as Aumale in the role of Nuntius reports, full of the "spirit's convulsions," compared to "a fierce and fire-given cannon" (IV, i, 11–39). He reads Renel a lecture from Epictetus on being pleased with one's place, another moralization, by implication, on his brother's fault, on the wisdom of not "resisting th' All" (III, iv, 48–75), commending by the way the Earl of Oxford for his "noblesse," contemning the perturbed life of public men, and proclaiming that Fortune cannot touch him, since he is obedient only to "the high and general Cause" and his discipline is to "join himself with th' Universe/ In his main sway," and so forth—a much-quoted speech based on Epictetus, *Discourses*, iv. Tributes are reverently placed on his plinth: Guise commends his "firm inexorable spirit," his "contempt of riches and of greatness," the "learning of his soul." He is summed up in "this Senecal man" (IV, iv, 14–46).

These sentiments elevate him not only in opposition to policy when kingship is corrupt (IV, iii, 41–46) but absolutely, "as something sacred fallen from the sky"—an unconscious reference to Bussy's fallen star? As the sermons and the testimonies multiply, their weight slows the play to a stop. "Alles Stoische ist untheatralisch." The hero being absolute, there is nothing to do but observe how absolute he is.

The revenge motif, re-introduced mechanically at the end of Act IV, raises a next-to-impossible dramatic problem: a set of principles arranged in a recurring rhetorical pattern (i.e. copied from the same page of the commonplace book) has to accomplish an act of blood. And an almost equally difficult ethical problem: an inner-directed complete man has to accept the conventional supernatural urging to that act. Chapman has, it is true, given his protagonist a paradoxical human dimension in making him the "creature" of a noble patron, and, it must here be added, in providing him with a noble mistress, the Countess of Cambrai, who blinds herself in weeping his betrayal. Guise notes:

> How strangely thou art lov'd of both the sexes;
> Yet thou lov'st neither, but the good of both.
>
> (V, i, 154–5)

To which Clermont replies that until enjoyment he is "passionate/ Like other lovers," but fruition past he then loves "out of judgement," proceeding then to develop a paradox against marriage, arguing that love cannot co-exist with "the bed's desire in blood" but rather in friendship "chaste and masculine." Guise, professing delight in these "paradoxes strange and too precise" for other men, would have Clermont his "mistress"; dying, he commends his love to Clermont (V, iv, 69–72). As for the Senecal man, it is not always observed that *his* dying speech is almost entirely an act of devotion to his patron:

> Shall I live, and he
> Dead, that alone gave means of life to me?
> There's no disputing with the acts of kings,
> Revenge is impious on their sacred persons;
> And could I play the worldling (no man loving
> Longer than gain is reap'd, or grace from him)
> I should survive, and shall be wonder'd at
> Though (in my own hands being) I end with him:
> But friendship is the cement of two minds,
> As of one man the soul and body is. . . .
>
> Guise, O my lord, how shall I cast from me
> The bands and coverts hind'ring me from thee?
> The garment or the cover of the mind,
> The human soul is; of the soul the spirit

The proper robe is; of the spirit the blood;
And of the blood, the body is the shroud.
With that must I begin then to unclothe,
And come at th' other. . . .

. . . now my master calls, my ship, my venture . . .
                    and I left negligent,
To all the horrors of the vicious time . . .
None favouring goodness, none but he respecting
Piety or manhood. . . .

I come, my lord! Clermont, thy creature, comes.
                    (V, v, 149–58, 168–75, 183–89, 193)

Hardly the last gesture of the self-sufficient man who is one with the All, but the passionate rejection of a world empty without his love. In one perspective Clermont is a character in love with a perfection he has himself created in the one to whom his devotion is vowed; in the other, he is a *persona* in an allegory of the Stoic sage.

The revenge is achieved by the second of these figures, in a solemn parody of the conventions of the genre. In an obvious attempt to solve the ethical problem. Chapman has the inciting Ghost (of Bussy) begin with what sounds like the exordium of an evangelical sermon, urging ignorant men to reform their "manless" lives, to consider the divisions in Christendom and to mend the world's proportion by seeing to it that not "any one ill scape his penalty" (V, i, 1–32). The way to "live to God," to strive to "be his image," is to supply "what corrupted law/ Leaves unperform'd in kings" (V, i, 79–99). Revenge, then, is commanded as a deed "to fit eternity"—a curious and paradoxical doctrine. Clermont takes this pretty calmly (though not with the same bathos as his arrest—"This heavily prevents/ My purpos'd recreation in these parts") and his calm is contrasted with the fiery "unmatched spirit" of his sister. But the revenge approved by "Christian" justice in the last scene is submitted by Clermont to the fortune of a duel with the poltroon Montsurry, and a painful performance it is, for Clermont has to breathe some D'Ambois spirit into his enemy, then offer to "set [his] life at large" if he will only put up a little fight, while at his fall he exchanges "noble and Christian" forgiveness, pronouncing a benediction, "Rest, worthy soul." Attended by a dance of ghosts, led by the shade of Bussy, amid the frenzied cries of his blind mistress and his sister, who decide to survive "in cloisters," this most non-conformist of revengers passes out of the world to rejoin his blessed patron.

I have abused chronology to discuss the two Bussy plays together, not only because the second is a confutation of the first, even to the contrasting tone and tenor of the last speeches of the protagonists, or because, as the dramatist's imagination is subdued to what it works in, the matter of Bussy imposed certain irregular limits upon Chapman's powers which neither allegorized Marlowe nor versified Epictetus could break out of, but because I am not altogether convinced that there is a clear line of development in Chapman's thought, passing comfortably from the Achillean to the Ulyssean ideal. The line is there, of course, and it passes through Byron's hollow greatness to the Stoic figure (albeit ambivalently conceived) of Clermont, but Chapman was writing plays, hoping to sell them as they were "outwardly" satisfying, while working towards a mode which would say his inward obsessions in the best way. I think he found his form in the Byron plays, and lost it thereafter.

The Conspiracy and Tragedy of Byron[24] is a fine dramatic poem, lucid and grand, if we take it on its own terms as a secular oratorio, set to a suite of limited themes, from which the ordinary business of the stage (so embarrassing in the Bussy plays) is almost entirely banished, leaving only a series of weightily arranged discussions, confrontations and soliloquies. Of plot—in the sense that we may speak of the plot of *Sejanus* or of *Coriolanus*, plays with a similar theme—there is little. Byron is flattered into treasonable associations against his king, Henry IV, by the Duke of Savoy and others; he is reconciled with the King (*The Conspiracy*). He is moved to renew his conspiracy by a sense of greatness imperfectly recompensed and by dreams of absolute power, is trapped by the evidence of his intimates, condemned and executed by the royal justice (*The Tragedy*). These events are not narrated in their smaller delineations, with exact indications of time and place, but projected as it were upon a macrocosmic backdrop, appearing in portentous images succeeding each other in majestic procession, so that the separation of the mythic from the ethical-political dimension virtually disappears, and the whole is a galaxy of metaphor.

The argument is heroic, treating one of the most important political subjects of the Renaissance. As the critical problem of mass democracy is the power of the demagogue, who comes to despise and manipulate the very "opinion" which created him and keeps him in power, so in the time of the would-be-absolute monarch, the problem was the abuse

[24]On date, text, sources, &c., see *Tragedies*, pp. 591 ff.

of power in men *raised* by royal recognition until they seemed to themselves to become indispensable and the source of the very power that raised them. For such persons analogues (not always exact) could be found in antiquity as interpreted by Amyot's Plutarch, and their careers were examined in terms of Virtue and Fortune as discussed in the *Moralia*, which Chapman had before him as he wrote the Byron plays.[25] For an Englishman of Chapman's generation, the two conspicuous examples were Robert Devereux, Earl of Essex and Charles de Gontaut, Duc de Biron, each of whom, seen in the perspective glass of history—and, it should be added, in the wisdom of contemporary statesmen like Robert Cecil and Henry of Navarre—may be considered as turbulent anachronisms in the development of the bureaucratic state.

The analogy between their careers did not go unnoticed. Witness a French work of 1607 (the year of publication of Edward Grimeston's *General Inventorie of the History of France*, which Chapman closely followed), *Histoire de la vie et mort du Comte d'Essex avec un discours grave et eloquent de la Royne d'Angleterre, au Duc de Biron sur ce sujet. La conspiration, prison, jugement, testament, & mort du Duc de Biron: Trahison mort & procez de Nicholas Loste, prison du Comte d'Auvergne & de madame la Marquise de Vernueil*, in which the moral of Byron's visit to the court of Elizabeth after Essex's execution is drawn:

[Byron] estoit hazardeux en guerre, ambitieux sans mesure, & qui eust finy sa vie plus heureusement s'il eust cru les remonstrances de la Royne Elizabeth d'Angleterre, & qu'elles eussent touché ses entrailles, quand elle luy fit voir la teste du Compte d'essex, & qu'elle luy dit, Si j'estois en la place du Roy mon frere, il y'auroit des testes aussi bien coupées à Paris qu'à Londre. L'exces de son ambition luy fit user de rodomontades sans jugement.[26] [Sigs. F-Fi]

Chapman makes much of Byron's "school[ing] by the matchless queen," reported at length in a scene which has been cut ("dismembered" is his word for these poems), and the hero himself is elsewhere made to recognize the parallel (*Trag.*, IV, i; V, iii). He could hardly have failed to follow Essex's career with passionate interest—who did not?—and especially since in 1598 he had committed himself

[25]Peter Ure, "The Main Outline of Chapman's *Byron*," *SP* XLVII (1950), 573–82. Note also the significant likenesses between Byron and Jonson's *Sejanus*, especially *Sejanus'* *hubris* (at V, 1–9).

[26]Byron was in England September 5–14, 1601. I have used the B.M. copy of the *Histoire*, 807 a. 25. Cf. Daniel's *Philotas* (1607) and its alleged connection with Essex's troubles (Chambers, III, 275–6).

very deeply in the dedicatory prefaces to his first essays in Homeric translation, terming Essex

Most true Achilles (whom by sacred prophecie Homere did but prefigure in his admirable object and in whose unmatched vertues shyne the dignities of the soule and the whole excellence of royall humanitie).[27]

By 1607–8, as Jacquot observes, "il a mesuré sa grandeur et sa faiblesse, et il a porté finalement un jugement rigoreux sur les ambitieux de son espèce."[28] Reading of Byron in Grimeston, he found him compared to "Achilles in battle"—and Henry IV compared to Ulysses (pp. 959, 968), that "he valued himself at an inestimable price," that Essex was an example of such a man as this, "possest with this violent passion of desire to be Masters, being no more capable of government" (pp. 961–2). And he would not have needed to know Essex personally to know, as everyone did, that in his last days he was alternately possessed of melancholy and choler, which Grimeston repeatedly characterizes as "those bad humours which did choake" Byron.

The political lesson was there, reinforced by bitter memory at home; it was plain and exemplary in common talk from across the narrow seas, and set down solemnly in Grimeston:

[Byron] had goodly parts, communicable to fewe, his Valour was admirable . . . of an invincible Courage. . . . He was extremely Vainglorious, yea, sometime, he would refuse his meate, and content himselfe with little to feede his Fantasie with Glory and Vanitie. . . . The excess of his Ambition made him to brave it without judgement. He became so presumptuous, as he thought that the King, nor France could not subsist without him.[29]

As for the King, he was described as righteous and just, generous and determined to preserve the laws which keep society in order and proportion. Grimeston described this quality in him in a passage explaining his bringing Byron to trial, which must have wakened an echo in the memory of the author of *Hero and Leander*, III: "He will have the Solemnities and lawfull Ceremonies observed, and that they [the conspirators] be judged by the rigour of the Lawes."[30]

Byron's fall was timely and sufficiently disturbing to serve as a parable, but he was also *excessive* and astonishing, awakening the poet's imagination to promote him from particular example to general tragic significance. One stage in this transformation may have been suggested

[27] *Homer*, I, 504.
[28] Jacquot, p. 31.
[29] *General Inventorie*, pp. 992–3.
[30] *Ibid.*, p. 968.

by Grimeston's observations about Byron's choler (which is emphasized in the poem), taken with these commonplaces from Coeffeteau's *Table of Humane Passions*:

[Choleric] men desire passionately to see themselves honoured, and they beleeve, that such as are inferior to them . . . are bound to yeeld them all sorts of duty and respect. . . . Hee which said that man was a creature which is passionate for glory, seemes to have discovered all the roots of Choler.[31]

The excessive desire for honour is a kind of self-idolatry, "tender of it selfe onely, making honour a triumph, or rather trophy of desire" (Fulke Greville), in which the great man, looking out upon the world, sees only an image of himself to "feede his Fantasie." In another place I have discussed this "humour" as it is reflected in Shakespeare's Achilles, Antony and Coriolanus;[32] the last two are presented with that peculiar detached sympathy which is Shakespeare's mark, a god in working, nothing left out. Chapman's powers are less subtle, he is more involved and sees less, but he can see something like a man fronting his own likeness "put in statue" (*Con.*, III, ii, 142), and it moves him to a fine amazement, even while he is troubled by the emptiness, absurdity and danger of the pose. Beyond that, he can see the contest between the King and Byron as a cosmic drama, a conflict between Olympian order and Titanic unrest. Henry is a sun-king (*Trag.*, IV, i, 92; V, i, 138–46), whereas Byron would turn all into chaos again and create another world (*Trag.*, I, ii, 29–31). In a related figure the analogy with Hercules appears: Byron is compared to Hercules in his triumph over Fortune (*Con.*, II, ii, 93), and he compares himself to that hero, in his "labours" for France. In his delusion that he has been indispensable in creating the present state, he says,

> I have Alcides-like gone under th' earth,
> And on these shoulders borne the weight of France.
> (*Trag.*, III, i, 151–2)

As Herculean hero, he also participates in that inflated absurdity which is part of the Hercules tradition. Byron is a hollow man, puffed-up, who, as the "Prologus" states, "bursts in growing great."[33] The Savoyards who would use him note that his humour of glory is blown up "with praise of his perfections" (*Con.*, I, i, 70–4); when he first appears he finds his state "full/ Of pleasure not to be contain'd in

[31]F. N. Coeffeteau, *A Table of Humane Passions . . . translated by Edw: Grimeston* (1621), pp. 568, 575.
[32]"Shakespeare and the Lonely Dragon," *UTQ* XXIV (1954–5), 109–20.
[33]Cf. *Revenge of Bussy*, I, i, 344–5; *Caesar and Pompey*, V, i, 181–6.

flesh"; he is like the shaft "shot at the sun by angry Hercules" which will be shivered by the thunder "if I burst"—a pride of images (*Con.*, I, ii, 28–9, 40–3); the King compares him to a poem "fronted" well with commendations, "puff'd with their empty breath," "passions of wind," since such "corrupted heralds" are "fitter to blow up bladders than full men" (*Con.*, III, ii, 247–66), and tells him that his veins have been swelled by whispers of others. These allusions virtually disappear in *The Tragedy*, as the tone grows more desperate and solemn, but reach their proper climax at the moment of Byron's arrest, in Epernon's comment:

> Farewell for ever! So have I discern'd
> An exhalation that would be a star
> Fall, when the sun forsook it, in a sink.
> Sho[w]s [Qq :shooes] ever overthrow that are too large,
> And hugest cannons burst with overcharge.
>
> (*Trag.*, IV, ii, 291–5)

This quality in the hero suggests the "humorous man," as Jacquot has noted,[34] and when we first hear the King's opinion of Byron's condition, he defines it clinically as flowing "with adust and melancholy choler," adding that "melancholy spirits are venomous" and that he intends to send his dangerous subject to England "to breathe a while in temperate English air" (*Con.*, II, ii, 42–9). This humour, a scorching and *feverish* (cf. *Trag.*, V, ii, 5–6) putrefaction, is purged only in his execution, when it flares up violently for the last time. But this burning, though a disease in state, also provides the metaphor which raises the hero to his loftiest pitch, to fly at Heaven. His valour is matchless, boundless, "more than human"; he is persuaded by the flatterer Picoté that he belongs with "hot, shining, swift, light and aspiring things . . . of celestial nature" (*Con.*, I, ii, 112–3); like Bussy he is full of "hot spirit," as the King perceives (*Trag.*, I, i, 71); to himself he has always been "a fighting flame," yet that flaming spirit is "amazed" at the shadow of death.

These images not only illustrate Chapman's familiar ambivalence but enforce the macrocosmic-microcosmic analogy which at once enlarges and unifies the design of the poem. Yet to isolate them so is to lose something of the majesty of the design. A comparison with *Paradise Lost* is not altogether fanciful. Here too we have the aspiring Adversary who would be highest, who sees the perfect order and

---

[34]Jacquot, p. 194.

decorum of the court's heaven in the "cozening" glass of his vanity as politic and inverted, and fed by adulation makes evil his good, descending from his glory to the fury of a trapped beast. It is time to look at the design as a whole, delineated as it is by the "shaddow and heightening" of "expressive Epethites."

The Conspiracy, unlike the Bussy plays, opens a window on the great stage of European diplomacy and war, with the paradox that mean men (the Duke of Savoy and his henchmen) are surveying it. For their designs they find the "newly-created" Duke of Byron (his autumnal star—see the "Prologus"—is still rising, in the *de casibus* tradition) fit, and observe that his ambition and "excess of glory" are sustained

> With an unlimited fancy that the King,
> Nor France itself, without him can subsist.
> *(Con.*, I, i, 81–2)

The main clue is thus planted at the beginning, and the contrast with his hell of policy (and also with the first scenes of *The Tragedy of Bussy*) is imaged in the appearance of the King, his sunny "aspect/Folded in clouds," banishing the decayed magician, litigant and politician La Fin, who is to be the "outward" agent of Byron's fall, from his court, which is, he proclaims, no "hive for drones," but a "society of noblesse," where such trouble-makers as La Fin are poison. After this instructive prelude, Byron is introduced at the Archduke's court in Brussels, where his "humours" are observed and a tempter (Picoté) set in his way. It is a grand entrance, making a heaven of hell, or glory out of policy. Before him, "for the sweet steps of his state," is spread a carpet figuring the "history of Catiline" (a sinister touch), and he enters to music, breathing the elevated accents of Vergil:

> What place is this, what air, what region,
> In which a man may hear the harmony
> Of all things moving? . . .
> The blood turns in my veins; I stand on change,
> And shall dissolve in changing; 'tis so full
> Of pleasure not to be confin'd in flesh:
> To fear a violent good abuseth goodness,
> 'Tis immortality to die aspiring,
> As if a man were taken quick to heaven;
> What will not hold perfection, let it burst;
> What force hath any cannon, not being charg'd,
> Or being not discharg'd? . . .

> happy Semele,
> That died compress'd with glory!...
>   They follow all my steps with music
> As if my feet were numerous, and trod sounds
> Out of the centre with Apollo's virtue. . . .
> They hide the earth from me with coverings rich,
> To make me think that I am here in heaven.
>   (*Con.*, I, ii, 22–51, *passim*)

Picoté goes to work to undermine his loyalty, i.e. his *virtue*, and though Byron resists his argument in a fine speech (I, ii, 137–64) which, in the choric manner to which Chapman's readers should become accustomed, asserts the value of "human noblesse" which flourishes in "the natural clime of truth" when we trust not "without men" but "the sure form in themselves," he is overcome by a set of puffers who set him up for the promises of La Fin in the next scene (II, i), which prompt him to reveal in soliloquy his passion to "handsel Fortune":

> If to be highest still, be to be best,
> All works to that end are the worthiest.
>   (*Con.*, II, i, 154–5)

So Byron makes *his* version of the choice of Hercules, putting off "into industrious and high-going seas"—a noble image he will use again—but taking the Machiavellian way: "So worst works are made good with good success." The King, hearing of this "state adultery," preserves his righteous calm, in this discourse:

> ... men whom virtue
> Forms with the stuff of Fortune, great and gracious,
> Must needs partake with Fortune in her humour
> Of instability, and are like to shafts
> Grown crook'd with standing, which to rectify
> Must twice as much be bow'd another way.
>   (*Con.*, II, ii, 26–31)

But he is moved to set the record straight when Savoy, fishing for some undervaluing of Byron from his lips, over-praises Byron's valour and indispensability in the King's wars. These tedious encomiums and accounts of battles are prefixed by another noble image, of the Duke riding the great horse:[35]

> Your Majesty hath missed a royal sight:
> The Duke Byron on his brave beast Pastrana,

---

[35]On riding the great horse as a symbol of human excellence, see *The Faerie Queene*, II, iv, 1; the exordium of Sidney's *Defence*; *Hamlet*, IV, vii, 85–91, &c.

Who sits him like a full sail'd Argosy
Danc'd with a lofty billow, and as snug
Plies to his bearer, both their motions mix'd;
And being consider'd in their site together,
They do the best present the state of man
In his first royalty ruling, and of beasts
In their first loyalty serving (one commanding,
And no way being mov'd; the other serving,
And no way being compell'd) of all the sights
That ever my eyes witness'd; and they make
A doctrinal and witty hieroglyphic
Of a blest kingdom: to express and teach
Kings to command as they could serve, and subjects
To serve as if they had power to command.
                                    (*Con.*, II, ii, 66–81)

The "first royalty" implies that Byron (like Bussy) is representative of man in his "native noblesse," but the perfection defined by the figure is precisely what Byron's passion destroys. Inflamed by admiration, he is prey to his passion to be "glorious," however well he may colour his breach of faith by a pseudo-rational attack on "those mere politic terms/Of love, fame, loyalty" as enemies of "all the free-born powers of royal man" (*Con.*, III, i, 25–31), and he is stirred to choler when he hears that the King thinks him a less competent soldier than the English veterans Norris and Williams. He topples into absurdity in his reception of his picture, his giantism prefiguring the megalomania of Mount Rushmore:

                          I will give you
My likeness put in statue, not in picture,
And by a statuary of mine own,
That can in brass express the wit of man,
And in his form make all men see his virtues:
Others that with much strictness imitate
The something-stooping carriage of my neck,
The voluble and mild radiance of mine eyes,
Never observe my masculine aspect
And lion-like instinct it shadoweth,
Which Envy cannot say is flattery:
And I will have my image promised you,
Cut in such matter as shall ever last,
Where it shall stand, fix'd with eternal roots
And with a most unmoved gravity;
For I will have the famous mountain Oros . . .
          with such inimitable art

> Express'd and handled . . .
> That, though it keep the true form of that hill . . .
> Yet shall it clearly bear my counterfeit.
> (Con., III, ii, 140–64)

Warned by the King against flattery, he proudly asserts himself one of those "in themselves entire"—"I build not outward, nor depend on props"—but at the end of the scene he determines to consult the stars, which, he later tells Queen Elizabeth, "are divine books to us." Provoked by the evil aspect (a Caput Algol)[36] revealed by the astrologer, he cries:

> I am a nobler substance than the stars. . . .
> I'll wear these golden spurs upon my heels,
> And kick at fate; be free, all worthy spirits,
> And stretch yourselves for greatness and for height,
> Untruss your slaveries; you have height enough
> Beneath this steep heaven to use all your reaches;
> 'Tis too far off to let you, or respect you.
> Give me a spirit that on this life's rough sea
> Loves t'have his sails fill'd with a lusty wind,
> Even till his sail-yards tremble, his mast crack,
> And his rapt ship run on her side so low
> That she drinks water, and her keel plows air.
> There is no danger to a man that knows
> What life and death is; there's not any law
> Exceeds his knowledge; neither is it lawful
> That he should stoop to any other law.
> He goes before them, and commands them all,
> That to himself is a law rational.
> (Con., III, iii, 109, 129–45)

This is magnificent, for Chapman means us to recognize that Byron is astonishing; for that moment, as the great figure of the ship dominates the poet's imagination, we forget that Byron is not a law rational to himself, but a tumult of disordered passions, that he does not know yet what life and death is. Byron's assertion that his *ad hoc* doctrine of practical politics is "the faith/ Of reason and of wisdom" (III, i, 63–4) is ironic; but here irony disappears in vision, and the undramatic character of the speech is indicated also by the fact that this assertion of absolute man comes between two evidences of belief in the stars' influence.

[36]J. Parr, "The Duke of Byron's Malignant *Caput Algol*," *SP* XLIII (1946), 194–202.

Queen Elizabeth's long lecture to Byron, reported by Crequi (IV, i),
which is climaxed by her warning—

> ... you have laid
> A brave foundation by the hand of virtue;
> Put not the roof to fortune—

and her ominous simile of the overhanging promontory, have no effect
on him, for he bursts with choler when the king refuses him the citadel
of Bourg, shouts, "I will be mine own king," is driven to fury at the
King's laughter, but calmed by the royal advice against his evil
flatterers and the encomium of Innocence, kneels penitently, and rises
"by absolute merit" (V, ii). The final scene of *The Conspiracy*, in
which Savoy is discovered courting his mistresses, effectively diminishes
the tempter as a diplomat, and the conspiracy seems in retrospect a
fancy only. Byron can be saved from himself by a good word, as his
treason seems to have been little more than swelling language.

The Byron of *The Tragedy* is the same man, but drawn in more
sombre and fatal colours; the King is the same man, but the religious
aspect of his kingship is emphasized, in contrast with the atheism
of Byron, who, it is said, "was of no religion" but would "mock and
jest at all" (*Trag.*, I, iii, 4–6), though he is made the mouthpiece for
a "deep discourse" which might have come better from Clermont,
on the decline of kings from their first growth on the "green tree"
of Religion (III, i, 1–48). The welfare of goodness with greatness
assumes a seriousness which troubles the whole state of nature, and
Byron is no more the sick man, his veins swelled by flattery, of Henry's
speech of reconciliation in *The Conspiracy*, but a beast who would be
a god.

His "traitorous relapse" astonishes the King, whose "sacred power"
is symbolized in his prayer for the young Dauphin's power, peace and
virtue (I, i, 109–48), and by the masque of Cupid (II, i), "an emblem
of discord resolved" (Ure). To Byron, this court of order and righteousness appears inverted, and he blasphemously cries:

> We must reform and have a new creation
> Of state and government, and on our Chaos
> Will I sit brooding up another world.
> I, who through all the dangers that can siege
> The life of man have forc'd my glorious way
> To the repairing of my country's ruins,
> Will ruin it again to re-advance it.
>
> (I, ii, 29–35)

He repudiates "the mizzling breath of policy," though he is himself
its tool—what we should nowadays call its "front"—and as his fate
hurries toward him on the King's commands he seems curiously
passive, full of *hubris*, losing what his valour has won "with a most
enchanted glory." The adjective is apt, for he is bemused and begins
to speak much of his "innocence" (a word Chapman was to work
upon in *Chabot*, with other implications). While he is so lost in his
dream of himself, it is not entirely out of character that he should cast
contempt on "the base fruits of a settled peace" when men "grow rude
and foggy" (IV, i, 1–10)—he too is an unemployed and distrusted
veteran. More suggestive is his captain's comment that he is bereft
of reason, and is left "but the spirit of a horse . . . only power to dare"
(IV, i, 109–10); indeed he is moved by the "ostentful" death of his
own great horse to envy the "noble happy beasts" who do not serve
each other. Against this descent of mind, which has its own grave
beauty too, is set the King's god-like charity—"I never lov'd man
like him"—his open and rational justice—"I like not executions so
informal"—his religious care:

> O Thou that govern'st the keen swords of kings,
> Direct my arm in this important stroke,
> Or hold it being advanc'd; the weight of blood,
> Even in the basest subject, doth exact
> Deep consultation in the highest king. . . .
> The soul's eye sharpen'd with that sacred light
> Of whom the sun itself is but a beam,
> Must only give that judgment.
>   (IV, ii, 63–7, 77–9)

So Byron is taken, protesting his innocence, and the bystander
Epernon observes: ". . . his state is best/That hath most inward
worth."

The hero's trial and execution succeed. As prologue to this, before
he is withdrawn to leave the stage to Byron, the King displays his
justice and sits in triumph "in [his] sun of height,/The circular splendour and full sphere of state," like the sun "at height and passive o'er
the crowns of men" (V, i, 138–41). Byron, in prison, is compared to a
bird in a closet, who, "amazed/And wrathful beats his breast from
wall to wall"—the contrast of images in the same scene is striking
indeed. The entrance of La Fin against Byron (V, ii, 130–5) makes all
"circular," as Chapman planned it, and from this begins the prolonged
Herculean rage of a glorious spirit fastened to a dying animal, the
furious wild boar at bay (V, iii, 229–37). His defence at his trial is a

continued descant upon the theme of trapped power; he has been bewitched and tempted by the "damn'd enchanter" La Fin, he who "did deserve too much," he who bears the scars of "five and thirty wounds" open for France. Now the "dunghill" of La Fin is to be raised on his own "monumental heap." This is still Byron besotted by his own image, but after he hears his sentence, the tone shifts, becomes more intimate and desperate as he approaches the irrevocable dissolution. One final titanic gesture, looking backward at his greatness—

> All France shall feel an earthquake; with what murmur
> This world shrinks into chaos—

and then the "amaz'd" gaze forward into death:

> Horror of death! Let me alone in peace.
> And leave my soul to me, whom it concerns;
> You have no charge of it; I feel her free:
> How she doth rouse and like a falcon stretch
> Her silver wings, as threatening Death with death. . . .
>
>   I know . . .
> That life is but a dark and stormy night
> Of senseless dreams, terrors and broken sleeps. . . .
> I . . . a little earth,
> Am seated like the earth, betwixt both the heavens,
> That if I rise, to heaven I rise; if fall,
> I likewise fall to heaven; what stronger faith
> Hath any of your souls? . . .
>
> Why should I keep my soul in this dark light,
> Whose black beams lighted me to lose myself?
> When I have lost my arms, my fame, my mind,
> Friends, brother, hopes, fortunes, and even my fury?
>   (V, iv, 26–72)

Terrifying the executioner, he still cannot accept that he should die thus, but (a brilliant touch, and not in Grimeston) he is helped out of his frenzy by the last-minute tribute to his "better Angel" from a soldier standing by (V, iv, 213–25), and rises finally out of himself to make the true Herculean discovery that he is one of the community of man:

> And so farewell for ever! Never more
> Shall any hope of my revival see me;
> Such is the endless exile of dead men.
> Summer succeeds the Spring; Autumn the Summer;
> The frosts of Winter the fall'n leaves of Autumn:

> All these and all fruits in them yearly fade,
> And every year return: but cursed man
> Shall never more renew his vanish'd face.
> Fall on your knees then, statists, ere ye fall,
> That you may rise again: knees bent too late,
> Stick you in earth like statues: see in me
> How you are pour'd down from your clearest heavens;
> Fall lower yet, mix'd with th' unmoved centre,
> That your own shadows may no longer mock ye.
> Strike, strike, O strike; fly, fly, commanding soul,
> And on thy wings for this thy body's breath,
> Bear the eternal victory of Death!

The play closes on this. Whether it was so concluded in the "scenical representation" or not we do not know.[37] Byron is made to point the moral of his fate in terms identical with those in the Prologue,

> He is at no end of his actions blest,
> Whose ends will make him greatest, and not best.
>
> (V, iv, 144–5)

thus anticipating the reference to "statists" in the final speech, but the only comment in the play worthy to stand after that speech is made earlier by Epernon:

> Oh of what contraries consists a man!
> Of what impossible mixtures! Vice and virtue,
> Corruption, and eternnesse, at one time,
> And in one subject, let together loose!
> We have not any strength but weakens us,
> No greatness but doth crush us into air.
> Our knowledges do light us but to err,
> Our ornaments are burthens, our delights
> Are our tormenters, fiends that, rais'd in fears,
> At parting shake our roofs about our ears.
>
> (V, iii, 189–98)

But Byron's speech is in another dimension from these horizontal paradoxes, spanning vertically the axis of the human imagination, from heaven to the unmoved centre. The image resolves and concludes perfectly the conception of one who was the whole universe to himself.

The Tragedy of Chabot, Admiral of France[38] is in some respects an "answer" to the Byron plays, though not in the strict sense that

[37] See *Tragedies*, p. 623.

[38] On date, text, source, collaboration with Shirley, &c. see *Tragedies*, pp. 631 ff.; Ribner, pp. 35 ff.

The Revenge of Bussy is a retraction of his *Tragedy*. One need not go all the way with Parrott when he says that "in *Chabot* we have a complete reversal of the situation and the problem of the *Conspiracy and Tragedy of Byron*,"[39] but there are some significant contrasts. Where Byron protests his "innocence" falsely, the Admiral's innocence, so continually asserted that it becomes a rather oppressive leitmotif, is of the kind eulogized by Henry IV in *The Conspiracy*:

> the sacred amulet
> Gainst all the poisons of infirmity,
> Of all misfortune, injury and death,
> That makes a man in tune still in himself . . .
> No strife nor no sedition in his powers.
> (*Con.*, V, ii, 85ff.)

(But it does not save Chabot.) Whereas Byron is puffed up by flatterers, and though disclaiming "outward props" is really propped up against oblivion by the delusion of his own indispensability—"I know they cannot all supply my place"—Chabot is "inwardly" certain of his virtue in his conscience. (But he too insists on his merit and his "service.") Byron is justly executed in the ceremony of righteous law; Chabot is destroyed by the "policy" of the King's ministers, given leave to make him acknowledge the King's "superior bounties." (But Chabot is destroyed by his own pride.)

The beginning reader finds the play full of echoes from the other tragedies and from Chapman's private vocabulary generally. Like Bussy, Chabot would die standing; like Clermont, he is compared to Brutus and amazes beholders with his inward virtue; much is made of his "piety," sacred and admirable like Strozza's; to outsiders, his assurance looks like "confidence," reminding us of the other force of that word in *The Widow's Tears*. These and other echoes seem to suggest that *Chabot* is a final testament, especially since the play is subtle, ambiguous, wise and well-constructed—as high opus numbers often are. But there are difficulties. It was long ago noted that the source for the play is Estienne Pasquier's *Les Recherches de la France* in the editions of 1611 and/or 1621, and more recently suggested that it was either written or revised after 1621 as an allegory of the fortunes of Somerset.[40] At some points, notably in the trial of the Lord Chancellor (i.e. Bacon), and perhaps in the characterization of Montmorency the younger favorite (i.e. Villiers), the allusions seem just possible,

[39] *Tragedies*, p. 636.
[40] See Norma Dobie Solve, *Stuart Politics in Chapman's Tragedy of Chabot* (Ann Arbor, 1928).

and characteristic of the loyal and intransigent old poet who scuttled himself on *Andromeda Liberata*. But the title-page of the 1639 quarto gives James Shirley as collaborator. Parrott's account, which minimizes the effect on the whole design of what we may take to be Shirley's revisions, remains essentially unchallenged; if we are willing to assign to the younger playwright some if not all of the neatness of the dramatic structure, we are surely safe in attributing to Chapman the driving notions and conclusions of the play, and, as I have noted, its characteristic vocabulary. Chabot's father-in-law, "no courtier," whose choric meditations on greatness seem to reflect the retired philosopher-poet's religious glance upon the outward world, appears in the Quarto's list of "Speakers" as "Father," but Chabot's wife does not so appear, and Parrott conjectures that that part was added by Shirley; the jealous by-play of Queen and Wife certainly seems uncharacteristic of Chapman.

There is nothing so simple here as the opposition of a bad king and a good subject, or vice versa, but there is the familiar contrast between inward "decrees" in Chabot and the "degrees and languages" of the servant of policy the Advocate, who pleads indifferently against Chabot, and when he is vindicated, against the Chancellor. The main ethical-political problem, however, is concentrated in the relation between Chabot and his king, who perhaps derives not only from the view of Francis I in Pasquier but also from some thoughts at a distance about the pedantry, dilettantism and emotionalism of James I.

The play opens with the usual prologue-discussion between courtiers, in this case Asall and Allegre, who is Chabot's man. The outward situation is simple, and the exposition consequently less oblique than in *The Conspiracy*. Chabot, like Bussy, Clermont and Byron, is a "raised" man, the "great and only famous favorite," and now he is on the way to being supplanted by Montmorency—no more than one might expect to happen to a virtuous man in "this vile, degenerate age," in which a man "fix'd in the sphere of honour,/And precious to his sovereign," has his actions "nay, very soul," exposed to "common and base dissection." Allegre then proceeds to analyze his master's qualities, and a very interesting analysis it is. The Admiral, it appears, is "not flexible" in causes of justice; if an unjust suit comes before him "his blood boils over"; seen "by the right laid line/Of truth" he is wise, just and good, but "lateral and partial glances" as in "a picture wrought to optic reason" ("perspective" again) may show him weak or monstrous. Above all, he is sensitive:

> ... There's no needle
> In a sun-dial, plac'd upon his steel

In such a tender posture that doth tremble,
The timely dial being held amiss,
And will shake ever till you hold it right,
More tender than himself in anything
That he concludes in justice for the state:
For, as a fever held him, he will shake
When he is signing any things of weight,
Lest human frailty should misguide his justice.

(I, i, 48–57)

This significantly "tender"—hence proud—personage is then formally reconciled with Montmorency, who, in spite of the Chancellor's advice to pursue "fashionable and privileg'd policy," turns out to be sensitive too, complaining of the "misery/Of rising statesmen" and troubled in his conscience that he may be the instrument of a good man's ruin. As the observing Father later observes, "Good man he would be, would the bad not spoil him," and he is described by Allegre, in one of Chapman's most sensitively worked out similes, as one who will sometimes dare to

Take fire in such flame as his faction wishes;
But with wise fear contains himself, and so,
Like a green faggot in his kindling, smokes;

then the Chancellor finds him apt to burn again,

And then the faggot flames as never more
The bellows needed, till the too soft greenness
Of his state habit shows his sap still flows
Above the solid timber, with which, then,
His blaze shrinks head, he cools, and smokes again.

(II, ii, 17–26)

We are presented, then, with a situation of considerable psychological complexity, and by an outward concord which is demonstrably unstable. If this play were in the style of *Byron* we should expect further scenes of reflection or illustrative tableau, but here the action emerges at once from the situation, and the sun-dial's needle shakes. No sooner has Chabot rejected the warning of his father-in-law and asserted his freedom of justice within the limits of the King's grace than he is presented with an unjust suit of Montmorency and in a passion tears the bill, thus exposing himself to the machinations of the Queen and Chancellor, being armed only with his "innocence, which is a conquering justice." Confronting the King, he exasperates his master by his insistence on his inflexible justice, which *he* alone will judge (II, iii, 90–1). With what the King describes as "so fine a confidence" and passion, and presuming on his services, which, he says, balance the royal favours and dignities, he moves the King (very naturally, one might think) to reflect that no man can be so "truly circular" as to have no "swellings-out," crooks and crannies, and to a determination to "sift" him by the Chancellor's agency. Chabot's pride, his confidence—"The more you sift, the more you shall refine me"—makes him vulnerable, not to discovery of any "oversights" of "capital nature," but to the delusion that it must be impossible for him to be doubted by the King, since he sees himself as the keeper of the King's conscience. He does not realize that he has an "outward prop" too: he assumes that the King's love for his innocence must be as absolute as his own.[41]

There are two turning-points in this play. The first, the outward one, comes at once (III, i),[42] before Chabot's trial. Chabot's wife and her father plead his innocence before the Queen. Like Chabot, his wife assumes the "privilege royal" of the free soul to lecture the Queen in asserting absolute truth. The difference is that the Queen, supported by Montmorency, who has observed the scene and been converted from his faction, is prepared now to plead Chabot's case before the King. The trial, with oratorical flourishes by the Advocate, is a mockery of justice, since the verdict, against the evidence, is forced by the Chancellor, and the King resists the appeals of Chabot's supporters, joying that "this boldness is condemned,"

> ... that I may pardon,
> And therein get some ground in his opinion,
> By so much bounty as saves his life.
>
> (IV, i, 167–8)

The King is *envious*, it appears, of Chabot's confidence (as the Queen was of his wife's pride and "greatness"); "I long," he says, "to see this man of confidence again," and to Chabot:

> And now you feel how vain is too much faith
> And flattery of yourself, as if your breast
> Were proof gainst all invasion; 'tis so slight
> You see, it lets in death.
>
> (IV, i, 215–8)

Invoking his absolute power he pardons Chabot. Chabot replies: "You cannot pardon me, sir." This is the second turning-point, and

---

[41]On this point see Ribner, pp. 39–44. My reading of the play differs in some essential points from Ribner and Ure (*Jacobean Theatre*, pp. 243–4).

[42]Parrott attributes this scene to Shirley, *Tragedies*, p. 643.

the essential one,[43] for this is a "prodigy" (the King's word) which inverts all "the loyalties and true deserts" by which the King has till then believed he governed, and it shakes his "frame of reason" as he recognizes too late that this was "too wild a way" to assault the inwardly justified innocence of his servant. The King's turning upon his Chancellor seems then like the act, however just, of one who must punish *someone*, and exhibits with considerable psychological subtlety the dilemma of power, which can only act, not be. The King can learn his lesson, can deliver a fervent panegyric of "blessed justice" proved "in wonder of this man" (IV, i, 421 ff.), can feel very bad indeed and continue to make comforting and anxious noises, but that is all he can do—and be a king.

If Chapman (or Shirley; see below) had here exercised the sure decorum of *The Tragedy of Byron*, he would have excluded the King from the long agony of Chabot, who already feels ice at his heart from "some apprehension of the King's unkindness." "The greatest souls are thus oft wounded," remarks the father-in-law significantly:

> 'Tis dangerous to play too wild a descant
> On numerous virtue, though it becomes princes
> To assure their adventures made in everything:
> Goodness, confin'd within poor flesh and blood,
> Hath but a queasy and still sickly state;
> A musical hand should only play on her,
> Fluent as air, yet every touch command.
> (V, i, 92–8)

An appropriately Herculean note is sounded for this hero, who has made his choice of the hard way of virtue—

> No centaur's blood could rankle so,

as does this wound of love, and he shows spirit and fortitude in refusing his bed,

> wishing he might stand and look
> His destiny in the face at the last summons.

The Queen, wondering how he can "in this show spirit, and want force/To wrestle with a thought," is answered by the father-in-law:

> We may have proof against the sword and tyranny
> Of boisterous war that threatens us; but when
> Kings frown, a cannon mounted in each eye,
> Shoot death to apprehension ere their fire
> And force approach us.
> (V, i, 35–9)

---

[43]Ure, in *Jacobean Theatre*, p. 244.

Good official Jacobean doctrine, but Chapman has probed more deeply and perhaps obscurely into the tragic relations of outward power and inward worth than this timely sentiment can quite take care of. He seeks to isolate the hero in his last phase, chiefly by insisting on his *piety*, by showing him passionate like a saint over the sufferings of his tortured servant Allegre, by his religious definition of his own hurt, wounded "past all the remedy of art or time." Yet carrying the perfect man out of the world over the threshold of unmerited suffering, the poet strains our sympathies and leaves us with an impression sentimental rather than tragic. The King's appeal—"Give me thy heart . . ./And in my heart the world shall read thee living"—is met by "My heart despairs so rich a monument." Chabot would die with no other object before his eyes than the king, and he dies *kneeling* in thanks for the royal pardon of the Chancellor, followed by the king's epitaph:

> He has a victory in's death; this world
> Deserv'd him not. How soon he was translated
> To glorious eternity!

This unhappily anticipates a purple death-bed scene from some uplifting Victorian novel.

This final scene, Parrott thinks, is "heavily overlaid" with Shirley,[44] and one would like to take it so, for Chapman's sake. Yet if Shirley contributed the sentimentality, if he emphasized the emotional relationship between Chabot and the King, and chose to play upon the piety of the hero, he was only painting in more garish colours the "heightening" which was the older poet's sign of working. We remember Clermont's farewell to this world. Is this paradox of the innocent and noble person, the man prompted by inward decrees and yet so committed to the love of his patron, to him who "raised" him, that he cannot live without him, with all that connotes of spiritual pride, a profound criticism of greatness, or is it merely the accidental result of a failure to modulate the rhetoric of climactic speeches?

Of the tragedies there remains, if we except *Charlemagne*,[45] *The*

[44]*Tragedies*, p. 648.

[45]*Charlemagne or The Distracted Emperor* has been edited by F. L. Schoell (Princeton, 1920) and by W. W. Greg and J. H. Walter in the Malone Society Reprints (no. 75; 1938). Schoell thought that it might be the play entered S.R. as Chapman's in 1660 with the title *The Fatall Love: a French Tragedy*, and made out an elaborate case for Chapman's authorship from parallel passages and the recognition of characteristic themes and images. This evidence did not impress the Malone Society editors, who suggest that the play reads like the "work of an amateur" influenced perhaps

Tragedy of Caesar and Pompey, which, in spite of some most interesting features, remains, *pace* Schwartz,[46] a dull piece of work. The text is corrupt,[47] and the date of composition a problem. Chapman's dedicatory epistle to the Earl of Middlesex in Q1 (1631) states that it was written "long since," and Rees, taking into account the reference to Bellamont in *Northward Ho* having written a tragedy of Caesar and Pompey, dates it before 1605, possibly 1603.[48] Parrott and Ornstein are inclined to put it about 1612–13 (about the time of *The Revenge of Bussy*) on internal evidence; if we assume that the first version of *Chabot* might well have been written c. 1611–12, then we may agree with Ornstein that *Caesar and Pompey* "completes the pattern of [Chapman's] tragedies."[49] It is possible to go along with this without claiming too much for the play in itself.

In the preface Chapman refers to the play as a "martial history," and its outward action has this form. Everybody knew the story, from Plutarch and Lucan, but Chapman did not have Shakespeare's gift of telling a familiar Roman story so that it seems rich and strange, or Jonson's power to re-create the marmoreal elegance, richness of allusion, and *point* of his Roman sources. The opposition of Caesar and Pompey was a great and exemplary matter. (It still is, for we too live in an age of private armies, beleaguered legislatures, and impotent men of good will.) Hence the fanfare of Cato's prologue:

> Now will the two suns of our Roman heaven,
> Pompey and Caesar, in their tropic burning,

---

by Chapman. It is true that the description of Charlemagne with his dead empress (II, i, 230 ff.) reminds one of the obsession of St. Anne in *Monsieur D'Olive*; Didier, the broken creature of Ganelon, might serve as a preliminary sketch for La Fin in *Byron*; and there are familiar themes, such as a disordered court where "vice onlye thryves and merryt starves," and the conflict of virtue with policy or fortune. But these are commonplaces, and the case for Chapman's authorship remains unproved. The play, which has been edited from MS. Egerton 1994, probably dates from c. 1604.

[46] Elias Schwartz, "A Neglected Play by Chapman," *SP* LVIII (1961), 140–59: "*Caesar and Pompey* ought to stand . . . next to *Byron* among Chapman's tragedies." According to Ure, "Chapman's only Roman play is [unexpectedly, considering the influence on him of Plutarch and Epictetus] a branch that takes us away from the main body of his work" (in *Jacobean Theatre*, p. 243).

[47] *Tragedies*, pp. 677 ff.

[48] *Tragedies of George Chapman*, pp. 128–33. Schwartz, "The Dates and Order of Chapman's Tragedies" (*MP* LVII [1959–60], 80–2), pushing back the dates of all the tragedies, puts *Caesar and Pompey* in 1604–5. His conclusions have been seriously questioned by Ornstein (*MP* LIX [1962–63], 61–4), and I should like more documentary evidence before rejecting the traditional dating of the tragedies.

[49] *Moral Vision of Jacobean Tragedy*, p. 79.

> With their contention all the clouds assemble
> That threaten tempests to our peace and empire,
> Which we shall shortly see pour down in blood,
> Civil and natural wild and barbarous turning.

But we get no impression of an important and world-changing march of events, rather of noise and muddle. A stormy scene in the Senate (I, ii) over the "admission" of Pompey's army is prelude to the war, of which the first events are narrated by a Nuntius (II, ii), and the subsequent alternations of Caesar's and Pompey's fortunes are concealed by conversations of the leaders with minor figures, Vibius and Brutus (II, iii; II, iv), and with discussions of Caesar's offer of peace (III, i). The battle of Pharsalia is even more condensed and confused than such alarums and excursions usually are, preceded by lengthy passages of self-exculpation by Caesar and Pompey (III, ii; IV, i), and ending with Caesar's eulogy over the body of his lieutenant Crassinius (IV, ii). With a relief which the reader can readily sense, Chapman turns to Pompey in defeat (IV, iii), and to an exploration of the implications of these events in the "inward" lives of Pompey and Cato, whose suicide provides the epilogue.

The inward action is focussed upon Pompey, who is shown moving from Fortune to Virtue, from greatness to goodness, from the "tumour and bile of rotten observation" to "solid grace." Defeated by Caesar, he wins another kind of victory, because in losing an empire he can become purely a disciple of Cato, not only in justice but in righteousness. The essential contest, then, is between Caesar and Cato; in morality terms they are good and bad angels contending for the soul of Pompey. In fact *Caesar and Pompey* is essentially a morality, "out of whose events is evicted this Proposition, Only a just man is a free man," as the first title-page affirms, and the appearance of Vice and devil in one curious scene (II, i), to be discussed below, contributes to the atmosphere of the genre, as does the perfunctory treatment of the familiar outward action. (Such elements do not necessarily point to an early date for the text we have.)

Caesar, Cato affirms at the beginning, is followed by "a flock of puttocks" (the "Ruffians" who shout "War, war, O Caesar" at the end of the Senate debate), all the cankers of the realm—

> Imposters, flatterers, favourites, and bawds,
> Buffoons, intelligencers, select wits,
> Close murtherers, mountebanks, and decay'd thieves—

as his "black guard and red agents." Against this outward and tyrannous power Cato has "inward guard" supported by the "firmness of [the gods'] endless being," a stoical assurance which undergirds him in the Senate, where Caesar's politic moves, which he, like Byron, justifies by his services—

> I have passed them all
> That by their acts can boast themselves to be
> Their country's lovers—

conflict with Pompey's protestations that Fortune is Caesar's "page," not his (he renounces her), and that he is devoted to the public good, that all Caesar's golden speech is but to "gild/A copper soul in him," that Caesar has

> a spirit too great
> For all his body's passages to serve it,

full of "blood's rank fire" denoting "some rude vice" within him.

Chapman's Caesar owes much to Lucan's, here as in his lonely daring during the tempest by sea (II, v);[50] he is *spirited* and *fortunate*, and has a Satanic splendour—"I, that should not, bear all"—ready to set a crown on all his actions by a master-stroke, defying night and fear (II, v). And Pompey, who calls Cato "truest friend and worthy father" (II, iv, 71), is at first vowed to the same alliance of confidence in nature and fortune as is his enemy: he prays to Fortune (II, iv, 129–42), invokes "the spirit of all [his] fortunes" (III, i, 4), commits the engagement to that goddess (III, i, 72–6), and seems under pressure the servant of omens and opinion (IV, i). A shifting and ambiguous figure in the turmoil of the war, seeming to listen to both his mentors, enemy and friend, he professes that he would "rather wish to err with Cato/Than with the truth go of the world besides" (III, i, 116–7)— which is the wrong kind of commitment to Cato—but displays a Caesar-like recklessness in committing his destiny to the fortunes of battle.

In the first phase of the play, then, Pompey may be said to be Caesar's "disciple," and therefore his victim. From the moment of his defeat he passes into the context of Cato, from outward fortitude to inward calm:

> Thus have the gods their justice, men their wills,
> And I, by men's wills rul'd, myself renouncing,

---

[50]William Blissett, "Lucan's Caesar and the Elizabethan Villain," *SP* LIII (1956), 553–75; J. E. Ingledew, "Chapman's Use of Lucan in *Caesar and Pompey*," *RES*, n.s. XIII (1962), 283–8.

> Am by my Angel and the gods abhorred,
> Who drew me like a vapour up to heaven,
> To dash me like a tempest gainst the earth.
> O, the deserved terrors that attend
> On human confidence!
>
> (IV, iii, 1-7)

Moving from "ominous confidence" to the light of reason and piety (IV, iii, 21, 44), *converted* in other words, he proclaims he is still himself: his passions flamed, but now his soul is unmoved, and he is not a Pompey or a Caesar, "but a man." At Lesbos, revealed in his defeat and flight to his wife Cornelia, he engages with her in a duet of rapture in goodness:

> O, Pompey, Pompey, never 'Great' till now!
>
> O, my Cornelia, let us still be good,
> And we shall still be great. . . .
>
> I will stand no more
> On others' legs, nor build one joy without me.
> If ever I be worth a house again
> I'll build all inward . . .
> And only look at heaven.
>
> (V, i, 180ff.)

Yet, dying, murdered by Caesar's emissaries, he accuses the gods' justice (V, i, 257-63).

Caesar's peripeteia occurs at the end of the preceding scene, where he vows to "preserve with balms and spices" the corpse of the good soldier Crassinius. At the end of the play he is busy with plans for a monument to Cato. This is all the outward man can do for the inward one; that, and profess that he fought for his country, hoping, as Caesar does, that he can also capture the intellectuals.

So each sun of the Roman heaven pays Cato the tribute that is in his power. Caesar pays the outward one of honouring his bones, and perhaps an inward one too. His revulsion against Pompey's murderers sounds like Henry IV's repudiation of Exton, but it is hard to resist the rhetoric of his response to Cato's death:

> O Cato,
> All my late conquest, and my life's whole acts,
> Most crown'd, most beautified, are blasted all
> With thy grave life's expiring in their scorn.
>
> (V, ii, 179-82)

Pompey pays the inward one of learning the master's lesson to be "fix'd and quiet."

It is impossible not to think that Chapman was well aware that the suicide of Cato was a crux in humanist ethics and a recurring subject of debate.[51] Cato could be thought of as a Christian hero;[52] Montaigne admired him; but for Anthony Copley (whom Chapman no doubt regarded as an ignorant vulgar) he was "a spirit of Despair & self-wisdom."[53] Chapman had himself proposed the Christian answer to suicide in *The Gentleman Usher*, where Cynanche gives her husband Strozza "divine advice" against his suicidal despair in his pain, salving "with Christian patience pagan sin" (IV, i). But Strozza does not have Cato's excuse, that the just man is free to refuse to live under tyranny.

In this play Chapman provides two preludes to the suicide, one burlesque, one philosophical. The former (II, i)—if Chapman wrote it[54]—introduces Fronto (*frons* = impudence; hence "confident"), a Vice-like figure, "with a halter in his hand," who since his knavish courses have been cut off by "wars and presses" cries "Despair, come seize me!" and offers to hang himself—an obvious parody of the position which Cato will assume. To him there appears the dragon-devil Ophioneus, who announces that this is "the only time that ever was for a rascal to live in," since the world is "out of frame," religion divided. Man is for this "immortal devil" a contemptible confused creature, whose suicide is the act of a galley-slave, and he commands Fronto to "rise by fortune" and "care for nothing hereafter." So Fronto puts himself in the devil's hands, to get "rich office." Schwartz thinks that this is Caesar's world;[55] I would not go so far, but it is the opposite of Cato's.

The second prelude (IV, v) discloses Cato's son hiding his father's sword, and Cato arguing by "apparent reason" that just men "enlarge their lives" by death, not destroying the soul but in the resurrection of the body restoring its proper "form." The argument begins on the Stoic level and ends on the Christian, and it is wholly absurd, for the Christian view undermines the Stoic, and is at the same time used to justify what Christian morals forbid. Here, as in the final scene,

---

[51]See S. E. Sprott, *The English Debate on Suicide from Donne to Hume* (LaSalle, Ill., 1961).

[52]So Zwingli; see Seznec, *Survival of the Pagan Gods*, p. 23.

[53]*A Fig for Fortune* (1596).

[54]See *Tragedies*, p. 667.

[55]"A Neglected Play," 146.

Chapman really evades the problem, or, rather, passes it on to his readers. Does Chapman's personal conviction of Christian immortality intrude upon the consistency of Cato? Or, does he believe that he ennobles Cato by imputing to him these pious affirmations? Or, is he still darkly working in his favorite figure of paradox, which seems to colour the final speeches of both Pompey and Caesar? (It is perhaps to consider too curiously to consider so.) In any case, the last scene is a disaster—even Schwartz does not like the bit about Cato plucking out his entrails—though there is a muddle of fine sentiments.

Cato, shown as before with a book, repeats the familiar sentence that the law is "made for a sort of outlaws," not for his subjection; death is terrible only to slaves, and in death he will "conquer conquering Caesar." In one way of thinking, his suicide is an act of spite, yet its prospect is given dignity by the philosopher Athenodorus:

> ... for this giant world,
> Let's not contend with it, when heaven itself
> Fails to reform it: why should we affect
> The least hand over it in that ambition?
> A heap 'tis of digested villainy;
> Virtue in labour with eternal chaos
> Press'd to a living death, and rack'd beneath it,
> Her throes unpitied, every worthy man
> Limb by limb sawn out of her virgin womb,
> To live here piecemeal tortur'd; fly life then,
> Your life and death made precedents for men.
> (V, ii, 76-86)

But that dignity is lost in Cato's abandonment of this world for a better, in true evangelical accents ("Shall we gather at the river," &c.):

> For we shall know each other, and past death
> Retain those forms of knowledge learn'd in life,

to which his last gesture gives the lie—

> Just men are only free, the rest are slaves.

He who looks forward to a continuance of human society beyond death is not free, but bound by that hope.

The vocabulary of the tragedies is so narrow and repetitive, so specialized, that even though the key-words which "evict the propositions" have obvious public meanings, they tend to take on the qualities of a private language, formulaic and obtrusive. As the reader will have observed by this time, past the point of tedium no doubt, the verbal pattern is antithetical ("inward"/"outward," &c.), usually established at the beginning of a play, hence incapable of modulation and essentially static. Against such patterns work the inventive hyperbole of panegyric and invective, and the long reach of the frequent similes,[56] either carrying the mind beyond categories (the great ship) or centripetally accurate (the green faggot). Here, as elsewhere in Chapman, and especially in the *Homer*, pedantic insistence upon preconceived propositions is at war with an imagination which responds to all magnificence, and to the paradoxes of human power and knowledge.

But it is a response to these qualities themselves, and not to their manifestation in various characters created, as Shakespeare's are, so as to give the illusion that they have an existence beyond what they say. Chapman's persons have no silences; when they cease to speak they cease to exist. They have nor youth nor age (we are told that Bussy is young, but little is made of that); consequently we miss the impression that the tragic experience is rooted in the rhythms of nature. These tragedies are *artificial*, moving to the rhythms, sometimes in harmony, sometimes in discord, of dialectic and vision.

[56]On Chapman's similes generally, see Pagnini, pp. 246 ff.

N THE SPRING of 1820 Keats borrowed a copy of Chapman's translation of Homer from **B. R.** Haydon; it was the edition "with the head" (i.e. the *Whole Works* [1616?] with the superb engraved portrait of Chapman). Keats lost it, or it was stolen, and he had to buy another copy for Haydon.[1] The result of this reading we know; indeed it is almost all that many cultivated persons, including most graduate students in English Literature, do know about "Chapman's Homer." Those who have sampled it, or even studied it attentively, have been sharply divided in their opinions of its merit, and the way back to it is strewn with contending prejudices, some of which I have assembled here by way of preface.

Samuel Sheppard will serve to lead off the encomiasts, with his fervent tribute to "Mr. Chapmans Incomparable Translation of *Homers* Workes":

> What none before durst even venture on,
> Unto our wonder is by *Chapman* done,
> Who by his skill hath made great *Homers* Song
> To vaile its Bonnet in our *English* tongue,
> So that the Learned well may question it,
> Whether in *Greek*, or *English Homer* writ,
> O happy *Homer*, such an able pen
> To have for thy Translator, happier then
> **Ovid*, or †*Virgil*, who beyond their strength
> Are stretcht, each Sentence near a mile in length:

*By *Golding*.
†By *Phaer*.

[1] *The Letters of John Keats*, ed. H. E. Rollins (Cambridge, Mass., 1958), II, 308, 318, 326.

> But our renoun'd *Chapman* worthy praise,
> And meriting the never blasted Bayes,
> Had rendered *Homer* in a genuine sense,
> Yea, and hath added to his Eloquence.[2]

And John Phillips praises Chapman in similar terms:

> But as reverent *Chapman,* who hath brought to us
> *Musaeus, Homer,* and *Hesiodus,*
> Out of the Greek, and by his skill hath rear'd
> Them to that height, and to our tongue indear'd,
> That were those poets at this day alive,
> To see their Books, that with us thus survive,
> They would think, having neglected them so long
> They had been written in the *English tongue.*[3]

But the translation fell harshly upon some ears in a more "refined" age. Dryden marks the transition:

The Earl of Mulgrave and Mr. Waller, two of the best judges of our age, have assured me, that they could never read over the translation of Chapman without incredible pleasure and extreme transport. This admiration of theirs must needs proceed from the author himself; for the translator has thrown him down as low as harsh numbers, improper English, and a monstrous length of verse [the fourteeners of the *Iliads*] could carry him.[4]

So also Gerard Winstanley, writing (in 1687) of Chapman as

one in his time much praised for the fluency of his verse, gaining a great repute for his translation of Homer and Hesiod, which in those times passed as works beyond compare . . . though since the translation of Homer is very far outdone by Mr. Ogilby.[5]

---

[2]*Epigrams Six Bookes* (1651), p. 162.

[3]"A Censure of the Poets" [1656], in G. E. Bentley, *Shakespeare and Jonson: Their Reputations in the Seventeenth Century Compared* (Chicago, 1945), 2 pt., 281. Cf. Sir John Myres' approval of "the naturalized Homer of George Chapman" in *Homer and his Critics* (London, 1958), p. 41.

[4]Dedication of *Examen Poeticum* (1693), in *Essays,* ed. W. P. Ker (Oxford, 1900), II, 14. Thomas Warton also found the "awkward, unharmonious and unheroic measure, imposed by custom . . . disgustful to modern ears." But he added, Chapman is "not always without strength or spirit." *History of English Poetry,* ed. W. C. Hazlitt (London, 1871), IV, 317–18. Pope, condemning Dryden's translation of *Iliad* I and part of VI, noted that he had "too much regard to Chapman, copying him or following him even where he wanders from the original." See *The Iliad of Homer, Translated by Mr. Pope* (1715), I, sig. F2v.

[5]Quoted in G. G. Loane, "Chapman's Homer," *Cornhill Magazine* CLVI (1937), 644.

It seems incredible that Ogilby's monuments to the conspicuous consumption of culture (*Iliad* in 1660, *Odyssey* in 1665) should have been preferred to Chapman, but gulfs in taste are hard to bridge, and, besides, I suspect that few *read* Ogilby, they just looked at the books, which resemble Blenheim palace done up in binding.

Pope, who is very penetrating upon Chapman's methods of translation, as we shall see, concludes:

In a word, the Nature of the Man may account for his whole Performance; for he appears from his Preface and Remarks to have been of an arrogant Turn, and an Enthusiast in Poetry. . . . But that which is to be allowed him, and which very much contributed to cover his Defects, is a daring fiery Spirit that animates his Translation, which is something like what one might imagine *Homer* himself would have writ before he arriv'd to Years of Discretion.[6]

Leaving modern Homeric criticism aside, the absurdity of the last clause in this notable judgment colours the whole comment, but Pope makes an important point for the criticism of this Homer. Going further than Warton, who noted that Chapman had "by no means represented the dignity or the simplicity" of his original, he asserts that "there is scarce any Paraphrase more loose and rambling" than Chapman's, and in effect invites his readers to think of Chapman's translation as something in its own way admirable but certainly not Homer. This line was followed by Coleridge, with a difference:

It is as truly an original poem as the Faery Queene;—it will give you small idea of Homer, though a far truer one than Pope's epigrams, or Cowper's cumbersome most anti-Homeric Miltonish.

Chapman wrote, he adds, "as Homer might have written had he lived in England in the reign of Queen Elizabeth,"[7] a remark which characteristically transfers the question to a different context, raising the whole complicated question of what a translation can properly do. Lamb is, as one might expect, simpler: "His Homer is not so properly a translation as the stories of Achilles and Ulysses re-written."[8]

Critics since have not all been prepared to accept this easy way out. Arnold's strictures are well known: between Chapman and Homer, he thought, there was interposed the mist of fancifulness of the Elizabethan age, entirely alien to the plain directness of Homer's thought

---

[6]*Iliad* (1715), I, sig. F2.

[7]*Miscellaneous Criticism*, ed. T. M. Raysor (London, 1936), p. 231.

[8]*Works*, ed. T. Hutchinson (London, 1908), I, 69. One is reminded of Hugh Kenner's description of an Ezra Pound translation: "a poem of his own following the contours of the poem before him." *The Translations of Ezra Pound* (London, 1953), p. 11.

and feeling; Chapman is "fanciful ... steeped in humours and fantas-
ticality. . . . All the Middle Age, with its grotesqueness, its conceits,
its irrationality, is still in these opening pages." Chapman's "ballad-
manner" is "pitched sensibly lower than Homer's."[9] (How wrong he
was! If Chapman had had a "ballad-manner," he would have come
closer to Homer than he did.) While Saintsbury, in a moment of
characteristic enthusiasm, declared that Chapman is "far nearer
Homer than any modern translation in any modern language," and
W. H. D. Rouse praised the Homer as "alive, vigorous, pleasant to
read aloud, generally quick and idiomatic, and omit[ting] little of its
original,"[10] Dr. Tillyard observes, damning with faint praise, that "to
do [it] at all was prodigious," for Sir Stanley Leathers it is "for the
most part very commonplace doggerel," and F. Seymour Smith returns
us to the old dilemma with his statement that "considered strictly and
solely as a translation, it is probably almost the worst."[11]

The judicious, beginning with Ben Jonson, have not made the
mistake of separating Chapman from Homer, nor of exercising their
rhetoric in total praise or condemnation of what is, after all, a large
and inevitably unequal performance. Jonson, we recall, penned some
sharp annotations in his copy of the *Whole Works*,[12] but confessed to
Drummond, in a canary mood, that he had by heart "a piece of Chapmans translation of ye 13 of the Iliads, which he thinketh well done."
Frederic Harrison, perceptive in this as in other matters, noted that
the translation is "rather archaic for ordinary readers and too loose
for scholarly readers," and Ezra Pound observes:

Chapman remains the best English "Homer", marred though he may be by
excess of added argument, and rather more marred by parentheses and inversions,
to the point of being hard to read in many places. And if one turns to Chapman
for almost any favorite passage one is almost sure to be disappointed: on the
other hand I think no one will excel him in the plainer passages of narrative, as
of Priam's going to Achilles in the XXIVth Iliad. Yet he breaks down in Priam's
prayer at just the point where the language should be the simplest and austerest.[13]

[9]*Essays in Criticism* (Boston, 1865), pp. 292, 301–23.
[10]In his edition of Arnold's *On Translating Homer* (London, 1905), pp. 11–12.
Rouse thinks Chapman's version of the *Odyssey* is "generally simple." He cannot
have read it.
[11]E. M. W. Tillyard, *The English Epic and its Background* (London 1954), p. 348;
Leathers is quoted in Loane, "Chapman's Homer," 644; F. Seymour Smith, *The
Classics in Translation* (New York, 1930), p. 16.
[12]Now in the Fitzwilliam Museum, Cambridge. See Percy Simpson's transcription
in *TLS*, March 3, 1932, 155.
[13]*Literary Essays*, ed. T. S. Eliot (London, 1954), pp. 249–50.

The few modern scholars who have really examined the Homer would agree in general with this appraisal, except for the claim that Chapman's *remains* the best translation. (Nothing can approach Lattimore's *Iliad*, for our time.) G. G. Loane, for example, whose many learned notes on Chapman's text are invaluable to the student, decides that "few famous works of poetry are so unequal as this Homer,"[14] and H. C. Fay, who has worked over the *Iliads* very carefully, attributes this inequality to

the two contradictory personalities that Chapman comprised: the one human, sensuous, robust, the countryman, sportsman, soldier and playwright, the friend and admirer of explorers; the other a myopic doctrinaire bemused by the close print of ill-comprehended volumes, vain, quarrelsome and lonely.[15]

The schizophrenia was hardly so stark as that, but any long reading of the Homer, prepared for by meditation on the tragedies, certainly tempts one to such a hypothesis.

The best, then, that can be said for this Homer is that if it is a masterpiece it is a flawed and eccentric one, and if it is a failure it is at least a monumental failure. On one point all agree: Chapman *translated* Homer, turned him into something strange (if not rich). But these opinions are, after all, pretty superficial. We need to submerge in Chapman's element, to acquire the sense of his imagination working upon the words, to puzzle over the motives and meanings of his commentary—always involved, and swinging from rapture to indignation—and, above all, to get away from the idea of "Chapman's Homer," as if it were one thing, which it is not, for the *Iliads* and the *Odyssey* differ in much more than metre, and Chapman was "translated" too, by Homer, as he went on in his great labour.

One cannot imagine Chapman beginning any literary enterprise, even if his motive was "outward," as in the two trial flights (*Seaven Bookes* and *Achilles Shield* of 1598) dedicated to Essex, without some theoretical justification. He did not choose to translate the *Iliad* merely because there was "a job there that needed doing," as we academics put it, or even because, simply, it was *Homer*—although

[14]"Chapman's Homer," 638.

[15]"Poetry, Pendantry and Life in Chapman's *Iliads*," *RES*, n.s. IV (1953), 21–2. I have found indispensable Mr. Fay's "Chapman's *Iliads of Homer*: A Critical Introduction, with a Specimen Edition of Book XI," University of London Ph.D. thesis, 1954. Rudolf Sühnel, in his *Homer und die englische Humanität: Chapmans und Popes Übersetzungskunst im Rahmen der humanistischen Tradition* (Tübingen, 1958), cites Fay but does not employ him as he might have done. His portrait of Chapman's translation is given a special turn by his general thesis on the nature of humanism.

from the first he was conscious of aiming high, and as the enterprise came to dominate his life he felt himself irradiated by the "free light" of which only Homer is the source. He had a choice of interpretations of his author before him, in the tradition, and for the most part represented in the commentary of the texts he used. As Bacon caustically noted, the Stoics made of Homer "a kinde of Scripture"; they especially made of Odysseus an "ideal *homo viator*," and for them the *Odyssey* "became a kind of Stoic *Pilgrim's Progress*."[16] They saved Homer from impiety in his presentation of the Olympians by reading such passages allegorically. So Heraclides, and this view was adopted by Arthur Hall in the preface to his *Ten Bookes of Homers Iliades* (1581)—and, incidentally, by G. M. Hopkins.[17] But the result of the Stoic allegorizing was to make the poems guides to good conduct, and to see the heroes as *exemplary* of vices and virtues. Neoplatonic allegorists, for whom the universe was "a great myth endowed with spiritual meaning,"[18] tended to find in Homer the very secrets of nature covertly expressed by one who, blind, saw with the soul's eye the stuff of *magia naturalis*; this was Pico's view,[19] and it is a deeper reading of "Scripture," by allegories "farre strained" of which Ralegh, while not doubting that Homer "had read over all the books of Moses," disapproved.[20] From what we have learned of Chapman's early fascination with "philosophical conceits," we might expect him to adopt the neoplatonic exegesis of "sacred" Homer with some enthusiasm, but he does not do so.

It is true that he makes many claims for the "mysteries" in Homer, by way of advertisement: "Seas, earth and heaven, he did in verse comprise," he writes; ". . . he was onely soule;/Saw all things spher'd in Nature, without eyes"; in those "sacred pages," that "deepe Fount of life,"

> The Nerves of all things hid in Nature, lie
> Naked before him; all their Harmonie
> Tun'd to his Accents;

"(Blinde) He all things sawe."[21] And he planned a "Poem of the

[16]W. B. Stanford, *The Ulysses Theme* (Oxford, 1954), pp. 121–6.

[17]For Heraclides, see Seznec, p. 84n. Hall's effort is described below, Appendix C. See the *Correspondence of G. M. Hopkins and R. W. Dixon* (Oxford, 1935), pp. 146–7.

[18]Seznec, p. 85.

[19]Quoted in J. W. H. Atkins, *English Literary Criticism: The Renaissance* (London, 1955), p. 28.

[20]*History of the World* (1617), I, 79, 382.

[21]See the prefatory poems in *Poems*, pp. 386, 390, 406, 416. Cf. *Blind Beggar*, I, 222–3.

mysteries/Reveal'd in *Homer*," an unfulfilled project, as his friend the mystagogue Henry Reynolds complained.[22] But just what this poem was to accomplish is not clear; from what he says of it, it sounds like a justification of his own insight into Homer's truth: he will there clearly prove that only "Poesie can open Poesie," and in another place he seems to equate the "mysteries" with his own revelation of the meaning of Homer in his translation.[23] If the translation and commentary gave some solid evidence of an effort to unfold a multiple allegory or to create a symbolic system out of the Homeric poems, we should be able to give more credit to these rapturous announcements. But the evidence is not there. Even in the prefaces, the prevailing recommendations emphasize the *exemplary* moral and political instruction breathed through Homer by the divine Muse. It might be well to examine the prefatory pieces, in what we may suppose to have been the order of their composition, and so put together Chapman's "Essay on Homer," beginning with the dedication of the *Seaven Bookes* to Essex.

He begins with the image of the soul "buried" in the body, awaiting "illustration" by the power of poetic genius. This opening passage is worth quoting at length, as little known, as central to the understanding of Chapman's ideals, and as a piece of dense and powerful prose.

How irrational and brutish an impietie so ever it be, not only to increase the curse of humanity in making the scum of the body the Crown of the soule, but to murther and burie her in it, none needs to be benumd with admiration, since her intellectuall blood is shed with such auctoritie, preferment and profession—and to be a perfect villanizer of her faculties is to seate Custome and Imputation (like Justice and Wisdome) on both sides of his Chaire, crowning him with honor. And this even of a plaguy necessitie must come to passe, since all the meanes we have to make her excellencie knowne to us and to forge out of that holie knowledge darts to enamour us with her unpainted bewties are held, with too true experience of their effects, the only Parasites to entangle our estates in miseries and massacres. Her substance yet being too pure and illustrate to be discernd with ignorant and barbarous sence, and the matter whereon she works too passive and drossie to propagate her earthlie residence to eternitie, shee hath devisde (in despight of that worm-eaten Idoll) another fruitles, dead and despised receptacle to reserve her apparence with unspeakable profit, comfort and life to al posterities—and that is this poor scribling, this toy, this too living a preservative for the deathful toombes of nobility, being accounted in our most

---

[22]See *Poems*, p. 393, and Henry Reynolds, *Mythomystes*, in *Critical Essays of the Seventeenth Century*, ed. Spingarn. I. 165. Cf. Phyllis B. Bartlett, "The Heroes of Chapman's Homer," *RES* XVII (1941), 257.

[23]*Poems*, p. 404.

gentle and complementall use of it onlie the droppings of an idle humor, farre
unworthie the serious expence of an exact Gentleman's tyme. So is poore Learning the inseparable Genius of this Homericall writing I intend; wherein notwithstanding the soules of all the recorded worthies that ever liv'de become
eternally embodied even upon earth and, our understanding parts making
transition in that we understand, the lyves of worthilie-termed Poets are their
earthlie Elisummes; wherein we walke with survival of all the deceased worthies
we reade of, everie conceipt, sentence, figure and word being a most bewtiful
lyneament of their soules' infinite bodies, and, could a beautie be objected to
sence, composde of as many divine members, and that we had sences responsible
for their full apprehension, they should impresse no more pleasure to such a
bodie than is sweetly enjoyde in this true manner of communication and combination of soules.[24]

So much has not often been claimed for the eternizing power of poetry,
here described as a very "translation" with the poet as psychopomp.
But this overpowering exordium, directed after all to the "outward"
eye of a vain and tempestuous nobleman, leads to no more than the
assertion that Homer is the "President of all learning, vertue, valour,
honor and societie," "so firme an Eternizer," who by "sacred prophecie" prefigured the unmatched virtues of Essex in Achilles; that
the *Iliad* sets out "the true image of all vertues and humaine governe-
ment" and "contaynes the true portraite of ancient stratagems and
disciplines of war." Homer is exemplary, then, but he is not "perviall"
("the plaine way to barbarisme," as the preface to *OBS* tells us):
"Homericall writing" is "the native deduction, image and true heire
of true knowledge," and this knowledge ("Learning") is the "proportion" of the soul, and "the soule an intellectual beam of God." No
"meare reader," he adds in his preface "To the Reader," may approach
"this Emperor of all wisdome." The poet, with god-like "invention"
irresistibly displays the perfect proportions of the "inward" man; this
is a prophetic function, and as prophetic mysterious; the translator,
seeking the "true sence and height" of his invention, must participate
in this soul-infused power of creation, be himself inspired. How easy,
then, for the translator to find Homer's wisdom coincident with his
own "Learning"!

If readers can accept the fact that, from the beginning, Chapman
was determined to be (and in the end was) *possessed* by Homer, so
that "Chapman's Homer" equals Homer's Chapman—if Arnold, for
example, had not merely sampled the verses but puzzled a while over
the cloudy preliminary matter—they will find the expansion and

[24]*Homer*, I, 503–4.

alteration of the text, and the commentary, not wholly ancillary and ill-informed but inevitable, even when, as in the dedicatory epistle to *Achilles Shield*[25] and elsewhere, Chapman enters into a conventional controversy in his opposition to Scaliger. They may even enjoy his vehemence. From Spondanus, out of Eustathius, he derives the allegory of the shield: a figure of "the universall world." Noting that Vergil's imitation of Homer in this passage reaches "an exceeding height of wit," and that "since . . . publication of the other seven bookes comparison hath beene made between Virgill and Homer," he introduces the comparison under the usual topics ("Homer's Poems were writ from a free fire . . . Virgil's out of a courtly, laborious and altogether imitatorie spirit"; "the silken body of Virgil's muse curiously drest in guilt and embrodered silver, but Homer's in plaine, massie and unvalued gold"), affirms once more that from Homer are deduced "all learning, government and wisdom," that he "hath his chiefe holinesse of estimation for matter and instruction," and then launches upon a fierce condemnation of "soule-blind Scalliger" for his "impalsied diminution of Homer."[26] Warming to this theme in the Commentarius to the Third Booke of the *Iliads*, he holds up to ridicule Scaliger's "French wit":

Putidus, ineptus, frigidus, puerilis (bieng terms fitter for a scold or a bawd then a man softened by learning) he belcheth against him whom all the world hath reverenced and admired as the fountaine of all wit, wisdome and learning. What touch is it to me, then, to beare spots of depravations, when my great maister is thus muddily dawb'd with it? But who ever saw true learning, wisdome or wit vouchsafe mansion in any proud, vaineglorious and braggartly spirit?[27]

The identification with his poet is, we observe, complete; he and Homer are of the soul's party; the fact that he understands the convention of Homer's formulaic epithets as little as Scaliger—who was objecting to the repetition of ποδάρκης 'Αχιλλεύς—is obscured.

In the epistle "To the Understander" prefixed to *Achilles Shield* he treats temperately of the didactic value of the Homeric poems, "so full of government and direction to all estates," for soldiers, counsellors, fathers, "husbands, wives, lovers, friends and allies having in him mirrors for all their duties." In the preface "To the Reader" before

---

[25]*Homer*, I, 543–7.

[26]The relevant passages from Scaliger's *Poetics* may be found conveniently in *Select Translations from Scaliger's Poetics*, ed. and trans. F. M. Padelford (New York, 1905), pp. 37, 73, 79. Cf. Samuel Sheppard, *Epigrams* (1651), pp. 176–99: "The Socratick Session, or The Arraignment and Conviction of Julius Scaliger."

[27]*Homer*, I, 88.

the *Iliads*,[28] having in the meantime experienced the "joy of soule" commemorated in *The Tears of Peace*, and Homer being then to him "Angell ... Starre, and Fate," "a Beame of *Homers* fre'er soule" shining within him, he returns to the elevated and prophetic strain. The chief end of man, he affirms, is to glorify God, and no art performs this "with so much excitation and expression as Poesie," which is not "of the world indeed, but (like Truth) hides it selfe from it," having "a perpetual commerce with the divine Majesty," like a sunflower turning to the source of all wisdom. In the Commentarius to *Iliad* I he further affirms that "the inward sense or soule of the sacred Muse is onely within eye-shot of a Poeticall spirit's inspection," fire finding out fire, and confesses that only when he had "driven through" the second half of the *Iliad* did he plumb "the main depth and [see] the round coming of the silver bow of our Phoebus, the clear scope and contexture of his work, the full and most beautiful figures of his persons," hitherto obscured by "Grammaticall Criticks."

But what did his "inspection" reveal? The inimitable truth of nature in the characters of the poem, the fashioning of "absolute" moral archetypes—not "farr fetcht Allegories."[29] When Chapman quarrels with other translators and commentators his purpose is almost always, as we shall see, to unfold the (until then) hidden truth of Homer's fiction, the *inspired reasonableness* of his images of the human situation. Considering Chapman's affirmation of the divinity of the human soul, this is not inconsistent with his conviction that Homer is a second scripture, expressed elegantly in the epilogue to the *Iliads*, where he prays to the divine mercy that "(ever most incomparably preferring the great light of his truth in his direct and infallible Scriptures) [he] may ever be enabled, by resting wondring in his right comfortable shadowes in these [i.e. the Homeric poems] to magnifie the clearenesse of his almighty apparence in the other."[30]

The ideal of Christian humanism has, I suppose, received no clearer expression than this, which Erasmus would have applauded, however much he might smile wryly at the polemical disturbance which surrounds its devotional calm.

The consequences of this idea of "shadowes" for the interpretation

[28]*Homer*, I, 14 ff.

[29]*Ibid.*, I, 43. Cf. Sheppard, *Epigrams*, p. 162; and Sühnel (pp. 52-3): "Das Ethische wird von Chapman weniger rational als mystisch gefasst: ethisches Handeln ist Ausfluss eines überindischen Impulses. Das Sittliche ist das spirituelle Ordnungsprinzip der Welt."

[30]*Ibid.*, I, 498.

of Homer are to be found in the most important and indeed final of
Chapman's theoretical statements: the prose passage of the dedicatory
epistle to Somerset prefixed to the *Odysses*.[31] Here he distinguishes (as
I have noted above) between *insania* and *divinus furor*, of which
"Homer hath ever bene both first and last Instance," creating an
"all-comprising Poesie," not "meere fictive,"

but the most *materiall and doctrinall* illations of Truth, both for all manly information of Manners in the yong, all prescription of Justice, and *even Christian
pietie*, in the most grave and high governed. [My italics]

The fiction, he continues, is the body, "the letter of historie," which
may seem "beyond Possibilitie to bring into Act," and the "Allegorie"
is the soul, intending "a more eminent expressure of Vertue, for her
lovelinesse, and of Vice, for her uglinesse, in their severall effects, going
beyond the life than any Art within life can possibly delineate." This
is very close to Sidney, and makes clear that what "mysteries" Chapman came to find in Homer were moral truths, the "soule" to be
revealed by the divine power exercised also in the translator of this
scripture, which has, moreover, its own old and new testaments,
making up between them the whole range of rational human possibility
(excluding the "great light" of God's truth in the Christian revelation).
Hence the following well-known exposition, which echoes and enlarges
Thomas Wilson:

And that your Lordship may in his Face take view of his Mind, the first word
of his *Iliads* is μῆνιν, *wrath*; the first word of his *Odysses*, ἄνδρα, *Man*—con-
tracting in either word his each worke's Proposition. In one, Predominant
Perturbation; in the other, over-ruling Wisedome; in one, the Bodie's fervour
and fashion of outward Fortitude to all possible height of Heroicall Action; in
the other, the Mind's inward, constant and unconquered Empire, unbroken,
unaltered with any most insolent and tyrannous infliction.[32]

(The resemblance to a preacher's "opening" of a sacred text is striking,
and not accidental.) The Odyssean testament is "preferred to his
Iliads," for it contains "the information and fashion of an absolute
man, and necessarie (or fatal) passage through many afflictions (accord-

---

[31]*Homer*, II, 4–6.
[32]Cf. Wilson's *Arte of Rhetorique* (1553), fol. 104: "For what other is the painfull
travaile of Ulisses, described so largely by *Homer*, but a lively picture of Mans
miseries in this life. And as *Plutarch* saieth: and likewise Basilius Magnus: in the
Iliades are described strength and valiantnesses of the bodie: In Odissea is set forth
a lively patterne of the minde."

ing with the most sacred letter) to his naturall haven and country."

Chapman's final vision of Homer presents us with a paradox by now familiar: the theory is utterly unoriginal, but he expresses it as a personal experience. He has built the epics into the ethical architecture of the late Renaissance, into that paradigm of complements—youth and age, passion and reason, storm and calm, outward and inward, body and soul—and rested, ultimately, in the figure nearest his heart, the much-suffering Ulysses, emerging from "the intangling of the wisest in his affections" to a peaceful wisdom and holy hope, guided and guarded the while by a "heavenly familiar," Athena who is wisdom, *Learning*. To the last he is surrounded by the monsters of the outward world, "supercilious wizards," drones, the "immane and mad Impietie" of men.

For the modern critic, Chapman "ascribed to Homer the background, both material and mental, of his own age."[33] For Chapman, this would be putting it the wrong way round: the sacred letter of Homer being eternal, first and last, no anachronism is possible, and it is Homer that "informs" the translation, makes it a revelation in English of the Greek. Certainly he could have little historical sense of the poems, of the characteristic culture of the heroic age as revealed in Homer, or the marks of oral composition, though he knows about rhapsodic recitation, and the stitching together of diverse elements within the *Iliad*.[34] But his Homer is *whole*, hence consistently exalted in the high manner of the maker, and to be translated so.

The letter is sacred, but that divinity will make no epiphany in a literal translation. In the controversy over methods of translation, very active in the Renaissance, that era of the great amateur translators, Chapman hurled himself with characteristic energy against the "grammarians." The traditional academic translation, word for word and phrase for phrase, the utilitarian crib, had earlier been challenged by liberal humanists with a strong sense of the dignity and eloquence of their own tongues, for example by Edmond Becke, in his preface to *Two dyalogs* of Erasmus (1549):

[What is most necessary is] to render the sence & the very meanyng of the author, not so relygyouslie addicte to translate worde for worde, for so the sence of the author is often times corrupted and depraved, and neyther the grace of the one tonge nor yet of the other is truly observed or aptlie expressed.

---

[33]Fay, "Chapman's *Iliads of Homer*," p. 51.
[34]Preface "To the Reader" in *Seaven Bookes, Homer*, I, 507.

The same view may be found in Etienne Dolet, in Thomas Wilson's preface to his *Three Orations of Demosthenes* [1570], and others.[35] The constant dilemma of translators, noted by Dryden and Pope,[36] between "rash paraphrase" and a "literal and close rendering," can be solved, if at all, only by a fine sense of the genius of each language; for the Elizabethan translator, trained at school in the "invention" and "flourishing" of themes by *copia*, the temptation to colour the construe and elaborate the rhetorical patterns was very strong. Chapman prefaces his task (as most translators do) with a statement of the ideal:

The worth of a skilful and worthy translator is to observe the sentences, figures and formes of speech proposed in his author, his true sence and height ["height = decorum], and to adorne them with figures and formes of oration fitted to the originall in the same tongue to which they are translated.[37]

This is all very fine, and one only wishes it were possible; besides, the word "adorne" is ominous, especially when we find him (in a preface to *Achilles Shield*) defending what others have called his "beyond-sea manner of writing," in other words his "inriching" of the English vocabulary by "good neighbourly borrowing" and "naturall Prosopopoeia."

He returns to the question in the rhyming preface "To the Reader" before the *Iliads*.[38] To render authors word for word is an error, for languages have "their sense and elegancie" bounded "in their distinguisht natures," and the literal translators lose "the free grace of their naturall Dialect/And shame their authors with a forced Glose." On this ground he defends his "needfull Periphrases" from the accusation of license. Poesy must be "opened" by poesy, but the "fit key of Nature" rather than the "down-right strength of Art" practised by other, grovelling translators, and English is "naturally" the tongue for the Muse's utterance. As for the needful periphrases, he hotly rejects the rumour of some "stupide ignorants" who affirm that his translation derives from the French, insists that he is "warranted" by the Greek, and invites his readers to compare the fullness and *expression* of his rendering with the "shortness" or "paraphrastical" license of the Latin versions of Valla and Eobanus Hessus. Then, citing Horace as authority, he repeats the definition of an ideal translation quoted

[35]See C. H. Conley, *The First English Translators of the Classics* (New Haven, 1927); Elizabeth J. Sweeting, *Early Tudor Criticism* (Oxford, 1940); F. A. Yates, *John Florio* (London, 1934), p. 223.
[36]Dryden, *Examen Poeticum*, in *Essays*, ed. Ker, II, 9; Pope, *Iliad* (1715), sig. E2v.
[37]*Homer*, I, 507. See Peter Green, *Essays in Antiquity* (London, 1960), p. 188.
[38]*Ibid.*, I, 9 ff.

above, confesses that his earliest attempts were "something paraphrastical and faulty," and turns his wrath upon "a certaine envious
Windsucker" who has spread the calumny that he translates from the
Latin only. (I cannot identify this "Castril," ambitious and with a
following of "associates"; I do not think it was Jonson.)

What all this comes to is that Chapman claims the freedom of the
poet to adorn his author with "elegancies," while insisting that he
conveys the sense and "height" of the original. As for the claim of
Nature above Art, in practice this means *interpreting* Homer in terms
congenial to the translator's spirit and convictions. The theory of
liberty in translation is, then, an asseveration in working terms of the
religious attitude to Homer with which Chapman began and in which
he continued to the end. The periphrases are more numerous, lengthy
and obtrusive in the *Odysses* than in the *Iliads* because there he found
more congenial scripture.

Thus much—and it is a great deal—prefaced by way of seeing
Homer through Chapman's eyes, we may turn to him at work upon
the task he was "born to doe."

The first question of course is, how good was his Greek? Some kind
of answer will emerge in the course of the general survey of the translation which follows; at this point it is sufficient to say that the three
scholars who have examined the *Homer* most carefully are agreed that
his Greek was rudimentary.[39] We can reconstruct from his commentary
the array of books on his table. He translated the *Iliad* and *Odyssey*,
Batrachomyomachia and *Hymns* from the text of Jean de Sponde
(Spondanus) with the parallel-column Latin version of Andreas Divus
(which Chapman took as Spondanus'); his dictionary was Scapula's
Lexicon Graeco-Latinum. In addition he consulted unsystematically
and sporadically the Latin versions of Valla and Eobanus Hessus, and
H. C. Fay has noted that he sometimes corrected the text of the *Iliad*
by reference to Henri Estienne's (Stephanus') edition.[40] As will appear,
he blocked out his translation from the Latin crib, keeping one eye

---

[39]See H. C. Fay's thesis, cited above; G. G. Loane, "Chapman and Scapula,"
N&Q, June 10, 1939, "Chapman's Homer," 637; Phyllis B. Bartlett, "Chapman's
Revisions in his *Iliads*," *ELH* II (1935), 106.

[40]I have used the following texts: (1) *Homeri quae exstant omnia Ilias, Odyssea,
Batrachomyomachia, Hymni, Poematia aliquot cum Latina versione . . . Io. Spondani
Maulionensis Commentariis . . . Basileae* [1583]; (2) J. Scapula, *Lexicon Graeco-
Latinum . . . Editio ultima* (1605); (3) *Homeri poetarum omnium principis. Ilias, per
Laurentium Vallam Latio Donato . . . Lugdini . . . 1541*; (4) *Homeri Iliados, de rebus
ad Troiam gestis, Libri xxiiii, impar Latino carmine elegantiis, redditi, Helio Eobano
Hesso Interprete . . . Basileae . . . 1549.*

uneasily on the Greek, and, enlightened by Scapula or by his own poetic intuition, worked out his own rendering, often marking the departure from the Latin by a defiant note in the margin or commentary. He seems to have had little knowledge of the accidence or syntax of Homeric Greek. I have not attempted to discover, by comparing his translation of Musaeus with the *Homer*, whether he was conscious of the peculiarities of the Homeric dialect, and I am not sure that this can be done. One suspects that he taught himself such Greek as he had: the Greek of the dictionary and of passionate inquiry, not of school exercises. Significantly, when at the very end of his labours, in the epilogue to the *Crowne of all Homers Workes*, he professes his capacity, he speaks slightingly of the learned who are angry that "one not taught like them should learne to know/Their Greeke rootes," and adds:

> Though he's best Scholler that, through paines and vows
> Made his owne Master onely, all things knows.

The reader will, I hope, hardly expect a detailed appreciation of the idiosyncracies, a census of the errors, a chrestomathy of the triumphs and failures, and a glossary of the "beyond-sea" epithets in the forty-eight books of Chapman's *Iliads* and *Odysses*, to say nothing of a continued test of his scholarship in the margins and commentaries. In my opinion, the *Iliads* is more interesting in its parts; the *Odysses*, far less faithful to its original, cabined and confined in heroic couplets where the *Iliads* moves loose and free in fourteeners, asks for more consideration as a whole poem. The periodicity of Chapman's syntax, characteristically involved and nourished besides by translation from the Latin versions, is more apparent in the *Odysses* because he was thinking the thing through as a moral poem "evicting" a proposition. The effect of this on the poem which above all others demands an easy, colourful and paratactic rendering is indeed unfortunate. Furthermore, having translated the 15,703 lines of the *Iliad* in 14,416 lines, he expands the 12,150 lines of the *Odyssey* to 16,663. The reduction in the first poem is only partly owing to the length of his line, and he makes numerous additions. He contracts the original sometimes by omitting or glancing at similes, and (frequently) by compressing speeches in indirect discourse. The expansion in the *Odysses* is owing chiefly to laborious workings-out of the implications of episodes or epithets. Here as elsewhere in this book I am resolved to engage Chapman on his terms, and accordingly I shall attempt to convey something of the quality of his *Iliads* through the accumulation of varied detail, and, while giving some attention to the translator's excellences and infidelities, focus in the *Odysses* upon his attempt to "expresse and approve the Allegorie driven through" the whole poem.

This is how Chapman begins:

> Achilles' banefull wrath resound, O Goddesse, that imposd
> Infinite sorrows on the Greekes, and many brave soules losd
> From breasts Heroique—sent them farre, to that invisible cave
> That no light comforts; and their lims to dogs and vultures gave.
>
> (*H*, I, 23)[41]

"To that invisible cave/That no light comforts" for Ἄϊδι (derived from Scapula on Ἀίδης) is a magnificent periphrasis, but also a warning of other elegancies, less apt, to follow, in which Chapman breaks up Homer's white light into his own varied spectrum. In fact he immediately produces a figure which diffuses the direct power of his original. The narrative begins (I, 8): "What god set these two to contend together?" Chapman has: "What God gave Eris their command, and op't that fighting veine?" (Margin: "Eris the Goddess of contention.") Nor is it long before we find the first impropriety, minor but ominous. Agamemnon warns Chryses (I, 26): "Let me not find you again, old man, by the hollow ships," for which Chapman, with a ring of the Rose theatre, "Doterd, avoid our fleet"—though this is a great improvement upon the *Seaven Bookes* version: "Hence doating Priest, nor let me find thy stay protracted now/In circuite of our hollow Fleete." But he manages the prelude well enough, and the reader begins to feel the great wave of Homer taking him, until, only 65 lines from the beginning, he collapses miserably in Calchas' (Chryses') speech to Achilles before the council (I, 74 ff.), apparently because the Latin is too literal and did not help him with the Greek syntax:

> Jove's beloved, would thy charge see disclosd
> The secret of Apollo's wrath? Then covenant, and take oth
> To my discoverie, that with words and powrefull actions
>   both
> Thy strength will guard the truth in me, because I well
>   conceive
> That he whose Empire governs all, whom all the Grecians
>   give

---

[41]References to Chapman's translation are to volume and page of Nicoll's edition, cited for brevity as *H*; references to the text of Homer are to book and line numbers, using capital roman for the books of the *Iliad*, lower-case roman for the *Odyssey*. Chapman's additions to his original are indicated by square brackets.

Confirm'd obedience, will be mov'd—and then you know
    the state
Of him that moves him. When a king hath once markt for
    his hate
A man inferior, though that day his wrath seems to digest
Th'offence he takes, yet ever more he rakes up in his breast
Brandes of quick anger till revenge hath quencht to his
    desire
The fire renewed. Tell me then, if, whatsoever ire
Suggests in hurt of me to him, thy valour will prevent?
                                        (*H*, I, 25)

This is certainly not poesy being opened by poesy but a painfully
construed crib, with the sense not missed but fogged by forcing. I
remember—and many readers will remember too—producing this sort
of thing out of Vergil, in my tender years, and wondering if it was
right; it seemed right, I had looked up all the words. Chapman has
more control than a schoolboy, but only just; later we shall find him
irrecoverably lost. When he has greater confidence—or temerity—he
begins to extrapolate, to impose a familiar psychology upon the sacred
text. Athene catches Achilles by the hair, and he cries, "Why are you
come again, daughter of Zeus ...?" and the goddess replies (I, 207–8),
"To stay your anger, if you will hear me, have I come from heaven."
So Chapman:

                    I come from heaven to see
Thy anger settled, [if thy soule will use her soveraigntie
In fit reflection.]
                                        (*H*, I, 29)

(The interpolated clause is not in the *Seaven Bookes* version.) And
Achilles responds:

                            Though my heart
Burne in [just] anger, [yet my soule must conquer th'angrie part
And yeeld you conquest,]

not in Homer's words (I, 216–8) but in an exemplary extension suggested by Spondanus' commentary, which runs *certamen istud in
Achille fuit Rationis & partis irascibilis*. Without warrant from Spondanus, and apparently without realizing how his sententious elaborations dilute the drama of the moment, he adds to Achilles' speech to
the heralds sent to bring Briseis to Agamemnon (I, 333–44) a moraliz-

ing passage (not in *Seaven Bookes*) which demonstrates also that he
did not need the Latin to complicate his sentences:

> But your king, in tempting mischiefe, raves,
> Nor sees at once by present things the future—[how like waves
> Ils follow ils, injustices, being never so secure
> In present times, but after-plagues, even then, are seene
>   as sure,
> When yet he sees not and so sooths his present lust—
>   which, checkt,
> Would checke plagues future, and he might, in succouring
>   right,] protect
> Such as fight for his right at fleete. [They still in safetie fight
> That fight still justly.]

(H, I, 33)

This "interpretation" of Achilles will concern us later; for the moment,
we may observe that although it is easy to show the first book in a
very discouraging light, there are flashes of mastery, promising better
things to come. Thus for βαρὺ στενάχων (I, 364), he has "sighing like
a storm"; for I, 481 ("And the wind blew into the middle of the sail"),
"The misens strooted with the gale," which has a fine blithe force to it.

As one begins, then, one gets the impression of a kind of heavy-footed
(figuratively and metrically) rendering, in which intuitions of the
speed, grace and mobility of the original are smothered by pompous
indirection; like the Queen in *Hamlet*, the reader calls for more matter
and less art, and this from a translator who in the Commentarius to
this first book swears (at length) that unlike the "Grammarians" he
uses no art at all, but gets at "the inward sense or soule of the sacred
Muse." If all others have "slept and bene dead to [Homer's] true
understanding," the least we can expect from Chapman is a fair degree
of fidelity in the translation of what the Greek—or even usually the
Latin—says.

It may be said in general that the reader is usually able to perceive
what is going on or what is being said in the poem, though sometimes
not without pain; but there are serious errors too, apart from incidental
infelicities of diction and syntax. One type is exemplified at V, 410ff.,
where Dione comforts Aphrodite wounded by Diomedes, and concludes (in Richard Lattimore's translation[42]):

> Then, though he be very strong indeed, let the son of Tydeus
>   take care lest someone even better than he fight with him,

---

[42]The University of Chicago Press, copyright 1951.

> lest for a long time Aigialeia, wise child of Adrastos,
> mourning wake out of sleep her household's beloved companions,
> longing for the best of the Achaians, her lord by marriage,
> she, the strong wife of Diomedes, breaker of horses.

It is a straightforward passage and the sense is in the Latin of Spondanus, but Chapman, changing the form to apostrophe as a preliminary work of supererogation, produces:

> Besides, hear this from me,
> Strength-trusting man: though thou be strong [and art in
> strength a toure.]
> Take heed a stronger meet thee not, [and that a woman's powre
> Containes not that superior strength,] and lest that woman be
> Adrastus' daughter, and thy wife, the wise Aegiale,
> When (from this houre not farre) she wakes, even sighing
> with desire
> [To kindle our revenge on thee] with her enamouring fire,
> [In choosing her some fresh young friend and so drowne all
> thy fame
> Wonne here in warre in her Court-peace and in an opener
> shame.]
>
> (H, I, 120)

Here he simply ignores the last four lines of the speech, and inserts, without comment, the account from the "Returns" of Aigialeia's infidelity, which he found in Valla's notes (cf. Valla: *non ita multo post in tenebris a somno excitata*, etc.). This differs in kind from most of his additions, which are designed to clarify (he thinks) or comment. In other places he is simply vague and confused; for example, in Agamemnon's speech to the council called by Achilles (XIX, 78ff.). The passage is not easy: Agamemnon has come late and reluctantly, speaks from his seat with some nervous embarrassment through the applause granted Achilles, and begins by saying that it is unseemly to break in on a speaker, even for a skilled orator; a man can neither hear nor speak effectively in an uproar, but he will speak to Achilles and let the others give heed. Chapman's version falters thus:

> Princes of Greece, your states shall suffer no indignitie,
> If (being farre off) ye stand and heare, nor fits it such
> as stand
> At greater distance to disturb the counsell now in hand
> By uprore, in their too much care of hearing. Some, of force,
> Must lose some words: for hard it is, in such a great
> concourse,

(Though hearers' eares be nere so sharpe) to touch at all
   things spoke.
And, in assemblies of such thrust, how can a man provoke
Fit powre to heare, or leave to speake? Best auditors
   may there
Lose fittest words, and the most vocall Orator fit eare.
My maine end, then, to satisfie Pelides with replie,
My words shall prosecute.

(H, I, 393)

Very bad, but it is not a flat misconception of the original, like the
most conspicuous mistranslation in the *Iliads*, at XXIV, 649–55,
where he seems to have been misled by Valla. Achilles speaks bitterly
(ἐπικερτομέων = jeering, sarcastic) to Priam: "Lie down outside, dear
old sir, for fear some of the Achaians may come here, as they keep
doing, to take counsel; if one of them were to see you and tell Agamemnon, there would be delay in ransoming the body" [of Hector]. For the
last clause Spondanus has *et dilatio redemptionis cadaveris fieret*, but
Chapman translates:

Good father, you must sleep without, lest any Counsellor
Make his accesse in depth of night—as oft their industrie
Brings them t'impart our warre-affaires—of whom should
   any eye
Discerne your presence, his next steps to Agamemnon flie,
And then shall I lose all these gifts.

(H, I, 493)

What persuaded Chapman to look over to Valla and find there *ut haec
munera restituam*? As he gives it, the speech hardly accords with his
conception of Achilles.

But there are moments when the divine rage triumphs over incom-
petence, pedantry and weariness. Such is Hector's defiance of the
augury (XII, 237ff.):

                ... yet light-wing'd birds must be
(By thy advice) our Oracles, whose feathers little stay
My serious actions. What care I if this or th'other way
Their wild wings sway them—if the right, on which the
   Sunne doth rise
Or to the left hand, where he sets? Tis Jove's high
   counsell flies
With those wings that shall beare up us—Jove's, that
   both earth and heaven,

> Both men and Gods, sustaines and rules. One augurie is given
> To order all men best of all—fight for thy country's right.
>
> (*H*, I, 245)

Or Sarpedon to Glaucus, a speech, says Chapman in the margin, "never equalled (in this kind) of all that have written" (XII, 322ff.):

> O friend, if keeping backe
> Would keepe backe age from us, and death, and that we might
>   not wracke
> In this life's humane sea at all, but that deferring now
> We shunned death ever—nor would I halfe this vaine valour
>   show,
> Nor glorifie a folly so, to wish thee to advance.
>
> (*H*, I, 248)

Here, as in the former purple passage, the heroic side of Chapman was moved, and not even the Latin "deferring" nor the monitory "vaine" and "folly" spoil the effect. He can manage, too, a phrase of extraordinary power in translating Zeus's contemplation of Hector's war-fury, as he dons Achilles' armour. The god says: "For the present I will give you great strength, to make up for it that you will not come back from the battle, and Andromache receive from your hands the glorious armour of Achilles" (XVII, 206–8). Thus Chapman:

> Yet since the justice is so strickt that not Andromache
> (In thy denied return from fight) must ever take of thee
> Those armes in glory of thy acts, [thou shalt have that
>   fraile blaze
> Of excellence that neighbours death]—a strength even to
>   amaze.
>
> (*H*, I, 353)

The periodic inversion of the sentence, the impropriety, strictly speaking, of the addition, are forgotten in the splendour of the words. Nor should we pass over Achilles' reply to Lycaon's plea for pity (XXI, 106–7):

> Die, die, my friend. What teares are these? What sad
>   lookes spoile thy face?
> Patroclus died, that farre past thee.
>
> (*H*, I, 424)

Yet take a touchstone passage, such as Hector with his son (VI, 466–73), and Chapman's latinisms and echoing ornaments, typical as they are of Elizabethan metaphrase and characteristic of his own style, try our patience:

> This said, he reacht to take his sonne, who (of his armes
>   afraid,
> And then the horse-haire plume, with which he was so
>   overlaid,
> Nodded so horribly) he clingd backe to his nurse and cride.
> Laughter affected his great Sire, who doft and laid aside
> His fearful Helme, that on the earth cast about it light.
> Then tooke and kist his loving sonne and (ballancing his
>   weight
> In dancing him) these loving vowes to living Jove he usde.
>
> (H, I, 150)

A short view of the eddies and runs of Chapman's great river does not, however, tell us much of its ordinary course. For the sound of that, we must examine some of his characteristic working devices in more detail, his treatment of the Homeric formulas, for example. He consistently varies the conventional repetitions "without which Homer would not be Homer" (Lattimore), and so of course makes Homer something else—though, we must add, any translation does that. Sometimes these variations are legitimate, as in his various translations of δαιμόνιος (cf. *H*, I, 40, 92, 152, 173); mostly they are not. He will not think of reproducing such a repeat as that in II, 13–15, 30–32; but translates the first as

> ... the heaven-housed Gods are now indifferent growne;
> Juno's request hath wonne them; Troy, now under imminent ils,
> At all parts labours,

and the second,

> No more the Gods dissentiously imploy
> Their high-housd powers; Juno's suite hath wonne them all
>   to her,
> And ill fates over-hang these towres, addrest by Jupiter.

And he extends himself absurdly in the epithets: thus for Ἀτρέος υἱὲ ἱπποδάμοιο we find "Atreus' tame-horse sonne"; Diomedes is "the skilfull horseman"; for the terrible ἀράβησε δὲ τεύχε' ἐπ'αὐτῷ "with much sound of his mightie armes", "his arms did eccho the resound," "his armes with him resounded, dead"; for μέγας κορυθαίολος Ἕκτωρ he has "the great Helme-mover," "the Helme-grac't Hector," and so on. As often as not he leaves out the epithet altogether, or changes and disputes it when it suits him to do so, especially when engaged upon his denigration of Menelaus.

Such variations as these few examples indicate diminish the clarity, the *ring* of the poem as one reads, and this smothering effect is deepened by the continual occurrence of words and phrases literally translated from the Latin version, or suggested by it. Not to speak of those which conspicuously affect the interpretation of character or action, it is possible to compile a really fascinating list of these renderings, of which the following is a fairly representative short selection.

Homer	Spondanus	Chapman
1. Ἀργεῖοι ἰόμωροι (IV, 242)	*iaculationi destinati*	"made for Buts to darts"
2. ποῖόνσε ἔπος φύγεν ἕρκος ὀδόντων [the formula]	*quale tibi verbum fugit ex septo dentium*	"How hath thy violent tongue broke through thy set [!] of teeth"
3. Ἀτρεΐδη κύδιστε	*illustrissimi*	"most illustrate king"
4. εἶς ὅ κέ περ Τροίην διαπέρσομεν (IX, 46)	*donec Troiam evertamus*	"till Troy be overcome with full eversion"
5. ἀριστήεσσι . . . καὶ βασιλεῦσι (IX, 334)	*optimatibus regibusque*	"to Optimates and Kings"
6. χάρμῃ γηθόσυνοι (XIII, 82)	*pugnae studio laeti*	"as over-joy'd with study for the fight"
7. Εὐρυνόμη, θυγάτηρ αψορρύον Ὠκεανοῖο (XVIII, 399)	*refluentis Oceanis*	"Eurynome, that to her father had/ Reciprocall Oceanus"
8. λύθρῳ δὲ παλάσσετο χεῖρας ἀάπτους (XX, 503)	*maculabat manus inaccessas*	"His most inaccessible hands in humane blood he died"
9. ἡ δ'ἐπεὶ οὖν ἔμπνυτο καὶ ἐς φρένα θυμὸς ἀγέρθη (XXII, 475)	*sed haec ut respiravit, & ad mentem animus collectus est*	"Then, when again her respirations found/ Free passes (her mind and spirit met")"

Since, in Chapman's phrase, "I am weary with beating this thicket for a woodcocke," I offer this gem as a climax to these examples of the "curious austeritie of belabouring art" (which Chapman professed to eschew):

10. ἐν νηῶν ἀγύρει (XXIV, 141)	*in navium congregatione*	"in eare of all the navall Station"

Comparable effects may be found in other places, where the fault

does not necessarily lie with the letter of the Latin version. One such
passage is in the translation of X, 131–47 (Nestor raising the leaders of
the host). The whole is worth quoting, partly because the first lines
illustrate what Arnold probably meant by "ballad-manner":

> Thus put he on his arming truss, faire shoes upon his feet,
> About him a mandilion, that did with buttons meet,
> Or purple, large and full of folds, curl'd with a warmefull
> nap.
> A garment that gainst cold in nights did souldiers use to
> wrap.
> Then tooke he his strong lance in hand, made sharpe with
> proved steele,
> And went along the Grecian fleet. First at Ulysses' keele
> He cald, [to breake the silken fumes that did his sences bind:]
> The voice through th' Organs of his eares straight rung
> about his mind.
> Forth came Ulysses, asking him: "Why stirre ye thus so late?
> Sustaine we such enforcive cause?" He answerd: "Our estate
> Doth force this perturbation; vouchsafe it, worthie friend,
> And come, let us excite one more to counsell of some end
> To our extremes, by fight or flight."

$$(H, \text{I}, 203)$$

("Mandilion" translates χλαῖναν; "steele" is for χαλκῷ; "to breake the
silken fumes that did his sences bind" is an added adornment.) Now
for ὅ τι δὴ χρειὼ τόσον ἵκει ("what need so great has come upon you?")
Spondanus' Latin has *an quia necessitas tanta advenit*, which is very
close; but Chapman produces the heavy phrase "Sustaine we such
enforcive cause," omits the formulas which follow ("Nestor the
horseman of Gerenia"; and "Zeus-born son of Laertes, Odysseus of
many wiles"), translates τοῖον γὰρ ἄχος βεβίηκεν 'Αχαιούς as "Our estate
doth force this perturbation," and, returning to Spondanus, renders
ἐγείρομεν as "excite" (*excitemus*).

His motive in such painful elaborations was undoubtedly to keep
up the "height" of the poem, but in raising the verses upon these
polysyllabic stilts he displays a real insensitivity to the Greek, while
professing in margin and commentary his insight into its beautiful
mysteries, for example in the matter of Homer's similes. He begins
early to comment on the "most inimitable Similes" of Homer, in the
Commentarius to the second book,[43] touching the bee simile at

---

[43]The commentarii leave off at III and return at XIII. The close of the Commentarius to III is characteristic: "And here haste makes me give end to these new

II, 87–93. Here he argues against Spondanus, who seems to think that between the two elements in the comparison there is only one point of application; this, says Chapman, is "as grosse as it is vulgar": in this case ἰλαδόν ("by companies") is not the only point of the comparison of the host to a bee-swarm, there is also their "infinite number" and "the everie where dispersing themselves." After this (truthful) pedantry, it is a disappointment to find him translating "frequent Bees" (*apium frequentium*) and for αἰεὶ νέον ἐρχομενάων the incredible "repairing the degrees of their egression," which is not in Spondanus at all. His marginal comment on the spinner ("Spinster poore") simile at XII, 433–5 as beyond admiration for "comparing mightiest things with meanest, and the meanest illustrating the mightiest, both meeting in one end of this life's preservation and credit," is just and eloquent; one asks why, then, does he leave out the striking brief simile immediately below, where Hector lifting the great stone before the gate is compared to a shepherd lightly bearing a ram's fleece?

But these excursions are minor in comparison with an elaborate commentary on XIV, 409–13, describing how Aias felled Hector with a stone. There is no difficulty with the simile in the original: ". . . he hit Hector on the chest near the neck, over the rim of the shield, and set him whirling like a top with the stroke, and he spun round and round" (στρόμβον δ'ὥς ἔσσευε βαλών, περὶ δ'ἔδραμε πάντῃ). Chapman translates:

> And shook him peecemeale—when the stone sprung backe
>   againe and smote
> Earth, like a whirlewind gathering dust with whirring
>   fiercely round,
> For fervours of his unspent strength, in settling on the
>   ground.

Then he proceeds, in the Commentarius, in full cry on a false scent, affirming that all the stupid interpreters, Valla, Eobanus, Spondanus, Salel, have been wrong in translating as I have above. Having firmly in his mind (from Scapula) that στρόμβον is to be taken in the sense of "whirlwind," and the stone, not Hector, likened to the whirlwind, he finds it "above the wit of a man to imitate Homer's wit" in giving such a "fierie" illustration of the force of the stone that it should turn

---

Annotations, deferring the like in the next nine bookes for more breath and encouragement, since time (that hast ever opprest me) will not otherwise let me come to the last twelve, in which the first free light of my Author entred and emboldened me." (*Homer*, I, 90).

on the earth afterward like a whirlwind; here is "where the conceit and life" of the simile lies. Homer does not speak of it, but "leaves it to his reader." "Notwithstanding he utters enough to make a stone understand it." What Chapman is looking for is hyperbole, and he finds it, un-"perviall" though it is:

But herein this case is ruled against such men, that they affirme these hyper-theticall or superlative sort of expressions and illustrations are too bold and bumbasted; and out of that word is spunne that which they call our Fustian, their plaine writing being stuffe nothing so substantial but such grosse sowtedge, or hairepatch, as every goose may eates oates through. Against which, and all these plebeian opinions that a man is bound to write to every vulgar reader's understanding, you see the great master of all elocution hath written so darkly that almost three thousand sunnes have not discovered him, nor more in five hundred other places than here—and yet all perviall enough (you may well say) when such a one as I comprehend them. [*H*, I, 295]

After such pleasures, who would put him to his Greek again?[44]

Chapman expands and contracts the *Iliad* like an accordion to play his own tune upon it. The contractions are less conspicuous, but they are constant; especially in the books of the battles the periodic structure, omission of formulas and reduction of speeches to reported discourse serve to compact if not to accelerate the Homeric style.[45] In the first books and the last, where the drama of the leaders more engages his attention, the additions are most frequent. They are everywhere, however, and not all of one kind. I have noticed some adornments and flourishes; many are *sententiae* ("Examples make excitements strong and sweeten a command"; "cursed policy was his undoing") added usually at the end of a speech. Some are explanatory, bridging an imagined gap in the narrative ("When Jove discerned him gone") or underlining a motive, as when to Euphorbus' boast to Menelaus over the body of Patroclus (XVII, 12–17) he appends

> [This mov'd him not but to the worse, since it renew'd the
>   sting
> That his slaine brother shot in him, rememberd by the king.]

Some of the more interesting ones are versifications of Spondanus' commentary inserted into the text, usually with a view to bringing Homer's psychology and physiology up to date. Agamemnon confesses

---

[44]Cf. other discussions of similes, *Homer*, I, 319, 368–9.
[45]Cf. the translation of XVIII, 94–6 (*Homer*, I, 375); and of XVIII, 356–67 (*Homer*, I, 381).

to Nestor that his heart "pounds through his chest" with fear for the Danaans (X, 94–5); Chapman puts it,

> my heart (the founte of heate)
> With his extreme affects made cold, without my breast doth beat,

drawing upon Spondanus, who has a long note based on Aristotle's *De Partibus* and *Problemata*.

But the additions and changes essential to Chapman's reading of the *Iliad* are those which he ventures upon in his characterization of the principal personages, "the full and most beautifull figures of his persons." It is hardly true, as G. G. Loane has said, that "Chapman tends to idealise all the heroes except Menelaus,"[46] but he presents the major figures as psychological archetypes as completely rationalized as his translation and marginal notes and commentary can make them, so that they lose the subtlety and emotional range which they have in the original, and become strictly exemplary. This for Chapman was the secret of Homer which he alone was empowered to reveal. Let us see what he does with Achilles and Hector, and finally consider the curious portrait of Menelaus.

The key to Achilles is, of course, his *wrath*, but while insisting in the preface to *Odysses* that the "Proposition" of the *Iliad* is "Predominant Perturbation" and "outward Fortitude," he justifies Achilles' anger in terms other than wounded pride, and suggests a contrast with the irresolute, arrogant and *politique* (*H*, I, 32) Agamemnon, as he contrasts the moral magnificence and stoical "generosity" of Hector with the effeminacy and concupiscence of "slick-haird" Paris. The Achilles of the *Iliads* is not the example cited by Clermont in *The Revenge of Bussy* (III, iv, 14–25). Thus when Athene catches Achilles by the hair and stays his anger (I, 194ff.), Chapman has her say that she comes to remind him of the "soveraigntie" of his soul, and Achilles replies:

> Though my heart
> Burne in just anger, yet my soule must conquer the'angrie part. . . .

To his speech receiving the heralds (I, 333ff.) Chapman adds six lines of moralizing on Agamemnon's lack of foresight and *injustice*. But Achilles weeps (I, 348–9, 357), which Chapman excuses in a long commentary (not without calling to mind the tears of Jesus over Lazarus), observing that "there are teares of manlinesse and magnanimitie," and that Homer did not make his heroes "blubber or sob, &c.,

---

[46]"Chapman's Homer," 643.

but in the verie point and sting of their unvented anger shed a few violent and seething-over teares." He will not admit the innocence (one might call it) of the hero's tears, but must rationalize all.

In the account of the embassy to Achilles (IX, 182ff.) he continues to fill out the portrait of the ideal hero. As the petitioners approach they find Achilles at his lyre, with the added comment, "And his true mind, that practise faild, sweet contemplation fed." The Renaissance ideal of lances and letters is imposed again in Phoenix' speech (IX, 440–3), where Chapman points the complementary powers of "skill of arms" and "habite of discourse." This "free and most ingenuous spirit," in his reply to Aias, in the original full of obstinate pride and defiance (IX, 644–55), is made to say:

> [My heart doth swell against the man that durst be so profane
> To violate his sacred place—not for my private bane,
> But since wrackt virtue's generall lawes he shamelesse did
>   infringe,
> For whose sake I will loose the reines and give mine anger
>   swinge
> Without my wisedom's least impeach. He is a foole, and base,
> That pitties vice-plagu'd minds, when, paine, not love of
>   right, gives place],
>
>   (*H*, I, 197)

an interpolation which attributes to Achilles a deliberation in his anger, and a well-developed sense of neo-stoic ethics. Chapman thinks it necessary to explain also Achilles' sending forth Patroclus, and adds to Zeus's prophetic speech to Hera (XV, 49ff.) a passage suggesting once more Achilles' thought for the general good. When the Achaeans fall among Achilles' ships,

> [. . . then the eyes of great Æacides
> (Made witnesse of the generall ill that doth so neare him
>   prease)
> Will make his owne particular looke out and by degrees
> Abate his wrath, that though himselfe for no extremities
> Will seem reflected, his friend may get of him the grace
> To helpe his countrey in his Armes; and he shall make fit
>   place
> For his full presence] with his death.
>
>   (*H*, I, 299)

Confronted with the tragic uncertainty of Achilles,—"Yet all this [the wrongs done him] we will let be, as over and done with; it was not in my heart to be angry for ever, yet I said that I would not cease my anger until the cry of battle came to my own ships. So, do you [Patroclus] put my glorious arms upon you" (XVI, 60–4)—Chapman blurs it badly:

> But beare we this as out of date; 'tis past, nor must we still
> Feed anger in our noblest parts; yet thus I have my will
> As well as our great king of men, for I did ever vow
> Never to cast off my disdaine till (as it fals out now)
> Their misse of me knockt at my fleete and told me in their
>   cries
> I was reveng'd and had my wish of all my enemies.
> And so of this repeate enough. Take thou my fame-blaz'd armes.
>
> (*H*, I, 324)

The deliberation and control with which Chapman qualifies the heroic spirit of Achilles are evident also in the translation of his speech before the leaders after his arming (XIX, 56ff.): where the Greek says simply, "Now I make an end of my anger, it is not fitting for me to rage unrelenting," we find an addition:

> [Tis for the senslesse fire
> Still to be burning, having stuffe, but men must
>   curbe rage still,
> Being fram'd with voluntrie powres, as well
>   to checke the will
> As give it raines.]
>
> (*H*, I, 393)

For such a moralist it is appropriate that when facing Hector in his "passion" (as Chapman marginally calls it), Achilles should cry, not ἐγγὺς ἀνὴρ ὅς ἐμόν γε μάλιστ' ἐσεμάσσατο Θυμόν ("Lo the man who has most struck my heart"), but "Here comes the man that most/ Of all the world destroys my minde," i.e. overthrows my reason; that he should lecture Hector (*H*, I, 446) on the requisite spirit for a soldier in much the same tone as a sergeant to a tame recruit at bayonet practice, and that his treatment of Hector's body (ἀεικέα = "insulting") should be termed in the text "a worke not worthy him," and excused in the margin by "his fury and love to his slaine friend."

Chapman's Achilles has had his edges rubbed off, so to speak, by the moralists, by the civilizers who took their terms out of Plato's myths, Aristotelian discipline and the *Offices* of Cicero. But he is not immortal, no more than Byron. Chapman professed the Christian hope, but his imagination rises to human fatality and if he "improves on" Homer anywhere, he does it in his version of Achilles' recollection (to Priam) of his doom, he the only son of Peleus:

> . . . his Name now (whose preservation here
> Men count the crown of their most good) not blest with powre
> to beare
> One blossom but my selfe, and I shaken as soon as blowne.

All this sophistication of Achilles tends to blur the distinction between him and Hector. Chapman will have none of anything beautiful and strange from the great sea of the heroic imagination, like Achilles in his wrathful despair sitting by the sea, ὁρόων ἐπὶ οἴνοπα πόντον, or Hector in his war-fury at the gate, νυκτὶ θοῇ ἀτάλαντος ὑπώπια. He will have his heroes immediately and entirely exemplary. In Homer there is a light all around them, and they are justified in their own being, but Chapman arranges the background, composes them into significant attitudes, frames them in principles drawn from the commentary which framed his text, and highlights them where his own emotions are most deeply engaged. He makes of Hector, accordingly, an austere figure, a centre of calm and stoic fortitude, and sets him against the concupiscent Paris—as perhaps he may have thought of him contrasted with the wrath of Achilles, though this is hardly explicit in the text. But his way of doing this is to put words in Hector's mouth which direct the reader to general principles; and this is what weakens the contrast with Achilles, who appeals to "virtue's generall lawes" too. For example, when Hector scorns Paris for his cowardice before Menelaus (III, 39ff.), Chapman has him say, "This spectacle doth make/ A man a monster," and

> [A rape
> Thou mad'st of nature, like their Queene. No soule, an
> emptie shape
> Takes up thy being;]

(*H*, I, 75)

and when Hector, returning from the battle, finds Paris "amongst the women" (not in the Greek, or in Spondanus), there is a long, admittedly "paraphrasticall" passage (*H*, I, 146) in which Chapman explains how "when the time so needed men," Hector went about persuading his brother to take up arms. One key passage for the understanding of Homer's Hector, where he answers Andromache, who has begged him not to go back to the battle,

> . . . yet I would feel deep shame
> before the Trojans, and the Trojan women with trailing garments

if like a coward I were to shrink aside from the fighting;
and the spirit [Θυμός] will not let me, since I have learned
    to be valiant
and to fight always among the foremost ranks of the Trojans,
                                    (VI, 441–5; trans. Lattimore)

Chapman makes to sound like a stoic "sentence" rather than a
revelation of character:

                            The spirit I first did breath
    Did never teach me that—much lesse since the contempt of
        death
    Was settl'd in me and my mind knew what a Worthy was,
    Whose office is to lead in fight and give no danger passe
    Without improvement. In this fire must Hector's triall shine.
                                                (H, I, 150)

Observe how this alters the Homeric tone: Θυμὸς = *mens*. Chapman
had already versified into his text a quite improper note of Spondanus
concerning Hector's being stung to the heart (δάκεδὲ φρένας Ἕκτορι μῦθος)
by the rebuke of Sarpedon (V, 493):

                    [. . . and yet, as every generous mind
        Should silent beare a just reproofe and shew what good they
            find
        In worthy counsels, by their ends put into present deeds,
        Not stomacke, nor be vainly sham'd, so Hector's spirit proceeds.]
                                                (H, I, 123)

Hector's wrath, like Achilles', is excused by an interjection—"his
friend's misse so put his powres in storme"—he is made to eschew the
vanity of leadership—"no such vaine Emperie/Did ever joy us"—and
to take account of the heavy expense of war for the Trojan citizens
(H, I, 379). But the final combat with Achilles inevitably overgoes
these footnotes: if Chapman can imagine the fatality of Achilles, he
can also rise to the terror of Hector's overthrow.

Chapman, says Loane, "pursues Menelaus with rancour"; that is
putting it mildly. I do not suppose there is a comparable example of
wrong-headedness, intransigence and sheer absurdity in the history
of Homeric interpretation. He begins the attack in the Commentarius
to the second book; having translated βοὴν ἀγαθὸς Μενέλαος as "at-a-
martial-crie/Good Menalaus" (in *Seaven Bookes*, "sweet-voic't Mene-
lay"), he affirms that the preferred translations *voce bonus Menelaus*
and *bello strenuus Menelaus* are "farre estranged from the mind of our

Homer," that the cry is "shrillie, or noisefullie, squeaking, howsoever in the vulgar conversion it is ... most grosslie abused," and proceeds:

In this first and next verse Homer (speaking scoptically ["by way of irrision"— so later]) breakes open the fountaine of his ridiculous humor following, never by anie interpreter understood, or touched at, being yet the most ingenious conceited person that any man can shew in any heroicall poem, or in any Comicke Poet ... viz. simple, wel-meaning, standing still affectedlie on telling truth; small, and shrill-voiced (not sweet or eloquent, as some most against the haire would have him) ... industrious in the field and willing to be emploied, and (being *mollis Bellator* himselfe) set still to call to everie hard service the hardiest ... what he wanted of the martiall furie and facultie himselfe that he would be bold to supplie out of Ajax—Ajax and he to any for blowes, Antilochus and he for wit ... sometimes valiant or daring (as what coward is not?), sometimes falling upon sentence and good matter in his speeches (as what meanest capacitie doth not?) [*H*, I, 71]

Homer, it seems, is very deep, very deep indeed; a superb ironist, he conveys wonders of ambiguity in the epithet αὐτόματος = "unbidden" (II, 408), whereby he opens the vein of Menelaus' "simplicitie," and follows the "true life of nature" in not following the "decorum" in this portrait that "some poore Criticks have stood upon."

What put him onto this I am unable to determine, apart from some confused reading in the commentators—a desire to seem singular, too much acquaintance with stage cuckolds, these are small provocations to such energy of persecution. At any rate he pursues the theme without respite, when the occasion for commentary presents itself, and when he remembers to be consistent. Thus he changes the epithet ἀρηΐφιλον (III, 52) to "weake," though the Latin is *bellicosum*, and alters violently the account of Menelaus' discourse in Antenor's description of the Greek princes (III, 212–5). Where Antenor says that Menelaus "spoke rapidly, with few words but clearly, since he was no lengthy, or rambling speaker, though younger" [than Odysseus], Chapman has (and it is not from the Latin):

> ... the speech
> Of Atreus' sonne was passing lowd, small, fast, yet did not reach
> To much, being naturally born Laconicall, nor would
> His humor lie for any thing or was (like th'other) old,
> (*H*, I, 80)

which, considered as a translation, is very poor, and taken with the Commentarius incredible. For there he adds that ἐπιτροχάδην means "fast, or thicke," and ἀλλὰ μάλα λιγέως is *valde stridulè*, "his utterance being noisefull, small or squeaking, an excellent pipe for a foole." As for οὐδ' ἀφαμαρτοεπής, that means he is no liar, and "affectedly" stands on that virtue; "it is impossible for the best linguist living to expresse an Author trulie, especially any Greeke author," and a good example of that is the translation of ἀρηίφιλος as *bellicosus*, rather *"cui Mars est carus*, because he might love the warre, and yet be no good warrior, as many love many exercises at which they will never be good."[47]

At times he either forgets his spleen in the labour of versifying, or perhaps leaves us to find Homer's ironies ourselves! The account of Menelaus' prowess at V, 561ff. is unchanged, and also his rebuke to the silent Greeks at Hector's challenge (VII, 96ff.); the marginal comment to Menelaus' counsel with himself over the body of Patroclus (XVII, 91ff.) is however obviously ironic: "Note the manly and wise discourse of Menelaus with himself, seeing Hector advancing towards him." With the return of the Commentary in XIII, Chapman returns to the theme, taking off from Menelaus' vaunt over the body of Peisander (XIII, 620ff.), getting into a lamentable tangle over the translation of κουριδίην ἄλοχον as *virginem uxorem* in his attempt to exhibit Menelaus as a ludicrous cuckold, and continuing to gather evidence of what he thinks are examples of his "pure imbecillitie" and of "how ingeniously Homer still giveth some colour of reason for his senslessnesse." He of course reads the whole speech as a kind of peevish complaint and so misinterprets it altogether. Again, when Menelaus departing from the body of Patroclus, and glancing warily about him, is compared to an eagle from whose keen gaze not even the crouching hare is unseen (XVII, 673ff.), Chapman divines that Homer is making sport with Menelaus, "resembling him intentionally to a harefinder, though for colour's sake he useth the word Eagle; as in all other places where he presents him (being so eminent a person) he hides his simplicity with some shadow of glory or other." So there he goes, says Chapman, "leering like a harefinder," though to keep decorum he has to be called an eagle.[48]

Homer, said Aristotle in a passage (*Poetics* 1460[a]) which might conceivably have come under Chapman's eye in a Latin translation, is the most impersonal of poets. He leaves the stage to his men and women, all with characters of their own. But just as we could scarcely

[47]*Homer*, I, 89–90.

[48]*Ibid.*, I, 370–1, with flourishes from Eobanus and Valla. See also Sühnel on Chapman's Menelaus, pp. 116–7, and Gosson, *Schoole of Abuse* (in Arber's *English Reprints* [1895], p. 48): *"Menelaus*, because he loved his Kercher better than a Burgonet . . . is let slippe without prayse."

expect Chapman to attempt to reproduce the style of the *Iliad* or the force of its conventions, considering the traditions in which he worked and the methods of translation he employed, so perhaps we should not be surprised to find him attributing to Homer the directing suasive moral precision expected in the heroic poem in his time. He sought to bring Homer home to the business and bosoms of Stuart Englishmen, as North did Plutarch for Elizabethans. But he went further than that, and the portrait of Menelaus is one conspicuous example of how he made the *Iliad* in some of its "accidents" a private poem, his own possession.

These savage sideswipes at Menelaus, like other details of interpretation, are based, as we have seen, upon professed insights into the true meanings of separate Greek words, which he has with pedantic tunnel vision looked up in Scapula and made into texts for wilful little sermons. In the matter of changes of tone in the *Iliad* he is not altogether trustworthy either. He does manage a lightness in his rendering of the theomachia in XXI: warned presumably by the laughter of Zeus, he uses such expressions as "they laid it freely," "thump-buckler Mars," "he slapt his lance on," "she dusted in the necke," and so forth. But he is far too heavy in his translation of the funeral games in XXIII: one cannot but admire his rendering of Antilochus' incitement to his horses (ἔμβητον, "Runne low"), and he can perceive the effect of the garrulity of Nestor, but he misses the tone of the exchange after Odysseus has with Athene's help beaten Antilochus in the footrace. Chapman was not much interested in Homer's gods, nor in the rituals, solemn, savage or aristocratic, which inform the *Iliad*. He sought his own kind of "inwardness" in Homer.

When he turned to the *Odyssey* he thought he had found it truly: "the information or fashion of an absolute man," the hero being exemplary of *wisdom* (πολύτροπον [i, 1] = "with his wisedome") and *piety*.[49] The pains of "that far-wandering Greeke" (as Spenser called him) are by "the divine inspiration" rendered "vast, illustrious and of

---

[49]For Chapman's Ulysses in the *Iliads*, see *Homer*, I, 50–1, 80, 142–3, 168. The last of these, his version of Odysseus "flight" back to the ships (VIII, 97–8), is of special interest. Diomedes calls to Odysseus to help him rescue Nestor from Hector, but "much-enduring great (δῖος) Odysseus paid no attention as he hastened to the hollow ships." The Latin of Spondanus has *nobilis* for δῖος and *patiens* for πολύτλας, but Chapman translates:

> He spake, but *warie* Ithacus would find no *patient* eare,
> But fled forthright, even to his fleet.

Even his Latin is faulty here, and what he gives to "Ithacus" in "warie" he takes away in "fled." For his exploitation of *patiens* in *Odysses*, see below.

miraculous composure," "deciphering the intangling of the wisest in his affections, and the torments that breede in every pious minde, to be thereby hindered to arrive so directly as he desires at the proper and onely true naturall countrie of every worthie man, whose haven is heaven and the next life, to which this life is but a sea in continuall aesture and vexation" (*H*, II, 14). This is the "Allegorie driven through the whole *Odysses*" and to point it out Chapman makes a significant addition to Athene's description of her favorite's plight (i, 45–62). Held by Calypso, who beguiles him, he is "possest/With so remisse a mind" and "in affection overcome" though "in judgement" he longs for home.

The growing piety of Chapman's temper, the disillusion with heroics, which we have noted in the tragedies, is here set out plainly. Characteristically he forgets that his own Achilles was not just informed with "Predominant Perturbation"; characteristically he chooses to alter drastically by additions and changes of emphasis the character of Odysseus, the man of many shifts, whom Athene cannot resist, he is so winning in speech, so intelligent, in a word so civilized.[50] I have counted twenty-five significant additions and alterations to the original, bearing on the character and situation of Odysseus, none of them suggested by the Greek and very few by Spondanus' translation or commentary, all of them tending in one way or another to the enforcing of this "Allegory."

Mr. Lord, in his interesting *Homeric Renaissance*, finds the *Odysses* generally consistent with Chapman's preliminary announcement of its "Proposition"; I am not so sure of this, nor can I go along with him when he contends (p. 15) that Chapman "was faithful to the essence of Homer's conception ... in presenting Odysseus' career as a moral evolution." Furthermore, as I have indicated earlier, what Chapman means by "allegory" is something very limited indeed. For him, the letter killeth—except where he uses it to blast Menelaus—but the spirit giveth life. He is for liberty of interpreting by the light of "Poesie," and the "Heav'n strong mysteries" in Homer are mysteries of character. So he passes without interest by the opportunities for esoteric exegesis; "the herbe Moly," he observes, "hath in chiefe an Allegoricall exposition," and he refers the reader to Spondanus; his Sirens are conventionally moralized as persuaders of the senses and will against reason and judgment; and he passes the Cave of the Nymphs without any addition or even a marginal note. But he certainly "moralizes" Odysseus. Let us trace this through the *Odysses*, remember-

[50]xiii, 330–2. I follow W. B. Stanford's interpretation of this superb passage.

ing that if the allegory is really "driven through," he will have to show an "overcoming" of faults in his Ulysses, and to present his triumph as a kind of glorification.

Ulysses' attributes of wisdom and piety are introduced at the beginning: Chapman's first marginal note (there are no Commentarii with the *Odysses*) states that πολύτροπος signifies *homo cuius ingenium velut per multas, et varias vias vertitur in verum*, and Ulysses' men who slaughtered the oxen of the Sun perished by reason of their "impieties" (Gr. ἀτασθαλίησιν; Lat. *stulti*). In the first addition to the text (*H*, II, 13), Pallas speaks to Jove of Ulysses' "more pious mind" which distinguishes him from Aegisthus and others who have perished by reason of evil deeds. In other words she puts the theological issue in terms more familiar to the Christian than to the Homeric audience: why do the righteous suffer?[51] The answer is implied in the added phrase already quoted: the hero is overcome by his "affections." This interpretation Chapman proceeds to justify as follows: δύστηνον ("unfortunate") has "a particular exposition" here, "to expresse Ulysses' desert errors" (a pun?), hence "homelesse-driven," and μαλακοῖσι λόγοισιν (i, 56: the "soft words" of Calypso) signify "*qui languide, et animo remisso rem aliquam gerit* [so in Spondanus] . . . being the effect of Calypso's sweete words in *Ulysses* . . . here applied passively to his owne sufferance of their operations."[52]

This is of course a gross misconception of the original, as Lord admits,[53] and it raises problems which Chapman cannot solve. If Ulysses is to grow in grace, then he must have "fallen," for Helen, it appears, remembers him as "good" (Gr. ταλασίφρονός = "stout-hearted"), and adds,

> [Since he was good, let us delight to heare
> How good he was, and what his suffrings were,]
> (*H*, II, 68)

this "patient" Ulysses, as she calls him here, and Menelaus later (translating the same epithet). Spondanus' Latin has *patiens* = "enduring," but Chapman avails himself of the ambiguity warranted by Cicero's *aures patientes*. But Ulysses is not "patient," for Chapman is forced to introduce him as Homer shows him, sitting by the "vext

[51]See Lord, pp. 56 ff. For Sühnel (pp. 120 ff., esp. 126), who does not cite Lord, Chapman's Ulysses is "the Senecal man."

[52]*Homer*, II, 14.

[53]Lord, p. 44. But in another place (p. 48) he considers Chapman's "basic interpretation" to be valid. I find my reservations about Lord's view of the *Homeric* poem supported by Lattimore's review, *MLN* LXXIII (1958), 60–4.

sea" in tears, "drown'd in discontent," and when he indicates distrust of Calypso's offer to send him off and her invitation to build a raft Chapman preserves the tone of his original, Ἦ δὴ ἀλιτρός γ' ἐσσί, &c., with "O y'are a shrewd one" (*H*, II, 94). The first important addition to Ulysses' speeches, however, is an assertion of piety. Cast up on the Phaeacian shore, he complains of his sad plight; practical as always, he wonders whether he should stay by the river or take refuge in the woods, being in peril either way (v, 465–73), but in Chapman he goes on:

> [Best appaid
> Doth that course make me yet; for there some strife,
> Strength and my spirit may make me make for life,
> Which, though empaird, may yet be fresh applied
> Where perill possible of escape is tried.
> But he that fights with heaven, or with the sea,
> To Indiscretion addes Impietie.]
>
> (*H*, II, 103)

The last lines are hardly evidence that "his rebellious, self-reliant spirit has finally been chastened."[54] For one thing, it is very difficult to impose what we call "character development" upon a narrative structure as complex as that of the *Odyssey*, and, for another, we haven't seen the rebellious spirit yet and never do see it. There is no doubt, however, that this bit of moralizing, dismal tag though it is, announces more of an eccentric interpretation of the poem than the shadings, emphases and variations in the portraits of Achilles and Hector.

There may be some hint, besides, of a "mystical" reading of Ulysses' situation in the figure added to Homer's simile of the hidden firebrand (v, 488–91), when he describes how the hero covered himself with leaves, "And thus nak't vertue's seed lies hid in leaves" (*H*, II, 104). The figure is from Spondanus' commentary, and how seriously we should take it is doubtful,[55] but at least it changes the emphasis of the original, for both the simile of the covered seed of fire and that of the mountain lion when Odysseus comes forth (vi, 130ff.) suggest the hidden and then manifest splendour of the shining (δῖος) and terrible (σμερδαλέος) hero. Nausicaa, commending him to her maidens, is made by Chapman intuitively to perceive his "inward" excellence:

> [This man is truly manly, wise, and staid,
> In soule more rich the more to sense decaid,

---

[54]Lord, p. 91.

[55]Lord (p. 92) calls it "a specific image of the hero's spiritual rebirth."

Who nor will do, nor suffer to be done,
Acts leud and abject; nor can such a one
Greete the Phaeacians with a mind envious;
Dear to the Gods they are, and he is pious.]
(*H*, II, 113)

And this beauty of soul is revealed when Athene puts grace (χάριν)
upon his head and shoulders, Chapman adding,

[when worke sets forth
A worthy soule to bodies of such worth,
No thought reproving th'act in any place,
Nor Art no debt to Nature's liveliest grace.]
(*H*, II, 114)

Lord thinks (p. 97) the suggestion of "spiritual rehabilitation" won
through suffering is suggested "obliquely and subtly" *by Homer*.
But Homer was not a Christian, and even Chapman's terms (soul/body,
thought/act, Art/Nature), though they are not Homeric, do little
more than give a kind of pedantic humanist emphasis to the original
at this point.

The case for a transformed Ulysses *in Chapman*, becomes stronger,
however, when we consider Chapman's interpretation of his tears at the
song of Demodocus (viii, 521–31). Homer compares his sorrow to that
of a woman wailing over the body of her husband as she is torn away
into captivity; Odysseus weeps because of his misfortune, not, as Lord
would have it (p. 102), because for the first time in his life he is
"identified sympathetically with the tragic victims of war rather than
the glorious conquerors"—that is flat sentimentalizing of the *Odyssey*.
But Chapman adds, before the simile, that the poet's art expressed the
slaughters at Troy "so lively" that the song "made him pitie his owne
crueltie,"

[And put into that ruth so pure an eye
Of humane frailtie]

that "in teares his feeling braine swet" (*H*, II, 146). Later, when
Ulysses begins what Stanford calls his model after-dinner speech, at
the banquet (ix, 1ff.), Chapman ruins it by a similar addition in which
Ulysses confesses that the repetition of past deeds has given him

[heartie apprehension
Of God and goodnesse, though they shew my ill.]
(*H*, II, 151)

This goes very badly with the straight translation, immediately following, of Ulysses' announcement of his name and fame, unless we are meant to believe that ″ος πᾶσι δόλοισιν ἀνθρώποισι μέλω (ix, 19–20) is equivalent to "I have had a very sinful past, as everybody knows." It could be argued that "The feare of all the world for policies," which is Chapman's version, has that force, remembering the significance of "policy" elsewhere.

How far the hero's narrative which follows goes to defining the lack of humanity and self-discipline which Ulysses "has finally over-come,"[56] is a question to be decided, finally, by what the reader brings to Chapman's *Odysses*. The translation, taking into account its latinized periodicity and its rhyming cramp, is close enough. Chapman notes marginally (*H*, II, 155) that "the descriptions of all these countries have admirable allegories, besides their artly and pleasing relation," but he does not in my opinion "open" these allegories, nor can I find much consistent indication that any changes of emphasis are more than the result of the imperfect "neoclassical" idiom of the rendering. For example, as Ulysses goes to find the Cyclops, he says he had a feeling that he would come upon a mighty man, a wild man who knew nothing of laws and dooms (ix, 213–5), which Chapman translates as

> . . . this heape of fortitude,
> That so illiterate was and upland rude
> That laws divine nor humane he had learnd.
>
> (*H*, II, 157)

Lord thinks that this has "an aura of snobbery"[57] but "heape of fortitude" is merely Spondanus' *ingenti fortitudine*, and "illiterate" suggests no more than Chapman's usual anachronism. And so with other passages. But if he is not consistent, he does remind himself from time to time of his allegory, and marks the place with a pious excursus by the hero. Thus when Odysseus calls up his men to explore Circe's isle, pointing out that they cannot know where the sun goes at night but at least they can see if any device will serve them at the moment (x, 189–97), Chapman's Ulysses adds:

> [Those counsailes then
> That passe our comprehension we must leave
> To him that knows their causes, and receave
> Direction from him in our acts as farre
> As he shall please to make them regular

---

[56]Lord, p. 103.
[57]*Ibid.*, p. 106.

And stoope them to our reason. In our state,
What then behoves us? Can we estimate,
With all our counsailes, where we are, or know
Without instruction past our owne skils) how
(Put off from hence) to stere our course the more?
I thinke we can not.]

(*H*, II, 175)

An admirable Christian sentiment, worthy of Milton's Raphael. Whether it represents "a new phase in Ulysses' self-knowledge" or is merely a "sentence" directed to the reader (like the choric comments in the tragedies) to remind him of the exemplary possibilities in the hero, is another matter. The margin (which Lord in commenting on this passage ignores) mentions that the "whole end" of this counsel was "to perswade his souldiers to explore those parts," and since he knew they would be timorous after their dreadful experiences, "therefore he prepares the little he hath to say with this long circumstance, implying a necessitie of that service, and necessary resolution." Ulysses shows a little more than Homeric "resolution" in his dealings with Circe: he is made to excuse his hot bath (x, 360ff.), though "something delicate," as fitting after his sorrows and troubles, and invokes "the rights of true humanitie" (for 'εναίσιμος) in his appeal for his comrades. His test of the Sirens' melody is altered here and there to set him apart from his "rude" followers (*H*, II, 214–6), who, being "students of the gut and life," giving way to "affection" of "the bellie's flame," brought all his resolution to naught in their slaughter of the oxen of the Sun.

Cast up once more, upon Ithaca, and Athene revealed to him, Odysseus, in one of the most delightful speeches in the poem, reproaches the goddess that she has forsaken him since Troy (xiii, 312–28). Chapman takes occasion to make this one of his chief demonstrations of Ulysses' piety, and turns his question into a meditation on what is due to the "inspired" wise man. In a long addition (*H*, II, 236), Ulysses argues that the righteous, "just and wise men" should not suffer wrong like evil men; all men think they know Athene (i.e. *wisdom*), but she appears in truth only to those who have "inspired light," a "free-given grace." The language carries us dangerously close to confusing Ulysses with one of the "elect," and this impression is sustained by the translation of 11. 320–2 as

But onely in my proper spirit involv'd,
Err'd here and there quite slaine, til heaven dissolv'd

> Me and my ill: which chanc't not, till thy grace
> By open speech confirm'd me.
>
> (p. 107)

"Err'd" is Spondanus' *erravi*: an example, says Lord, of the "happy ambiguity" of the word in the *Odysses*. It may be so, though a confession of sin rarely follows so hard upon an assertion of the inward powers, in Chapman's heroes. At any rate Athene's reply does not provide much opportunity to frame an answer to Ulysses' questioning of the divine will, though she is made to add to her assurance (xiii, 393), "Nor must thou faile, but do thy part with me."

The final drama begins. Odysseus, in his own house, having knocked out Irus, is pledged by Amphinomus, and warns that young man (xviii, 125–50). This is one of the great moments in the *Odyssey*: the speech is a repudiation of force and an assertion of the principles of law and *pietas*, but it is not, *in Homer*, "Ulysses' most self-critical speech," thus giving warrant for Chapman's "erring" reformed character.[58] Odysseus speaks, it is clear, as an old beggarman, an awful warning, and says: "I was once in the way of prosperity among men, and in my strength did many reckless deeds, trusting to my father and my brothers," but (elliptically) look at me now, and besides, the man of the house is "very near," so may some god put it in your mind to be off home. Chapman gives to the speech a tone of explicit Christian exhortation. After 1. 129 he makes Ulysses enforce his warning to the son of Nisus by telling him of the "miseries/That follow full states, if they be not held/With wisedome still at full," and translates 11. 136–7 (". . . for the spirit [νόος] of men upon the earth is such as the father of gods and men brings upon them") as

> The Minde of Man flyes stil out of his way,
> Unlesse God guide and prompt it every day.
>
> (*H*, II, 317)

He emphasizes Ulysses' account of his supposed sins, "what for Lust/Or any pleasure" he has committed, and the peril of soul in which they placed him.

If after all the labour of the translation Chapman ever really thought back to his hero with "so remisse a mind" in the toils of Calypso, it was here. If he did see his "circular" man completing his "absolute" course, he was not afraid of inconsistency. His Ulysses, the pious moralist, is, like his Homeric original, pleased that his wife

---

[58]Lord, p. 86. Cf. Phyllis B. Bartlett, "The Heroes of Chapman's *Homer*," 271, which Lord cites in support of his view.

collects the wooers' gifts and beguiles them with gentle words (xviii, 281–3):

> Divine Ulysses much rejoic't to heare
> His Queene thus fish for gifts and keepe in cheare
> Their hearts with hope,
>
> (*H*, II, 321)

and he demonstrates through all stages of his recognition and destruction of the wooers his canny control of the situation, though Chapman cannot bear that his man should have a thief as his grandfather, and accordingly softens xix, 395–6 to

> Autolycus, who th' Art
> Of Theft and swearing (not out of the hart,
> But by equivocation) first adorn'd. . . .
>
> (*H*, II, 340)

He puts stress also upon the chastity and gravity of the united wife and husband.

Is the hero, then, glorified? Lord thinks that he is, in a glorious transformation, reaching his "true form over the deforming passions which have for so long beset him."[59] Odysseus is bathed and anointed by Eurynome; then the poet repeats the description of the splendour cast upon him by Athena in Phaeacia (vi, 229–35; xxiii, 156–62), and forth he comes, in form like the immortals. Chapman translates this as straightforwardly as his usual limitations permit, until the simile of the goldsmith suggests to him something of a metaphysical conceit:

> Looke how a skilfull Artizan, well seene
> In all Arts Metalline, as having beene
> Taught by Minerva and the God of fire,
> Doth Gold with Silver mix [so that entire
> They keep their selfe distinction, and yet so
> That to the Silver from the Gold doth flow
> A much more artificial luster than his owne,
> And thereby to the Gold it selfe is growne
> A greater glory than if wrought alone,
> Both being stuck off by either's mixtion:
> So did Minerva hers and his combine;
> He more in Her, She more in Him did shine.]
>
> (*H*, II, 296)

This, being interpreted, can be made to mean that divine grace married to human responsibility produces the glory or transfiguration of the

[59] *Ibid.*, p. 117.

"absolute" man in whom the divine power of wisdom achieves its own glory. The passage ends, Lord suggests, with an echo of the Anglican office of Communion.

The point is well made, though I would be happier about it if Chapman had reinforced it by a marginal note—these notes cease at xxi, 33. That the "ethical significance" is suggested by the original, as Smalley implies,[60] I refuse to accept; nor can I find any consistent indication of the imperfect made perfect or any allegory of "heaven and the next life." In fact the doom of Zeus (xxiv, 483–6) is given an added emphasis in Chapman:

> Peace, Feastivall
> And Riches in abundance be the state
> [That crownes the close of Wise Ulysses' Fate.]
>
> (*H*, II, 419)

The reader will be convinced by now that Chapman's *Odysses* has considerably less of the spirit of its original than his *Iliads*. It is even more definitely a poem by George Chapman. The oceanic, fabulous *Odyssey*, with its vivid and kaleidoscopic surface and variations of tone and atmosphere, has been harnessed not only by densely constructed couplets but by the pressure of a religiously stubborn and stubbornly religious temper. There are many mis-translations, even of single words, some of them egregious, like "In Lacedaemon now, the nurse of whales" for Λακεδαίμονα κητώεσσαν (iv, 1)—Spondanus has *cavam Spartam amplam*, but Chapman found in Scapula that κητώεσσαν "signifies properly" *plurima cete nutrientem* (κῆτος = whale). Or "Unworthy breath!" for σχέτλιε (xi, 474) in the greeting of the shade of Achilles to Odysseus, a very curious and damaging error—Spondanus has *infelix*. Bathos and bad taste are not infrequent: e.g. "She cast a white shirt quickly o're his head," for iii, 467, or "she hath bene/ Gadding in some place" for vi, 278, or "For since he did with his Calypso part/He had no hote baths," for viii, 450–2. Experimental compounds of doubtful force appear in increasing numbers; thus for γέρων ἅλιος νημερτὴς, (iv, 401) we find "the old Sea-tell-truth," for ἀίδηλον (viii, 309), "this all-things-making-come-to-naught," for γήραι ὕπο λιπαρῷ (xi, 136), "onely-earnest-prayr-vow'd age" (λιπαρός signifies literally "oily," that is sleek, prosperous; but Chapman, to save the piety of Ulysses, will have it, out of Scapula, from λιπαρῶς "signifying *flagitanter orando*"), for γυνὴ Φοίνισσ' . . . καλή τε μεγάλη τε καὶ ἀγλαὰ

---

[60]Donald Smalley, "The Ethical Bias of Chapman's *Homer*," *SP* XXXVI (1939), 190.

ἔργα ἰδυῖα (xv, 417–8), "the Phoenician great-wench-net-layer." And
the style is even more rigid than that of the *Iliads* with semi-translated
Latin: "eate egregiously" for ἐσθιέμεν (*egregie comede*); "from compari-
son/Exempt in businesse navall" for ναυσικλειτοῖο (*celebris in re
navalis*); "How many infinites/Take up to admiration all men's
sights!" for ὕσσα ταδ' ἄσπετα πολλά σέβας μ'ἔχει εἰσορόωντα (*quanta haec
infinita multa, admiratio capit inspicientem*).

The translation, conceited and confused as it is, is "pointed" by
italicized *sententiae*, some of them composed out of more casual
statements in the original (e.g. "You are not he that sings/*The rule
of kingdomes is the worst of things*" for i, 391; "*Bashfull behaviour fits
no needy man*" for xvii, 347; "*It is no piety to bemone the proud*" for
xxii, 412); some added (e.g. "*Death evermore is the reward of Death*"
at iii, 308), and occasionally ornamented by figures of a "metaphysical"
cast. Eumaeus greets Telemachus, Ἦλθες, Τηλέμαχε, γλυκερὸν φάος
(xvi, 23), but Chapman has

> Thou yet are come
> (Sweet light, sweet Sun-rise) to thy cloudy home.

And when Odysseus instructs Telemachus to put away the arms and
deceive the wooers with gentle words (xix, 4–6), Chapman adds,

> [And to the wooers make so faire a sky
> As it would never thunder.]

These are small matters, though they have a cumulative effect.
Far more damaging to sound and sense is Chapman's undramatic
habit of abbreviating speeches in indirect discourse. There is a very
distressing example of this in the translation of Telemachus' speech
after he has taken his father for a god (xvi, 194ff.), which appears as

> His sonne
> (By all these violent arguments not wonne
> To credit him his Father) did deny
> His kinde assumpt, and said some Deity
> Fain'd that joye's cause to make him greeve the more,
> Affirming that no man, &c.
> (*H*, II, 283)

Other examples may be found in the translation of xxi, 140ff., where
the speeches of Antinous, Leiodes and Eurymachus are all reduced in
this way, but the worst instance is the version of the recognition of
Odysseus' scar by Eurycleia (xix, 467ff.). In Homer, Odysseus, holding

her by the throat, whispers, Μαῖα, τίη μ'ἐθέλεις ὀλέσαι ("Mother, would you destroy me?"), but Chapman produces

> Ulysses, noting yet her aptnesse well,
> With one hand tooke her chin, and made all shew
> Of favour to her, with the other drew
> Her offer'd parting closer—askt her why
> She, whose kinde breast had nurst so tenderly
> His infant life, would now his age destroy,
> Though twenty years had held him from the joy
> Of his lov'd country.
>
> (*H*, II, 342)

Sometimes his sentence structure is so confused as to be virtually impenetrable; such is the rendering of Menelaus' speech to Helen, observing the likeness of Telemachus to his father (*H*, II, 65), which one might have thought easy enough, Spondanus' Latin being clear; such is his version of Alcinous' courteous remarks at vii, 299–301—the passage is short enough for complete illustration:

1. (Loeb translation):
"Stranger, verily my daughter was not minded aright in this, that she did not bring thee to our house with the maidens. Yet it was to her first that thou didst make thy prayer."
2. (Spondanus):
> *Hospes, certê quidem hoc decenter non consideravit*
> *Filia mea, quod te neutiquam cum ancillis foeminis*
> *Duxit in nostram domum, tu vero primum supplicisti.*

3. (Chapman):
> Guest! my daughter knew
> Least of what most you give her, nor became
> The course she took, to let with every Dame
> Your person lackey, nor hath with them brought
> Your selfe home too, which first you had besought.
>
> (*H*, II, 128)

Or the sense may be clear enough, but the proper effect lost, as in the opening of xiii, the silence through the shadowy halls (κατὰ μέγαλα σκιόεντα, Lat. *per domos umbrosas*), which Chapman diminishes into

> He said, and silence all their Tongues contain'd
> (In admiration) when with pleasure chain'd
> Their eares had long been to him.
>
> (*H*, II, 225)

Some effects, not quite bathos, though indecorous by any standards, have a kind of clownish charm. We may be very close to the translator

working off a few lines after a heavy dinner. Such is the account of the
Phoenician woman (xv, 478–9), who, struck by Artemis, "fell with a
thud into the boat, as a seagull" (κήξ) dives,

> who into the pumpe
> Like to a Dap-chicke div'd, and gave a thumpe
> In her sad setling.
>
> (*H, II,* 274)

"Remisse" though he may show himself in such places, Chapman,
as always, can rise to magnificence. His phrase for Ulysses cast up on
Phaeacia—"The sea had soakt his heart through"—is justly famous
(such diverse persons as Keats and Professor Bush have found it
especially moving), and such fine things as "a cruell habit of calamitie"
or "And beate the aire so thinne they made it shine," stick in the mind;
nor can we fail to admire the polished rhetoric (an important bridge
between the Elizabethan and neo-classical styles) of

> So cut she through the waves, and bore a Man
> Even with the Gods in counsailes, that began
> And spent his former life in all misease,
> Battailes of men, and rude waves of the Seas,
> Yet now securely slept, forgetting all.
>
> (*H,* II, 228)

His finest moment, and even a justification of his syntax, is his translation of Anticlea's description of the state of the shades (xi, 216–22):

> "O Sonne," she answerd, "of the race of men
> The most unhappy, our most equall queene
> Will mocke no solide armes with empty shade,
> Nor suffer empty shades againe t'invade
> Flesh, bone, and nerves; nor will defraud the fire
> Of his last dues, that, soone as spirits expire
> And leave the white bone, are his native right,
> When, like a dreame, the soule assumes her flight."
>
> (*H,* II, 193)

In *The Tears of Peace,* Euthimya tells the poet that

> Homer tould me that there are
> Passions, in which corruption hath no share;
> There is a joy of soule.

I think we do not strain these words too much if we apply them to
what Chapman conceived his *Iliads* and *Odysses* capable of "opening"
to the judicious reader: the tragedy of noble passions and the comedy
of the progress of the "inward" man. The first he coloured by justice,
the second by piety. Each says something about the dignity of man.

Chapman's translation of the *Batrachomyomachia*, the "Homeric" *Hymns* and *Epigrams*, published as *The Crowne of all Homers Worckes* [1624?] marks not only his completion of what he believed to be the final works in Homer's "circular" progress as a poet, but also the climax of what Nicoll calls his "self-identification with Homer," symbolized by the juxtaposition of the two bearded bards on the title-page (*H*, II, 502), the one blind and laureated by divinities, the other mitred by the motto *Conscium evasi diem*—which takes us back circularly to *The Shadow of Night*. The epistle to Somerset in his disgrace (cited above) extols the powers of high poetry in "this Verminous time," and in an explanatory note Chapman adds that Homer "liv'd unhonord and needie till his death," yet "to his last accent incomparably singing" his "observance and honor of the Gods" in the Hymns, as he had, after his epics, "writ in contempt of men" the Battle of Frogs and Mice, "this ridiculous Poem of Vermin." The analogy with the translator's situation and temper is very clear.

The Widener Library copy of *The Crowne* has a manuscript dedication to Henry Reynolds, his friend the author of *Mythomystes*, in which he warns that "if at first sighte he seme darck or too fierie he will yet holde him fast (like Proteus) till he appears in his propper similitude and he will then shewe him self"—but not to the vulgar reader. Hidden truths are promised to one apt to seek them. Similar claims had been made by William Fowldes, in his "Paraphrastically done" *The Strange, Wonderfull, and bloudy Battell between Frogs and Mise . . . Covertly decyphering the estate of these times* (1603). This, writes Fowldes, he did for his "owne exercise at vacant houres" in the hope that it might be "a spurre to the riper wits of our time, that the golden works of this & other famous Poets may not still lie hidden, as under a vaile or mysterie, from the weake capacitie of meaner judgements" (sig. B 1v). After this persiflage, he continues: "There are many mysteries in this writer, which uttered in English, would shew little pleasure, and in mine opinion, are better to bee untouched, then to diminish the grace of the rest with tediousness & obscuritie" (sig. B 2). From another remark—

> Here thou shalt have fit matter for eche state,
> If thou consider what hereby is meant—

it appears that he had some notion of politically topical application of the burlesque, or at least a warning against "trifling jarres and foolish enmity"; the mice and frogs fight until Zeus sends "blacke Crabs" to help the frogs, and Fowldes adds that this will be small gain to the victors. All this is pretentiously obscure.

Chapman makes no reference to this production, and in any case there is no basis of comparison so far as translation is concerned, for *The Strange Battell* is a free paraphrase in "heroycall verse." Nor does Chapman marginally indicate any "allegory," but contents himself with expounding the burlesque epithets which distinguish the tiny champions of each party. The translation has no distinction—if distinction in such an enterprise is possible. Chapman expands the 303 lines of the original to 444, but usually by periphrases and line-filling phrases, not by additions, though he signs his version, as it were, by intruding an occasional characteristic phrase, such as "Yet am I not so sensuall to flie/ . . . fields embattaild," or "a triple flame/ Of life feele put forth in three famous sonnes" (for ἐπέι τρεῖς παῖδας ὄ-λεσσα), or "Cried 'Peepe', and perisht" for κατέτριξε. It is difficult to tell how effectively he reproduces the mock-heroic tone, for in this poem especially translation from the Latin tends to depress the verse with ponderous polysyllables. Note the effect, for example, of "did much deprave/ Unprofitable penitence" (*inutilem poenitentiam accusabat*) for ἄχρηστον μετάνοιαν ἐμέμφετο, though ". . . did before it beare/His universall entrails to the earth" (*universa intestina*) for χαμαὶ δ'ἔκχυντο ἄπαντα ἔγκατα, &c., is rather satisfying, in its way.

The text is corrupt, the Latin obscure, the translator uncomfortable, the result unfortunate.

The *Hymns* constituted a different kind of challenge, for the major ones, to Delian Apollo, to Hermes, to Aphrodite, are eloquent and interesting, but Chapman grinds through them, for the most part heavily uninspired. There are a few typical additions and interpretations. In the hymn to Hermes (in which he manages occasionally the comic tone of the original) he adds to Hermes' speech to the tortoise (11. 30–8), when the god says the tortoise must first profit him,

> [Goods, with good parts got, worth and honour gave;
> Left goods and honors every foole may have.
> And since thou first shalt give me meanes to live,
> I'le love thee ever. Virtuous qualities give
> To live at home with them enough content,
> Where those that want such *inward* ornament
> Fly out for *outward*, their life made their lode:
> Tis best to be at home; Harme lurks abroad.]
>   (*H*, II, 547; italics mine)

Clearly this is a private meditation, and meant too for the eye of his patron Somerset, whose virtuous retirement, as Chapman was pleased to call it, he had commended in his dedication to *The Crowne*. Where Hermes, having slaughtered the cattle of Apollo, reluctantly decides not to partake of the meat (11. 130–4), Chapman gets fearfully mixed up, seeming to interpret the episode as the god's submission to his inferior powers, and adding,

> [Even heavenly Powre had rather have his Will
> Than have his Right; and will's the worst of All,
> When but in least sort it is criminall,
> One Taint being Author of a Number still.]
>
> (*H*, II, 551)

This gloomy observation is no more characteristic than the expansion of Hermes' commendation of the lyre well played (11. 482–9),

> ... whoever rudely sets upon
> Of this Lute's skill th'Inquest or Question
> Never so ardently and angrilie,
> [Without the aptnesse and habilitie
> Of Art and Nature fitting, never shall
> Aspire to this, but utter triviall
> And idle accents, though sung ne'er so lowd,
> And never so commended of the Crowde,]
>
> (*H*, II, 565)

which, though the reference is obviously to poetry, echoes interestingly the assertion of a conservative taste in music, and condemnation of all "late flashes" in the sonnet prefixed to *Parthenia* [1611?].[61]

The hymn to Ares ("To Mars," *H*, II, 585), with its concluding Orphic(?) prayer, obviously appealed to him. Thus he translates ψυχῆς ἀπατηλὸν ὑπογνάμψαι φρεσὶν ὁρμήν as "keepe off . . . that false fire, caste from my soule's lowe kinde," and gives to the concluding prayer for peace a personal note:

> Give me still
> [Presence of minde to put in Act my will,
> Varied, as fits, to all Occasion;]
> And to live, free, unforc't, unwrought upon,
> Beneath those Lawes of Peace [that never are
> Affected with Pollutions Populare
> Of unjust hurt,] by losse to any One;
> And to beare safe the burthen undergone
> Of Foes inflexive and inhumane hates,
> Secure from violent and harmefull Fates.

In the other hymns, especially the shorter pieces, there is little to hold our attention. In the short hymn to Aphrodite ("To Venus,"

61 *Poems*, p. 364.

H, II, 586), he translates δὸς δ' ἱμερόεσσαν ἀοιδήν as "Informe my song with that celestiall fire/That in thy beauties kindles all desire," and in the hymn to Pan, where the god is described as delighting in high-pitched songs (1. 24), Chapman has, "he/With well-made songs maintaines th'alacritie/Of his free minde" (*H*, II, 591), a fair description of his own ideal of the poet's life. The final conspicuous signature is in the translation of the "Epigrams," which one might expect to be otherwise a dim anticlimax to the "endless [i.e. *circular*] works of Homer." Chapman gives to "Cuma, Refusing His Offer t'eternize Their State, though brought thither by the Muses" (*H*, II, 606; his version of epigram iv [Loeb]: Οἵη μ' αἴσῃ δῶκε, &c.) an autobiographical turn, beginning with

> O to what Fate hath father Jove given O're
> [My friendles life, borne ever to be Pore?],

and betraying his usual emphasis in "The sacred voice which I averre is Verse."

The task was finished. On that note, the epilogue to *The Crowne* (*H*, II, 614–6) breathes the familiar accents of piety, lonely resolution, and scorn of the ignorant multitude and the learned-ignorant critics. "Avant ye Haggs!" he cries,

> Your Hates and Scandalls are
> The Crownes and Comforts of a good Man's care;
> By whose impartiall Perpendiculare
> All is extuberance and tumor All
> That you your ornaments and glories call.
> (*H*, II, 614)

He heaps contumely upon the "supercilious wizerds," and (alas for his own defence!) upon the ostentation of such a one as "some sharpe-browd Doctor (English borne)" who can adorn a verse with "much learn'd Latine Idioms" but has a "bastard soule" within. From "Men's knowledges their Lives'-Acts flowe" and "lives and Learnings" should be "concomitant." What have these narrow academics to do with one whose warrant is "dantless labor, constant Prayer, and Grace"? He who would be a good translator of Homer must be in his life a true poem, and "lives obscure the starriest soules disclose." The *original* metaphor, of light shining in darkness, emerges for the last time.

VI · THE MINOR TRANSLATIONS*

HAPMAN, AS WE KNOW, filled his commonplace books with *sententiae* and elegant set-pieces out of his reading, some of them to be incorporated into the plays, some appropriate for inclusion in a kind of work in progress or bundle of poetic *fasces*, such as the volume of 1612, *Petrarchs Seven Pentitentiall Psalms . . . With Other Philosophicall Poems*,[1] dedicated to Sir Edward Phillips, the Master of the Rolls, "the end of it all" being "Good life, and the true feeling of our humane birth and Being." This little collection contains one original poem, "A Hymne to Our Saviour on the Crosse" (discussed above), a fragment of *The Tears of Peace*, sundry pieces versified from Hieronymus Wolfius' translation of Epictetus' *Enchiridion* and *Discourses* (Chapman's bedside book for many years), "Virgils Epigram[s] of a good man," "of Play," "of wine and women," "of this letter Y," and the title piece. The "Vergilian" pieces, translated from Ascensius' *Virgilii Maronis . . . Universum Poema, &c.* (1566),[2] do not deserve much attention, except to note that Chapman makes forty-six lines of the twenty-five of the "Vir bonus," which especially appealed to him, finds in Ascensius' comment on *teres atque rotundus* of line 5 ("est orbicularis, & sphaerica") either source or corollary for his favorite epithet "circulare," and, with typical wrong-headedness and ill-placed pedantry, takes Ascensius to task over the punctuation of lines 5–6.[3] The Psalms, "paraphrastically translated," deserve a longer look.

We do not know what text of the *Psalmi Poenitentiales* Chapman had before him, nor does it much matter; perhaps he read them in the

*An earlier version of this chapter appeared in *Modern Philology* LX (1963), 172–82 (Copyright 1963 by the University of Chicago Press).

[1] *Poems*, pp. 201–50.   [2] *Ibid.*, p. 447.

[3] *Ibid.*, p. 227. Cf. the text in *Appendix Vergiliana sive Carmina minora Vergilio adtributa*, ed. R. Ellis (Oxford, 1907).

edition of 1600 with the *Secretum*, a work that interested and influenced him, and that he drew on elsewhere.[4] The relation of Petrarch's *Psalmi* (which were written in great agony of spirit on a single day)[5] to their models, the seven penitential psalms appointed for the Lenten season (nos. vi, xxxii, xxxviii, li, cii, cxxx, cxliv—including the *miserere* and the *de profundis*) does not here concern us; they are written in the rhythmical pattern and in an approximation of the language of the Vulgate. Chapman "paraphrastically" converts them into English metres, following, presumably, the tradition of metrical paraphrase already well established in English verse; it is just possible that he had seen in manuscript "The Psalms of David" by Sir Philip Sidney, with their metrical variety.[6] He was normally no great metrist, as Jonson was, which makes these verses rather unusual: I and VII (*heu mihi misero* and *cogitabam stare*) paraphrase the original in six-line stanzas, *aabccb*, with a fascinating combination of stress patterns pivoted on a central feminine rhyme; II (*invocabo quem offendi*) is in eight-line stanzas, *ababcdcd*, alternating between four- and five-stressed lines, prevailingly iambic; III (*miserere Domini*) is in "common metre," *abab*; V (*recordari libet*) repeats the pattern of II, and V (*noctes meae*) varies it; VI (*circumvallarunt me inimici*) is in quatrains, *abab*, with the fourth line pentameter. I is also "more strictly translated" in a combination of pentameter quatrains and couplets. Since the question of "strictness" in translation was a matter of great concern to Chapman, it is of interest to compare the two versions of I with their original; for example, the opening:

> Heu mihi misero, quia iratum adversus
> me constitui redemptorem meum, et
> legem suam contumaciter neglexi.
> Iter rectum sponte deserui; et per invia
> longe lateque circumactus sum.

> (i) O me wretch, I have enrag'd
> My Redeemer; and engag'd
> My life, on deaths slow foote presuming:
> I have broke his blessed lawes,
> Turning with accursed cause,
> Saving love to wrath consuming.

---

[4] E.g., in *Monsieur D'Olive* III, i. *The Tears of Peace* (1609) also, in my opinion, owes much, in form and content, to the *Secretum*. For relevant editions of the *Secretum* with the *Psalmi* see Cornell University Library, *Catalogue of the Petrarch Collection* (London, 1916), pp. 59, 61–2.

[5] See E. H. Wilkins, *Life of Petrarch* (Chicago, 1961), pp. 37–38.

[6] *The Complete Works of Sir Philip Sidney*, ed. A. Feuillerat (Cambridge, 1923), III, 187–246.

Truths straite way, my will forsooke,
And to wretched bywaies tooke . . .

(ii) O me accurst, since I have set on me
(Incenst so sternely) my so meeke Redeemer;
And have bene proud in prides supreme degree;
Of his so serious law, a sleight esteemer.

I left the narrow right way with my will,
In bywaies brode, and farre about transferred . . .

One can see what "more strictly" means, though the second version is by no means literal nor pretends to be; the first version is obviously much better here and so continues, but in the second attempt the translator indulges the idiosyncrasies of his private vocabulary too; for example, for "inter lustra ferarum habitatio mea" he has

Even in the dens of savage beasts I err'd,
And there my manlesse mansion house erected;

"manlesse" is a favorite word, and the echo "manlesse-mansion" is a stylistic signature. What point could he have wanted to make in the repetition? For

Quid mihi procuravi demens? Catenam meam ipse contexui,
et incidi volens in insidias mortis,

we have, in the first version,

Mad wretch, how deare have I bought
Fetters with mine owne hands wrought?
Freely in deaths ambush falling,

and in the second,

Mad wretch, what have I to my selfe procured?
Mine owne hands forg'd, the chains I have endur'd.
In deaths black ambush, with my will I fell.

Possibly the second version was an ironic gesture in the direction of literal translation, possibly just an exercise to pad out a thin volume. But his real motive in composing these verses was surely not technical at all, in spite of the demonstration of his facility, but had something to do with his recognition of a kindred spirit, melancholy, learned and pious. Thus he paraphrases Petrarch's

Intus et extra mihi ipse sum molestus; utrobique
hostes domesticos inveni, qui me pessundederunt (V),

as

No outward light, my life hath graced,
My mind hath ever bene my onely Sunne:

> And that so farre hath envie chaced,
> That all in clouds her hated head is runne.
> And while she hides, immortall cares
> Consume the soule, that sense inspires:
> Since outward she sets eyes and eares,
> And other joyes spend her desires.

Here his usual paradigms of "inward" versus "outward," "sense" versus "soul," and his obsessive image of the true light smoldering in clouds of detraction, are worked out of the stark spiritual dilemma of the original. This translation belongs, in fact, to Chapman's "inward" world and must be judged in that frame of reference. The other translations, which follow the Homer, are in a different category; they are exhibitions of learning, not confessions of anxiety.

It was natural enough that Chapman should have sought to consolidate his reputation as England's Hellenist by completing the translation of what for him and his contemporaries constituted the trinity of "first" poets, Musaeus, Hesiod, Homer. With other scholars of his age, he identified Musaeus "the grammarian" with the legendary Orphic seer Musaeus,[7] and he was obviously attracted to Hesiod not only by his literary importance but by his piety and gravity. Besides, to return to the Hero and Leander story, after so many years, must have aroused even in his crusty spirit a certain nostalgia, though he protested that "the Workes are in nothing alike; a different character being held through both the style, matter and invention."[8]

[7]See Musaeus, *Hero and Leander, The Greek Text with Introductory Notes, Annotations, Translation, and Index,* by E. H. Blakeney (Oxford, 1935), p. 6; and Chapman's prefatory note "Of Musaeus," in *The Divine Poem of Musaeus. First of All Bookes. Translated according to the Originall by Geo: Chapman . . . 1616.* The unique copy is in the Bodleian; I have used the reprint of Elizabeth Story Donno, in *Elizabethan Minor Epics* (New York, 1963). Miss Donno believes that Chapman translated it before completing *Hero and Leander* (p. 16). Chapman's "Of Musaeus, out of the worthy D. Gager's Collections," begins: "Musaeus was a renowned Greek Poet, born at Athens, the son of Eumolpus. He lived in the time of Orpheus, and is said to be one of them that went the Famous Voyage to Colchis for the Golden Fleece. He wrote of the Gods' Genealogy before any other; and invented the Sphere. Whose opinion was, that all things were made of one Matter, and resolved into one again. Of whose works only this one Poem of *Hero* and *Leander* is extant." *Homer's Batrachomyomachia,* &c., trans. George Chapman, ed. R. Hooper (London, 1888). J. C. Scaliger, who put Vergil above Homer, put Musaeus above Homer too (Blakeney, p. 6).

[8]Hooper, p. 213. Moses Hadas (*A History of Greek Literature* [New York, 1950], p. 225) refers to the Marlowe-Chapman *Hero and Leander* as a "translation" of Musaeus. Abraham Fleming claimed to have published a translation c. 1577. See Bush, *Mythology and the Renaissance Tradition* (rev. ed., New York, 1963), pp. 123, 316.

For the translation of Musaeus, dedicated to Inigo Jones (since "ancient Poesy, and ancient Architecture [require] to their excellence a like creating and proportionable rapture ... alike overtopt by the Babels of our modern barbarism"), Chapman seems to have used the text, with Latin translation, of Marcus Musurus,[9] for, however he might inveigh against detractors who claimed that he turned his Greek "out of the Latine onely,"[10] he always availed himself of the ease of a bilingual edition. In this case, as so frequently in the Homer, his notes are designed to assert the short-comings of "the mere verbal translation of the Latin, being in the sense either imperfect, or utterly inelegant ... passing poor and absurd ... not expressing so particularly ... not enough expressing," and so forth,[11] but neither Greek nor Latin saves him from frequent lapses in taste if not in accuracy. For example, of Leander drowning, where the Greek has

$$καὶ \quad ποτὸν \quad ἀχρήιστον \quad ἀμαιμακέτου \quad πίεν \quad ἄλμης$$

(1. 327)

and the Latin *potum inutilem*, Chapman translates

And drink went downe that did him farre from good.

And for

$$ἄκρα \quad δὲ \quad χιονέης \quad φοινίσσετο \quad κύκλα \quad παρειῆς$$

(1.58)

he has

The Top-spheres of her snowy cheekes puts on
A glowing rednesse,

which is inelegant, to say the least.

Indeed he is most precious and absurd when he protests his accuracy and insight. He translates lines 59ff. thus:

You would have saide, in all her Lineaments
A Meddow full of Roses she presents.
All over her she blush't; which (putting on
Her white Robe, reaching to her Ankles) shone,
(While she in passing did her feet dispose)
As she had wholly bene a mooving Rose.
Graces, in Numbers, from her parts did flow,

---

[9]*Musaei opusculum de Herone & Leandro, quod & in latinam linguam ad uerbum tralatum est* [1494]. I have also used the bilingual Aldine edition of 1517.

[10]*Homer*, I, 17.

[11]Donno, pp. 73, 75.

and comments:

colore enim membrorum rubebat. A most excellent Hyperbole, being to be understood, she blusht al over her. Or, then followes another elegancie, as strange & hard to conceive. The mere verball translation of the Latine, being in the sence either imperfect, or utterly inelegant. . . . The words are

νισσομένης δὲ καὶ ῥόδα λευκοχίτωνος ὑπὸ σφυρὰ λάμπετο κούρης.

Euntis vero
Etiam Rosae candidam (indutae) tunicam sub talis
splendebant puellae.

To understand which, that her white weede was al underlin'd with Roses, & that they shin'd out of it as shee went, is passing poore and absurd: and as grosse to have her stuck all over with Roses. And therefore to make the sence answerable in heighth and elegancy to the former, she seem'd (blushing all over her White Robe, even below her Ankles, as she went) a moving Rose, as having the blush of many Roses about her.

This is very heavy going; Chapman reverses Ophelia's madness, and Musaeus' favour and prettiness he turns to thought and affliction— though he finally gets through to something like the original metaphor. Other translators have not troubled themselves so gravely with this conceit. Francis Fawkes, who incidentally did not know of Chapman's translation,[12] has a casual couplet,

> A flowery Mead her well-turn'd Limbs disclose,
> Fraught with the blushing beauties of the Rose;

and F. L. Lucas,[13] with more accuracy, "heighth and elegancy"—and a touch of plagiarism:

> . . . there seemd to blow
> A meadow full of roses through all the loveliness
> Of her young limbs; and under the pure white of her dress
> Rosy shone her ankles, as she glided on her way,
> Grace in her every motion.

If Chapman tramples heavily among the roses, he is hardly happier where one might expect his Homeric talents to find their exercise, in the rapidity and force of the poem's conclusion, with its evocation

---

[12]*The Works of Anacreon, Sappho, Bion, Moschus and Musaeus. Translated from the Original Greek* (1760), p. 296.
[13]*In Greek Poetry for Everyman* (London, 1951). See also the translations by F. E. Sikes (London, 1920), and A. S. Way, in *The Homeric Hymns, with Hero and Leander in English Verse* (London, 1934).

of the savage sea. He turns to a conventional Elizabethan hyperbole
to convey the description of winter's storms (11. 294–300):

> ... when the frosty winter kept his Justs,
> Rousing together all the horrid Gusts,
> That from the ever-whirling pits arise,
> And those weake deepes, that drive up to the skies,
> Against the drench't foundations, making knocke
> Their curled forheads,

and, making the best line of his poem, echoes his *Hero and Leander*
(III, 154) in translating

$$σιγὴ \ παυτὸυ \ ἔπηξεν \ ἐνυμφοκόμησε \ δ'ὀμίχλη,$$

(1. 280)

as

> Silence the Roome fixt; Darknesse deck't the Bride;

(The Latin is *silentium thalamum fixit, sponsum vero ornavit caligo*).
But in general the translation ends as it began, unhappily, carrying
over little of the sentiment, grace, and pathos which we must grant
its original.

With Hesiod he was, perhaps, more at ease. Certainly the commendatory verses of his friends, Michael Drayton and Ben Jonson,
prefixed to his translation of the *Works and Days*,[14] suggest a comparison with the *Homer*. Drayton begins:

> *Chapman;* We finde by thy past-prized fraught,
> What wealth thou dost upon this Land conferre;
> Th'olde Grecian Prophets hither that hast brought,
> Of their full words the true Interpreter. . . .
> Thou hast unlock'd the Treasury, wherein
> All Art, all Knowledge have so long been hidden:
> Which, till the gracefull Muses did begin
> Here to inhabite, was to us forbidden
>
> (sig. A4),

---

[14] *The Georgicks of Hesiod, by George Chapman: Translated Elaborately out of the
Greek: Containing Doctrine of Husbandrie, Moralitie, and Pietie; with a perpetuall
Calender of Good and Bad Daies: not Superstitious, but necessarie (as farre as natural
Causes compell) for all Men to observe, and difference in following their affaires. Nec
caret umbra Deo. . . . (1618).* (I have used the B.M. copy, C. 34. g. 32.) On the phrase
"as natural Causes compell," reflecting a thorny problem for the Christian humanist,
see his note on 11. 765 ff. (the auspicious days): "Of the rest, he makes difference;
shewing which are unfortunate, and which auspicious; and are so farre to be observed,
as naturall cause is to be given for them; for it were madnesse, not to ascribe Reason
to Nature; or to make that Reason so farre above us, that we cannot know by it,
what is daily in use with us; all beeing for our cause created of God" (sig. F2v).

and Jonson concludes:

> Whose worke could this be, *Chapman*, to refine
> Olde *Hesiods* Ore, and give it us; but thine,
> Who hadst before wrought in rich *Homers* mine?
>
> (sig. A4v).

With his conviction that "divine Poesie" is the fountain of all wisdom, and supported by the reverence paid to Hesiod as prophet and sage by Melanchthon,[15] Chapman was happy to pronounce (in his dedicatory epistle to the Lord Chancellor Bacon) "this auncient Authour, as the most Authentique, for all wisdome, crown'd with *Justice* and Pietie," of all "these most wise, learned, and circularly-spoken *Grecians*."[16] One imagines him, then, approaching the Boeotian sage with a not inappropriate reverence, the air of one about to interpret oracles, and the intention to apply Hesiod, wherever possible, to the general and present state of man, and, incidentally, to the prejudices of the translator. The margin is rich in such animadversions. Commenting on lines 176ff. (the iron age), for example, he writes:

> This fift Age he onely prophecied of: almost three thousand years since; which falling out in this age especially true, showes how divine a Truth inspired him: And whether it be lawfull or not, with Plato and all the formerly learned; to give these worthiest Poets the commendation of divine. [sig. C1]

He moralizes in conventional Renaissance terms upon lines 238–47 (how a πόλις may suffer for the violence and presumption of a bad man):

> For law being soule to every such politicke Bodie; and Judges; as if Essence to that soule, in giving it forme and Beeing ... the bodie politicke, of force must fare well or ill, as it is governed, well or ill. [sig. C2]

Affirming that Hesiod's view of man as distinguished from beasts by δίκη (11. 274–79) is "truly religious and right Christian," he develops out of Melanchthon (p. 80) a little essay on the nature of man couched in neoplatonic language (sig. C3), and he follows Melanchthon too in making Hesiod's precepts on friendship (11. 706–14) the basis for a sermon on the degeneracy of human relations in modern times (sig. F1). But he needs no help from anyone to compose his highly characteristic comment on φήμη (11. 760–64):

> Intending with deserving a good and honest fame amongst men, which knowne to himselfe impartially, and betwixt God and him; every worthy man should despise the contrary conceit of the world. According to that of Quintilian writing

---

[15] Ἡσιόδου ... Ἐργακαι Ἡμεραι. *Una cum praefatione ac ... enarrationibus P. Melanchthonis* (1532).

[16] Sig. A2.

to Seneca, affirming he cared no more what the misjudging world vented against him, *quam de ventre redditi crepitus.* [sig. F2]

So much for the margin as rostrum; it is also, of course, an interpreter's desk. Chapman translated from the text with Latin translation and commentary of Spondanus;[17] he had also, as noted above, the Melanchthon text, and his dictionary, the invaluable Scapula.[18] The annotations are excused in a preliminary note (sig. B1) as necessary "to approve [his] difference from the vulgar and verball exposition; and other amplifications, fitt and necessarie for the true rendring, and Illustration of [his] Author." Given his view of Hesiod, and his reception of the tradition of moralizing and allegorizing comment in humanist texts, it is not surprising that his commentary is very rich, if not at most points original. Thus he has a note on the myth of Prometheus (11. 42–58), "wisdome-wresting, Iaphets sonne," whose stealing of Jove's fire

figures learned mens over-subtile abuse of divine knowledge; wresting it in false expositions to their own objects. Thereby to inspire, and puffe up their owne prophane earth. Intending, their corporall Parts; And the Irreligious delights of them. But for the Mythologie of this; read my Lord Chancelors Booke *de sapientia veterum,* Cap. 26. being infinitely better. [sig. B2][19]

Hesiod, as everyone knows, says (*Works and Days,* 1. 82) that Zeus gave to men, ἀντὶ πυρὸς, Pandora, πῆμ' ἀνδράσιν ἀλφηστῆσιν, which Chapman translates, continuing his moral, as "to be the bane of curious minded men" (following Spondanus' *hominibus curiosis*); then he notes that Epimetheus figures "mans corporeall part" and headlong affections, and launches finally upon a kind of peroration to the whole series of notes, taking off from line 94 (Pandora opening the πίθος):

ἀλλὰ γυνὴ, of this came the proverbe ... the plague of women, And by the woman is understood, Appetite, or effeminate affection; and customarie, or fashionable

---

[17]*Hesiodi Ascraei opera et dies. I. Spondanus Rupellanae provinciae Praefectus recensuit, & commentariis illustrauit. Rupellae* . . . 1592. (I have used B.M. copy, 681.a.8.)

[18]Joannes Scapula, *Lexicon Graeco-Latinum.*

[19]He is following Melanchthon here, and working up a compliment to Bacon too, so forgetting the other interpretation of Prometheus given long before in *The Shadow of Night* (1594):

> "Therefore* Promethean Poets with the coles
> Of their most geniale, more-then-humane soules
> In living verse, created men like these, &c.

*He cals them Promethean Poets in this high conceipt, by a figurative comparison betwixt them, that as Pro. with fire fetcht from heaven, made men: so Poets with the fire of their soules are sayd to create those Harpies, &c." (*Poems,* p. 22).

Indulgence to the blood; not onely in womanish affectations; but in the generall fashions of Mens Judgements and actions. . . . The common source or sinke of the vulgar; prevailing past the Nobility, and pietie, of humanity and Religion. [sig. B3]

The other annotations do not display this kind of continuity, but in general they constitute a short view of the state of scholarship in Chapman's sources and the use he makes of it. For example he has a note on the δαίμονες of lines 121–23, drawn from Plutarch's *De oraculorum defectu* through Spondanus, observing that such beliefs are "discredited now" (sig. B4); he notes that the account of the smooth and hard roads, the Pythagorean Υ (11. 286–92) has been imitated by Vergil, and worries obscurely about the obscure "four quarters and eight slices" of line 442, which he thinks too "pinching a diet for an able Plowman" (sig. D3v). Forsaking Spondanus, he indulges a favorite theme in a long note on line 560, with special attention to εὐφρόναι ("the kindly time") as an epithet applied to night, "intending in studies and labours of the soule," adding that "Verball Expositors slubber up these divine expressions" (sig. E2). On lines 588 ff. he has a long note (from Spondanus) on how the Greeks diluted their wine with water, and on the instructions concerning urination (11. 727–32) observes, following Melanchthon:

He would have no contempt against the sun; either directly, or allegorically intending by the sun, great & reverend men [sig. F1v],

adding that even today among the Turks the behavior condemned by Hesiod is abhorred.

The translation, in the decasyllabic couplets by then almost habitual with him, also owes a good deal, as we might expect, to the Latin version, and is often very faulty and confused, as if the translator dodged uneasily from the Greek to the Latin column and developed a kind of poetic astigmatism. He always looked at the Latin to get his bearings (as we have seen in the *Homer*), but sometimes he looked at the Latin too hard. The Greek of lines 33–34 says, "When you have enough wealth (i.e., Demeter's grain) then you can begin to dispute about the goods of others"; the Latin, *Quo satiatus, lites ac rixam moveas? de facultatibus alienis*; and Chapman:

> With which, when thou art satiate; Nor dost know
> What to do with it: Then, to those wars go,
> For others Goods,

which, though awkward, is reasonably clear. So much cannot be said for the translation of line 202, introducing the fable of the hawk and the nightingale:

Νῦν δ'αἶνον βασιλεῦσιν ἐρέω φρονέουσι καὶ αὐτοῖς

Sed nunc fabulam regibus dicam, tametsi ipsi sapiant;

But now to *Kings*, a Fable Ile obtrude,
Though cleere, they favor all it can include.

At one point he has a most interesting interpretation, probably but not necessarily wrong. Hesiod says (1. 694), μέτρα φυλάσσεσθαι. καιρὸς δ'ἐπὶ πᾶσιν ἄριστος ("keep due measure; proportion is best in all things"); the Latin has *mediocritatê observa* and then, following the *first* meaning for καιρός given in Scapula, that is, *occasio*, continues *occasio vero in omnibus optima*; but Chapman translates:

The *Meane* observ'd, makes an exceeding state,
Occasion tooke at all times, equalls Fate.

Yet the translation is not to be rejected out of hand, except by purists. True, Chapman cannot resist the habit of translating the gloss into the text, and seeking to improve on it as he does so; for line 706 ("Take care to avoid the anger of the deathless gods"), he has

The Gods forewarnings, and pursuits of Men,
Of impious lives, with unavoided paine;
Their sight, their rule of all, their love, their feare,
Watching, and sitting up, give all thy care,

which has a strong old Testament ring, not altogether inappropriate. True he makes a fearful mess of the Hesiodic maxims at lines 214 ff., though managing one good line:

Wrong touches neer a miserable Man;
For (though most patient) yet he hardly can
Forebeare just words; and feele injurious deeds;
Unjust loads, vex; He hardly beares that bleeds.
And yet hath *Wrong*, to Right; a better way:
For, in the end, will Justice winne the *Day*.
Till which, who beares, sees then, Amends arise:
The foole first suffers, and is after wise;

and the lines on friendship (707–14) are very opaque indeed, though this is not so difficult a passage as the former:

Give never to thy friend an even respect,
With thy borne brother; for, in his neglect,
Thy selfe thou touchest first, with that defect.

> If thou shalt take thy friend with an offence,
> By word, or deed; twice onely, try what sense
> He hath of thy abuse, by making plaine
> The wrong he did thee: and if then againe
> He will turne friend, confesse, and pay all paine
> Due for his forfaite; take him into grace:
> The shameless Man shifts friends still with his place.
> But keepe those friends, forgive, and so convert,
> That not thy looke may reprehend thy heart.

But give him a straightforward passage of description, and there are many such, where the exigencies of his rhyme scheme, the heavy literalness of the crib, and his own determination to moralize do not combine to clot his language and twist his syntax, and he comes out fairly well. Here is one example, where the north wind, making the old man bend, touches not at all the fair virgin within doors (11. 518–24):

> He [Boreas] makes the olde Man trudge for life, to finde
> Shelter against him, but he cannot blast
> The tender, and the delicately-grac't
> Flesh of the virgin; she is kept within,
> Close by her mother, carefull of her skin;
> Since yet she never knew, how to enfolde
> The force of *Venus* swimming all in golde.
> Whose snowie bosome choicely washt and balm'd,
> With wealthy oils; she keepes the house becalm'd.

And, besides these easier stretches, there are memorable isolated passages, where we realize that here is a poet at work, as well as a pedant. Thus Hesiod's γυνὴ πυγοστόλος (1. 373) becomes a "neate-girt Dame, that all her wealth Laies on her waste," and for κηριτρεφέων ἀνφρώπων (1. 418) he has "hard-fate-fosterd Men," adding in the margin, "The most fit Epithete of Man." Across acres of pedantic exegesis, up and down ladders of false etymologies, and suspect allegories, one strong and bitter spirit can get through to the other.

Chapman's translation of Juvenal's Fifth Satire has received little or no attention,[20] though it is not wholly without merit. It appeared in 1629, as part of a little quarto entitled *A Justification of a Strange Action of Nero; In burying with a solemne Funerall, One of the cast Hayres of his Mistresse Poppaea. Also a just reproofe of a Romane*

---

[20]G. L. Brodersen, e.g., in his review of seventeenth-century translations of Juvenal (*The Phoenix*, VII [1953], 57–76), lists it, and quotes from the epistle "To the Reader," but does not comment on its quality.

smell-Feast, being the fifth Satyre of Juvenall, dedicated to one Richard Hubert, Esq.[21] The "Justification" is a mock-eulogy, toothlessly witty, one of the illegitimate progeny of the *Encomium Moriae*, of the kind collected by Caspar Dornavius in his *Amphitheatri Sapientiae Socraticae Ioco-seriae* (1619), and the whole volume was intended, so Chapman says in his dedicatory epistle, as a tale of a tub, exposing these "slight adventures" to the "vulgar Leviathan," to distract attention from his "maine adventure," some "ensuing intended Translations" (sig. A3). What these were to be we do not know; this is Chapman's last published translation, and his only translation of a Roman author.

One can see how Chapman would regard the stoic conservative Juvenal as something of a kindred spirit, like him contemptuous of poetasters and the conspicuous consumption of parvenus. But in selecting for translation a satire preparatory (perhaps) to other satires one might have expected him to pick Satire VII, that savage complaint of the fallen state of letters, containing many passages for which Chapman's prefaces and incidental remarks in poems, plays, and glosses provide close parallels, rather than V, which bitterly pictures the foul treatment of a client by his wealthy patron, and is richer in local color, shall we say, than VII. (Part of Joseph Hall's *Virgidemiarum* [1599], V, ii, is based on Satire V). At least the author of *The Widow's Tears* did not choose Satire VI. Satire V has 173 lines, VII has 243, and VI has 661.

In his "Preface to the Reader" he continues his earlier attacks on literal translation, and anticipates Dryden's argument in his strictures upon Holyday's and Stapleton's translation of Juvenal.[22] This "asinine error . . . that men must attempt it as a mastery in rendring any originall into another language, to doe it in as few words, and the like order" (sig. A3v) ties the poet-translator to a "verbal servitude," and it is "the outward not the inward virtue that prevails. The candlestick more then the candle, is the learning with which blind fortune useth to preferre her favorites" (sig. A4v). Here, as elsewhere, it is hard to tell just who those critics were who thought his former "conversions" were "licenses, bold ones, and utterly redundant" (sig. A3), though one may suspect some pretty sharp remarks from Jonson. The final grounds of his defence ("inward" versus "outward"; true versus false "learning") are constant.

How much liberty Chapman took in this case "to clothe and adorne" the "materiall things" in his author "with words and such a stile and

[21]I have used B.M. copy, C. 30.e.5.
[22]Quoted in Brodersen, 60.

forme of Oration as are most apt for the language into which they are converted"[23] may be learned from a few typical passages (noting also that his version runs to 307 lines). For *fructus amicitiae magnae cibus* (1. 14) he has

> O 'tis the fruit of a transcendent love,
> To give one victualls,

which underscores the irony; *vos aliam potatis aquam* (1.52) becomes

> But now remember it belongs to you
> To keep your distance in your water too

which certainly conveys the tone of the passage. If the client gets a jewel-studded cup at all, says Juvenal, there will be a guard to count the gems and *ungues observet acutos* (1. 41); Chapman translates:

> To watch the close walks of thy vulturous nails;

not often is so much made of a single adjective. The habit of translating marginal commentary into the text holds here too: thus *zelotypo iuvenis praelatus Iarbae* (1. 45) becomes

> ... our young Trojan Peere
> That made Iarbus jealous (since in love
> Prefer'd past him by Dido);

sometimes the amplification is, characteristically, to enforce the moral lesson: so *hoc agit ut doleas* (1. 157) becomes

> No: 'tis to greeve
> Thy greedy liquorous appetite.

Chapman probably used Farnaby's edition of 1612,[24] at least the margin of that text helps to explain some of his interpretations. For example, *calicem ... quassatum et rupto poscentem sulpura vitro* (1. 48) appears as

> And is so craz'd, That they would let it passe
> To them that Matches give, for broken Glasse,

where Farnaby's margin has *rupta vitrea sulphuratis permutabunter.* (Stapleton[25] translates:

> And going to the glasse-house every day
> For scraps of brimstone to be truckt away.)

---

[23] *Homer*, I, 17.
[24] *Iunii Iuvenalis et Avli Persii Flacci Satyrae: cum Annotationibus ad marginem,* &c. (1612).
[25] *Juvenal's Sixteen Satyres* (1647).

While Virro eats fruit like that of the Hesperides, the miserable client will be treated to a rotten apple (*scabie mali*—Chapman calls it "spaky fruit"):

> quod in aggere rodit
> qui tegitur parma et galea, metuensque flagelli
> discit ab hirsuta iaculum torquere capella
> (11. 153–55).

Chapman's version runs:

> . . . of that sowre sort
> That fresh-trained-souldiers feed on in their fort,
> Bestow'd on them in practise of their Art
> At a stuft goat-skin, to bestow a dart,
> Fearing for their default, the scourges smart.

Here we are lost without Farnaby's note to *discit*: *a centurione qui exercet tyrones, hirsuto instar capellae, vel induto fago Cilicio, &c.*

The general impression is of a strong, roughly textured version, often inaccurate, oftener awkward, but occasionally firm and eloquent, from the Restoration couplet with which it opens—

> If, of thy purpose yet, thou tak'st no shame,
> But keep'st thy minde, immutably, the same—

to the swift epigrammatic line which ends it:

> Thou'rt worthy such a feast, and such a friend.

I conclude by testing it twice more, against a near-contemporary translation, exhibiting in larger proportions its failures and successes. That superb picture of the sucker Trebius rushing off in the grim dawn to the long-awaited banquet (11. 19–23) Chapman renders thus:

> This grace to Trebius, enough ample is;
> To make his start from sleepe before the Larke,[26]
> Poasting abroad untrus'd, and in the darke
> Perplex'd with feare, lest all the servile-rout
> Of his saluters, have the round run out
> Before he come; whiles yet the fixed Starre
> Shewes his ambiguous head;[27] and heavens cold Car
> The slow Bootes wheeles about the Beare.

Stapleton, less expansive, is more accurate; for example, "break's sleep, and run ungarter'd and untrust"; "when the sev'n starrs do roll/Their cold and sluggish waine about the pole." But by Stapleton

---

[26]For *quod rumpere somnum.*
[27]For *sideribus dubiis*, apparently!

in another place our ears "in the first place are mortally offended" (Dryden's phrase); his version of the service of lobster and shrimp (11. 80–85), though in some details more correct, more literal, is intolerable, and misses altogether the snarling exuberance of the original:

> See how the charger bends with thy lord's fish,
> What sparagus begarnishes the dish;
> And how his tayle the table seems to scorne,
> When he's ith' hands of the tall servant borne.
> Thy Crab, with halfe an egge about it shred,
> Comes in a plate, a supper for the dead.

Chapman is verbose perhaps, but otherwise splendid:

> Observe the lobster serv'd to Virro's messe
> How with the length of his extended limbs[28]
> He does surcharge the Charger: how the brims
> With lust-full Sperage are all over-stor'd?
> With what a taile, he over-tops the bord?
> In service first borne-up betwixt the hands
> Of that vast Yeoman.[29] But, for thee there stands
> A puny Cray-fish, pent in half a shell,
> The dish not feast enough for one in Hell.

In the comparison of translations the critic is tempted to descend quickly from scholarly considerations to expressions of taste or confessions of sentiment, especially when the translation itself has chiefly an antiquarian interest, and when its edges have not been rubbed bright by constant citation, as with North's Plutarch or even Goldring's Ovid. But whatever else Chapman's translations are, they are not "quaint," and since he had the temerity to demand that his versions be judged by their originals, that is the judgment we must apply, however damaging it may prove to his reputation as a linguist, or whatever it may incidentally reveal of the shortcomings of Renaissance editors and lexicographers in knowledge of grammar, dialectal forms, or comparative mythology. Chapman's texts certainly did not help him to improve his Greek—or even his Latin; if he had been a better scholar he would not have needed to depend on them so much, but if he had been a better scholar he might well have been a worse translator. *Nec verbum verbo curabis reddere, fidus interpres*, said Horace the preceptor; it is not the business of the translator, remarked Sir John Denham, "to translate language into language, but poesie into

[28]Farnaby reads *distendat*.
[29]*Excelsi ministri*.

poesie,"[30] and in another century Edward Fitzgerald added, "Better a live sparrow than a stuffed eagle." But Chapman tried for a live eagle, and, if not in the *Iliads* and parts of the *Odysses*, certainly in these subsidiary efforts he generally failed. He failed not only because he was not as good a scholar as he liked to think, nor because he was wrong to eschew a literal rendering and to exercise the genius of his native tongue, but because he was committed to an attitude toward his originals and to a method of composition in its own way as rigorous and dangerous as those he condemned. First, as his prefaces to the Homer show, he was trained in school to regard his *auctores* as treasuries of wisdom, of *sententiae* (what he calls "materiall things"); an author is deified because he is *sententiarum floribus repletus*.[31] Then, the ideal in composition—and this includes translation—is to "clothe and adorne" these themes with the "forme[s] of Oration" appropriate to them, to "lymn, give luster, shaddow, and heightening" with "expressive Epethites."[32] The emphasis upon *ornatus* (Quintilian) in Renaissance rhetoric is the source of that curious involved copiousness which makes Chapman's translations so dense for the unacquainted reader, as the emphasis upon "point," upon the persuasive working word, contributes to their occasional gnomic power.

[30]Quoted in A. F. Tytler, *Essay on the Principles of Translation* (Everyman, n.d.), p. 35. Tytler, while condemning the "literal and servile transcripts" of the sixteenth- and earlier seventeenth-century translators of the classics, including Jonson, does not mention Chapman.

[31]Said of Ovid by Hugh of Trimberg; quoted in E. R. Curtius, *European Literature and the Latin Middle Ages* (London, 1953), p. 58.

[32]*Poems*, p. 49.

VII · CONCLUSION: *SIBI CONSCIA RECTI*[1]

HEN, READING CHAPMAN, you come upon a passage which seems especially significant, a "proposition" worked out, a finished image, an intricate simile, a silencing aphorism, you should be aware of Professor Schoell, who has probably found in some moralist of antiquity or in one of the handbooks of Renaissance educators the original from which it was copied or adapted. If he has not found it, the insinuation is firmly planted that there is an original somewhere: for example, I am poorly read in neo-Latin poetry, and so incompetent to trace those sources, but I uneasily feel they must be there. If Schoell has indicated the most important sources for the matter of Chapman's learning, I think I may claim to have suggested some distinguishing characteristics of its form.

We might expect one who contemned so fiercely the art of "Artsmen," and asserted his own dependence on the awakening of the secret natural fire of the soul, to display a discontinuous, tentative and visionary turn of mind and corresponding style. But he thinks in contraries, through antitheses and paradoxes: we can imagine his commonplace books organized in the conventional way, so that on facing pages we would find "effects of Virtue" and "effects of Fortune," examples of *sapientia* and examples of *fortitudo*, *copia* (i.e. different ways of expressing) for the operations of sense and *copia* for the influence of soul, and so on. The habit of opposition of elements, either in the equilibrium of contrast or paradox, or the disequilibrium of a

---

[1] *Aeneid*, I, 604: *mens sibi conscia recti*. It is ironic that Chapman's most revealing motto (see below) should come not from Homer but Vergil.

baroque surprise, is a constant characteristic of the style. It is to be found on almost every page:

> . . . he that curb'd with vertues hand his powre,
> His youth with continence; his sweet with sowre,
> Boldnes with pious feare. . . .

> The bribde, but incorrupted Garrison,
> Sung *Io Hymen*. . . .

> . . . like Hercules Furens, breaking forth,
> Biting the grene-cloth, as a doge a stone,
> And for the ridiculous shaddow of the bone
> Hazard the substance.

(The first is from the description of Prince Henry, the second of the surrender of the chaste Eucharis, the third of Ben Jonson.) The similes by which Chapman enlarges and points his "propositions" are frequently formulated by contraries:

> . . . . as Earths grosse and elementall fire,
> Cannot maintaine it selfe, but doth require
> Fresh matter still, to give it heate, and light;
> And, when it is enflam'd, mounts not upright;
> But struggles in his lowe impure ascent. . . .

> Much like a dung-hill Mastife, that dares not
> Assault the man he barks at, but the stone
> He throwes at him, takes in his eager jawes,
> And spoyles his teeth because they cannot spoyle.

These examples are picked at random from the poems, but what is to be found everywhere in the smaller elements of composition, in single words ("manlesse"), in brief phrases ("my desert fortunes"), in argument and simile, also constitutes the fundamental "in-forme" (Chapman's own word is appropriate) of the works, and obtrudes, as we have seen, into the *Homer*. The play of opposites and the disproportion of "humours" is the very stuff of comedy, in which an "outward" resolution suffices to complete the design. In fact the genius of comedy is disputation and sentence, its social analogue being a trial at law. But in tragedy, which treats of "inward" fulfilment, and for which the social analogue, human sacrifice, is archaic, the intellectual habit of working through opposed qualities to a decision tends to reduce the tragic hero to either a partisan or a miracle, or a muddled and paradoxical combination of the two.

But the prisoner in a frame of "wit," sentenced by his books, is a visionary too. The landscape of Chapman's heroic imagination is filled with images of freedom, of torn clouds and stormy sea, of rugged promontories and streams rushing and broadening into great rivers, of blazing comets and falling stars, of a titanic, Promethean world. And in his melancholy mood he conjures up the grisly furnishings of romantic despair. First, as malcontent, he imagines the "Pallace of Ruth, made all of teares, and rest," among furies, adders, night-ravens, bones and relics of the dead, until, in an apocalyptic climax, the world returns to an "indigest" lump, in ruins murmuring his miseries. Later, as sage, having rejected "the clamorous game-given world," and prayed to Christ to "quiet his bodies powers," he can subdue the savagery of such images to the solemn ritual of the funeral of "Humane Love" showing how "Poesie," treading upon the breast of Death, sings "the Funerall Oration,"

> and on a Furie leane;
> How, to her Fist, (as rites of service then)
> A Cast of Ravens flew; On her shoulders, how
> The Foules, that to the Muses Queene we vow,
> (The Owle, and Heronshaw) sate, how, for her hayre,
> A haplesse Comet, hurled about the Ayre
> Her curled Beames: whence sparkes, like falling starres,
> Vanisht about her.

Unlike Robert Burton, who also saw "dizzards" everywhere, Chapman never exorcised his dark humour, which is dispelled more satisfactorily by a busy disinterested industry than by pious meditation. Chapman became a minor prophet, narrow and intense, with an unresonant message. His vision grew upon him: cleared of its early obscurity, it appeared as the "whole scope" of his "poore life." But what was it when it did appear? The second vision of Homer (*Tears of Peace*, 11. 33 ff.), which reminds us, in its likeness and differences, of the apparitions of the masters in Dante and Eliot, holds the key. In his first "prompting," by Hitchin, that "spirit Elysian" moved his disciple to English him, and bequeathed to the translator his "true sense"; in his second and stranger appearance Homer is a divine presence, "transparent"—a glass through which the sacred fire delivers instruction. And what he inspires is *confidence*, for the poet's only study and the basis of his inward worth is *man*,

> For what hast thou to looke on, more divine,
> And horrid, then man is; as he should shine,
> And as he doth?

To reveal man's true nature and possibility is a sacred task, and "informes" the maker in his working. This is powerfully platonic, whatever Christian colouring it is given, that the chief beauty and excellence of a man lies in the perfecting of his craft.

But Chapman came to think of his integrity as an end in itself, and that conviction at once sharpened his intolerance and dulled his style. His Chabot buzzes "innocence" like an insect in a glass-house of policy, and the later non-dramatic poems record the same dismal refrain. The curiously constricting portrait of Odysseus, in which the most various of all heroes is generally interpreted in terms of interpolated copy-book maxims of righteousness, is another case of the same thing. Chapman's imaginative vision seems to have closed rather than opened to more variety and surprise. We may find that hard to admire, partly because the impulse came out of books no longer read, from neo-Stoic platitudes coloured by general ideas of Christian fortitude and Protestant individualistic piety.[2] In this context the Christian element diminishes the elegance, the "bravery" of the pagan ideal, and the Stoic ἀπάθεια cuts off the tenderness, the *caritas* of the Christian way. All that is left is a school-room conservatism which subsists upon a heritage of "great thoughts," an anthology of ethical monuments, continually rediscovered by visionary passion.

The central elements in Chapman's style, then, are the "evincing" of a limited number of propositions, by a rhetorical elaboration designed to image them as monumental, in their true magnitude and "composure," which is an "outward" or affirmatory process, and the "inward" wrestling with images marking the "struggle for birth" of the "genuine formes" of the poet's "hid soule," "under the clawes of this fowle Panther earth." In the later Chapman the first element largely though never completely dominates the second.

The result, even in the early verse, is not like anything we have come to understand as "metaphysical" poetry. Everyone in my generation of English scholarship remembers Mr. Eliot's "In Chapman especially there is a direct sensuous apprehension of thought into feeling, which is exactly what we find in Donne," supported by citing *Revenge of Bussy*, IV, i, 137–46. Other readers, encouraged or not by

[2]For contemporary statements of neo-Stoic ethics, see Guillaume DuVair, *The Moral Philosophy of the Stoicks . . . Englished . . . by T.J.* (1598); F. N. Coeffeteau, *A Table of Humane Passions . . . Translated by Edw: Grimeston* (1621), with a commendatory sonnet by Chapman. On the reconciliation of Stoicism and Christianity, see Joseph Hall, *Heaven upon Earth*, ed. R. Kirk (New Brunswick, N.J., 1948), and cf. DuVair, sig. A5v: "No kinde of philosophie is more profitable and neerer approching unto Christianitie (as S. Hierome saith) then the philosophie of the Stoicks."

this association, have quoted "the downward burning flame of her rich hair," and so forth, to support this dubious bit of classification.[3] One of the more interesting revisions in the second edition of Douglas Bush's *History* virtually dissolves the link with Donne and aligns Chapman firmly with Daniel and Greville, attributing to all three an "ethical urgency," though properly discriminating among their styles. An unchanged passage deserves quotation:

While Chapman has a lucid gnomic strain, his characteristic texture is tough and knotted with emblematic images and symbols sought for their philosophical expressiveness, and, as in many poets of our own day, these tend to become a semi-private code. Yet Chapman works in a great tradition and his symbols are not merely personal and miscellaneous, nor are they, like Donne's, largely realistic, scholastic, and scientific; much of his imagery comes, along with his ethical ideas, from such favourite authors as Plutarch, Epictetus, Ficino, Erasmus, and the allegorical mythographer Natalis Comes.[4]

It is especially in this matter of *expressiveness*, as I have sought to show, that the difference manifests itself most clearly: where Chapman is "witty" he is usually "evicting" a paradox; for the most part, instead of focussing upon the conceit, he has the imaginative habit of finishing, even forcing, an analogy, exhausting his image. He is orator and emblematist.[5]

I have noted above that for Chapman the genres are instrumental, to be spoken through, dislocated, rather than rested in. (Unless my reading of the comedies is completely off the mark, this is true even of those more apparently conventional productions.) Here he differs not only from the humanist poets in Latin and the vernacular (stuffed with degrees and languages), but also from his great contemporary, friend, collaborator and (perhaps) mentor, Jonson. What Marston did to blur the accepted modes by broad burlesque and extravagance, Chapman accomplished, in his way, by an inveterate seriousness and almost solipsistic attachment to a narrow range of primary images. Those formidable spirits, *hommes engagés* we should say, Marston (a clown, but with a clown's *sensibilité*, Skelton's successor in a different idiom), Greville, who turned the rhetoric of a sonnet sequence into a record of intellectual experience and hid his political opinions under

[3]T. S. Eliot, *Selected Essays* (London, 1949), p. 286. G. M. Story, troubled by the "metaphysical" label, calls Chapman a "mannerist." Introduction to *The Sonnets of William Alabaster*, (Oxford 1959), p. xxxii.

[4]Douglas Bush, *English Literature in the Earlier Seventeenth Century, 1600–1660* (2nd ed., Oxford, 1962), pp. 96–7. Cf. Pagnini, pp. 40–2.

[5]So Pagnini (following Mario Praz), pp. 245–6.

the veil of Senecan plots—and distrusted poetry, the Daniel of the *Civil Wars*, *Philotas* and *Musophilus*; and Chapman: these share, whatever their differences, and they are great, an intellectual habit of some interest for the understanding of the poetic process in their time. They all start with something to say, something to be put into verse; they want to be heard, not overheard, by their "private friends" or anybody. Chapman, denied the afternoon's repose of a quiet vicarage (Marston), a great fortune (Greville), or a happy patronage (Daniel), working in the troubled midnight of his poor estate, was incomparably the finest imagination of them all, but he was possessed —even in the sense of demonic possession—by a body of ideas, "philosophical conceits" he calls them in his neoplatonic phase, "grave and permanent" inventions, "genuine forms" of learning, or, in more public language, "propositions." With no little anguish of spirit, he sought to translate them into a language of power. Even the clear light of Homer becomes prismatic in his passionately twisted "perspective" glass. He could leave nothing as he found it; he had to work it out.

As I read over what I have written about him, I am struck by how much of it is qualification, reduction. There is an uncertainty in his achievement that makes one careful—too careful perhaps. One may claim much for him: the invention of humours comedy, derived from his interest (via the Florentines and others) in the relations of soul and body; the invention of a tragi-comedy with an incidental religious significance; the development of heroic tragedy with its monumental exhibition and analysis of the passions;[6] the re-creation of the vision poem in an age hostile to or just too sophisticated for that sort of allegory; the naturalization of Homer for pre-Civil War gentlemen; anticipations of the landscape poetry and the cult of the irrational in the romantic movement. In one way, he is an old Elizabethan, rich with the glamour of the re-discovered ancients seasoned by the salt of voyages and the savour of "noblesse"; in another, he is the inquiring seventeenth-century man, a virtuoso, insatiable in the search for "forms," trying everything the enchanted numbers of poetry can do. We remember, finally, the device on the title-page of *Ovids Banquet*: the gnomon bent in water, and the motto: *sibi conscia recti*.

[6] Cf. *ibid.*, p. 58.

APPENDIX A · CHAPMAN'S *MASQUE*

The Masque of the Middle Temple and Lincoln's Inn was performed at
Whitehall on February 15, 1613, as part of the wedding festivities of
the Princess Elizabeth and the Elector Palatine, and rushed into print
shortly after.[1] It was "invented, and fashioned, with the ground, and
speciall structure of the whole worke," by Inigo Jones, and must have
been what Chapman calls it, a "noble and magnificent performance,
renewing the ancient spirit and honour of the Inns of Court." The
procession of the masquers and their attendants from the house of the
Master of the Rolls to Whitehall was extraordinarily rich and strange,
and the "novel, conceitful and glorious" presentation which succeeded
apparently achieved a peculiar elegance.

Any discussion of the argument of Chapman's libretto must now
necessarily follow D. J. Gordon's definitive commentary, in his "Le
'Masque Mémorable' de George Chapman,"[2] to which I am deeply
indebted in the following discussion.

In a characteristic preface, Chapman answers "certain insolent
objections made against the length of [his] speeches and narrations,"
affirming generally, as I have noticed above, the primacy of *divinus
furor* in poetical composition, and specifically the decorum necessary
in such "courtly and honouring inventions" as this,[3] a decorum so well
preserved in the *Masque* itself that, as Gordon observes, it may serve
as an archetype of the form. Jonson must have seen how his friend's
imagination was emblematic, formal; hence his commendation of
Chapman as a masque-maker; and judging from the terms of his

[1]See Chapman's complaint of "the unexpected haste of the printer," *Comedies*,
p. 442, and STC entry 4981.
[2]In *Les Fêtes de la Renaissance*, ed. Jean Jacquot (Paris, 1956), I, 305–17.
[3]*Comedies*, p. 444.

quarrel with Jones, and his own careful use of the mythographers in the composition of masques, one can imagine him approving of Chapman's preface.

Even when, as here, we have a detailed account of the "inventions" of the designer and choreographer, we have to make a considerable effort of the imagination to get at what the masque must have been like in the performance. Chapman would think of that effort as "outward," (for all his pride in the spectacle); he, whatever the spectator might make of it, had a message for the searching spirits, and he attached great importance to what he had put on a page, even in this genre, so much an affair of the moment.[4]

The "works," i.e. the set for the masque, consisted of an "artificial rock, whose top was near as high as the hall [the great hall in Whitehall Palace] itself," within which were contrived "two winding pairs of stairs" for the masquers; to one side, "eminently raised on a fair hill," was erected a Temple of Honour, on the other side a "vast, withered and hollow tree, being the bare receptacle for the baboonery." The presentment began with a "low induction" by Plutus, god of Riches, and the curious figure Capriccio, "strangely habited, half French, half Swiss," in which the theme of the riches of Virginia was introduced. This was followed by the first anti-masque, an "antic and delightful" dance of baboons (appropriate to a masque of the "Indies"); then the chief masquers "were advanced to their discovery."

The action of the masque proper may be described very briefly. Plutus, before a heavy, blind, dull worldling, having come to adore the goddess Honour, the "miraculous cause ... of his sight and wit," invokes Eunomia ("or the sacred power of Law") to invite Honour to "the sacred nuptials." Honour in turn announces the presence of the "princes of the Virgin land," who, after a song by the "Phoebades" or priests of the sun ("the choice musicians of our kingdom" so attired), appear "in a mine of gold" (cf. De Guiana, 1. 18). The Phoebades then address their musical "observance" to the King, and Eunomia directs the Virginian princes to turn their devotions to "this our Briton Phoebus," who is "enlighten'd with a Christian piety." After a second anti-masque by the torch-bearers, Honour introduces songs of love and beauty in honour of the bride and bridegroom, and Plutus closes the masque with a prophecy of the union of Honour and Riches.

There is an apparent relation between this courtly spectacle and the utopian vision in the De Guiana of 1596, and in one sense the masque

---

[4]Cf. his slighting reference to Middleton's The Triumphs of Truth, a Lord Mayor's show of 1613, in Homer, II, 5-6.

is propaganda for a joint-stock company seeking to trade in, colonize, and make Protestant the New World; in a characteristic gesture, too, Chapman, while in the act of adulation of James, was engaged in spectacular figuring of Raleigh's main dream. Gordon writes: "Il est pour moi hors de doute que les projets de colonisation et les idées politiques de l'entourage de Raleigh sont presentés dans ce masque." The marriage of the princess to the Elector Palatine seemed to most Englishmen a symbol of united Protestantism; here, as in *De Guiana*, Chapman anticipates an Atlantic Protestant (and wealthy) empire.[5]

Such a vision, in which "Honour having golde would rob golde of honour" (*De Guiana*, 1. 75), typically paradoxical, has also its ethical implications.[6] If for Honour we read one of Chapman's favorite words, "noblesse," we can see that in the *Masque* he is figuring the association of "noblesse" with Virtue (here Eunomia or law), "the subject and materiall cause of honour," as Robert Ashley expressed it. In Chapman's dedicatory sonnet to *Nennio*,[7] a treatise proving "that the nobilitie of the minde is farre more true, and for more perfect, then the nobility of the blood conjoyned with riches," he celebrates his discovery "whence Noblesse sprung," and in *Byron* he invites us to see in the fall of that hero,

> how honour's flood
> Ebbs into air, when men are great, not good.

Remembering his fulminations against "students of the gut and life," it is perhaps harder to accept his reconciliation of virtue with riches, but Chapman, like others after him, looked for miracles from a "new frontier." The *Masque* itself was very expensive.

[5]For other publicity for the Virginia Company, see *The Paul's Cross Sermons, 1534–1642*, p. 230; and Gordon, 314–5.
[6]This discussion generally follows Gordon, 307–11.
[7]*Poems*, p. 353.

APPENDIX B · HALL AND OGILBY

Chapman affirmed his translation to be a rebirth of Homer, sound and "solide" in all his parts, "wherein before he should have beene borne so lame and defective as the French midwife hath brought him forth."[1] The reference is to Arthur Hall's *Ten Books of Homers Iliades, translated out of French* (1581). In his prefatory epistle to Sir Thomas Cecil, Hall modestly admits that his translation is a poor thing, having his "wares at the seconde hande, as by Fraunce out of Greece, because I am not able to travaile so farre for them, not understanding the language" (sig. Aiij v). He translated from the French of Hugues Salel, *Les dix premiers livres de l'Iliade d'Homere* (1545). (Incidentally, it has been established that Salel depended entirely upon the Latin version of Andreas Divus, which Chapman used.)[2]

Like Chapman, Hall commends Homer as teacher of all ages and estates, and he excuses his "fonde fabling of the Gods" as having probably "some peculiar meaning" (i.e. allegorical significance) which frees him from the charge of impiety. The translation is in lumbering fourteeners, and is fairly represented by its opening:

> I thee beseech, O Goddess milde, the balefull hate to plaine,
> Whereby Achilles was so wrong, and grewe in such disdaine,
> That thousands of the Greekish Dukes, in hard and heavie plight,
> To Plutoes Courte did yeelde their soules, and gaping lay upright,
> Those senselesse trunckes of buriall voide, by them erst gaily borne,
> By ravening curres, and carreine foules, in peeces to be torne.

---

[1] *Homer*, I, 546.

[2] A minor point, but of some interest. See Ph. Aug. Becker, in *Zeitschrift für französische Sprache und Literatur*, LIX (1935), 385–90. Ezra Pound considered Salel "a most delightful approach" to the *Iliad*. "Lie quiet, Divus."

Less then fifty years after the publication of the *Whole Works of Homer*, Chapman's translation was sufficiently demoded for that enterprising Scot John Ogilby to see an opportunity for a modern rendering. He therefore produced in 1660 *Homer His Iliads Translated, Adorn'd with Sculpture, and Illustrated with Annotations*, suitable for a wealthy gentleman's library, and dedicated to Charles II in terms he thought appropriate. Homer "appears a most constant Asserter of the Divine right of *Princes* and Monarchical Government . . . on the other side, all Anti-monarchical Persons he describes in the character of Thersites." The margins are heavy with the accumulation of traditional commentaries, and the poetry, as Pope justly observed, "too mean for criticism." Then in 1665, still onto a good thing, he came out with *Homer His Odysses Translated, Adorn'd with Sculpture*, &c. Ogilby, by this time Master of his Majesty's Revels in the Kingdom of Ireland, dedicated this volume to Prince James as "the most Ancient and Best Piece of Moral and Political Learning." The translation, from the evidence of Winstanley, and Hobbes (who "had no hope to do it better") was standard for its time. Mean though it is, a short sample will not utterly corrupt us, and may serve to remind us of the vagaries of taste in these matters. Here is Ogilby's version of Odysseus' famous greeting to Nausicaa (vi, 149–55):

> If thou art Mortal or Celestial Blood,
> Pitty great Queen, but if sprung from a God
> Who plants the Sky, *Diana* th'art, Joves race,
> Such thy majestick Person, *Mien*, and Face:
> But if that thee some Earthy Princess bare,
> Ah! then thrice happy thy relations are.

INDEX